Using Computer Graphics

Malcolm Richardson

Department of Innovation Studies
University of East London
Essex, UK

BLUEPRINT
An Imprint of Chapman & Hall

London · Glasgow · Weinheim · New York · Tokyo · Melbourne · Madras

**Published by Blueprint, an imprint of Chapman & Hall,
2—6 Boundary Row, London SE1 8HN**

Chapman & Hall, 2—6 Boundary Row, London SE1 8HN, UK

Blackie Academic & Professional, Wester Cleddens Road, Bishopbriggs, Glasgow G64 2NZ, UK

Chapman & Hall GmbH, Pappelallee 3, 69469 Weinheim, Germany

Chapman & Hall USA, 115 Fifth Avenue, New York, NY 10003, USA

Chapman & Hall Japan, ITP-Japan, Kyowa Building, 3F, 2-2-1 Hirakawacho, Chiyoda-ku, Tokyo 102, Japan

Chapman & Hall Australia, 102 Dodds Street, South Melbourne, Victoria 3205, Australia

Chapman & Hall India, R. Seshadri, 32 Second Main Road, CIT East, Madras 600 035, India

First edition 1995

© 1995 Malcolm Richardson

Printed in Great Britain by Alden Press, Oxford

ISBN   1 85713 003 0

A catalogue record for this book is available from the British Library

∞ Printed on acid-free text paper, manufactured in accordance with ANSI/NISO Z39.48-1992 (Permanence of Paper).

Using Computer

Graphics

Contents

Introduction

Key points
- *the purpose and structure of the book*
- *two different types of computer graphic images*
- *using graphics to control computers*
- *other applications of computer graphics*

What is 'Computer graphics'?

It is not very long since the term 'computer graphics' meant only one thing - CAD. CAD (computer-aided design) software was (and still is) used, usually by engineers, in the design of manufactured objects - anything from washing machines to space shuttles. The reason that the terms computer graphics and CAD were synonymous was mainly to do with cost. At that time graphics needed the most powerful computer systems available and these were very expensive. They also needed expensive specialist 'peripheral' equipment such as graphics displays and plotters. Because of this need for the most processing power possible, special computers called 'graphics work-stations' were made, in which everything was optimised for the distinctive requirements of graphics.

In the past 15 years, all that has changed. The cost effectiveness of computer graphics using the modern micro is such that it is no longer the preserve of professional groups like engineers or computer specialists. This has meant that a whole range of different types of computer graphic software has evolved and every profession has felt its impact.

This book has been written in the belief that increasing numbers of people from all walks of life would like to explore the use of computer graphics in their own profession or hobby and want to know what is possible. This introduction provides a quick, bird's-eye view of the many types of graphics software now available, all of which are explored in more detail in later chapters. At the end of all those chapters which describe a type of software, there is a table, listing some of the major commercial packages, together with some brief comments which are designed to help the reader choose software which suits their purpose (and price bracket).

Graphical user interfaces   The first use of computer graphics which most modern users now meet is in the software interface. The term 'interface' has come to mean those parts of the system which enable a user to communicate with the computer. The hardware interface consists of such tangible components as the keyboard, the screen and the mouse. The software interface consists of all the effects generated by computer programmes which enable the user to give instructions to the computer and receive messages back from it. The majority of these effects are communicated to the eye, via the screen, and this is where graphical interfaces have come into their own.

Early computers used 'command-line' interfaces. These consisted of text-based instructions and messages and often required the user to have considerable technical understanding because of the jargon which was involved. They also required a willingness to deal with abstract concepts and with what looked like algebraic formulae.

Graphical user interfaces (GUIs), on the other hand, use pictures and intuitive, mouse-based, pointing and dragging actions to produce an interface which has proved much easier to use (see Plate 1). This type of software was pioneered in the Apple Macintosh computer but has now spread to most computer systems. Most of the software described in this book uses GUIs. The key to the GUI is the use of small stylised pictures (called icons) to represent both parts of the computer system and the tools, or facilities, which are available to the user. It also depends on the development of easily-understood actions which the user can perform directly on these icons by means of a mouse.

This 'direct-action' style creates the illusion that the user is interacting directly with the task, rather than with the computer, in a way that seems very natural. This means that skills and relationships which have been learnt in the 'real' world can be transferred to the world of the computer. The GUI has been a big step forward in making the power of the computer available to ordinary people, but could not have happened without many of the techniques of computer graphics described in this book.

Computer-aided design   CAD (see Plate 2) software was designed to provide a computer-based replacement for the traditional engineering draughtperson's drawing board and pencil. The pencil is replaced by a mouse or an electronic stylus device such as a: light-pen or graphic tablet (see chapter 3 for details of graphics hardware). The drawings appear on the computer screen and are stored on disc. When the drawing is completed, a 'hardcopy' (a copy printed on paper) can be obtained using a plotter or printer. Once learnt, this system provides benefits, many of which are common to all types of drawing software. For example:

- mistakes in the drawing can be corrected easily, and with no sign of any alteration having been made;
- changes of mind can therefore be accommodated and it is quite practical to explore a much wider range of alternative designs;
- standard features which appear in many drawings can be saved in a 'library' and reused, again without redrawing;
- laborious tasks, like filling a shape with a pattern, can be fully automated;
- the drawing can be viewed at different magnifications so that very fine details can be drawn with ease.

Developments from CAD

It was soon realised that many of the benefits of this type of drawing system would be appreciated by other professional groups. It is not only engineers who draw diagrams, and so a whole range of drawing packages has evolved from CAD. They have a common core of drawing facilities together with special features which are appropriate to one particular type of application. Illustration software, Business presentation software, 3-D modelling software and even DTP (desktop publishing) can be thought of as developments of CAD since all of them store and handle the graphical shapes in a similar way.

Line-based graphics

There is an important distinction between CAD and the other packages just referred to, when compared with Paintbrush packages (described later). The former are based on line-drawings, and the latter on patterns of coloured dots (called 'pixels'). This distinction is elaborated in the theory section of the book (chapter 2) but the essence of the matter is that all the components of the drawing are stored as mathematical descriptions of lines within the computer. The final image, as seen on the screen or on a printout, is generated from those line definitions. It is therefore possible to use the computer like a microscope - to zoom-in on details of the drawing which, though stored in the computer, may not be displayed at all at a low magnification (see Plate 3a and b).

Pixel-based graphics

Though paint packages also have a zoom facility, it works in a different way and produces very different results. Because the images are created and stored as the pixels which make up the final displayed image, any magnified image shows little, if any, extra detail. All that can happen is that the pixels are shown larger than normal (see Plate 4).

Illustration software   Illustration software provides the graphic designer or commercial artist with their own CAD-like drawing tools (see Plate 5). Some of the differences between this and engineering-CAD are obvious. For example, instead of libraries of images of engineering components there will be 'clip-art' libraries of drawings of everyday objects which can be incorporated into designs. Other differences are of a more fundamental nature. For example, there are facilities for distorting the shapes of objects for artistic effect, like fitting text around a circle or along a curve. There are options for creating a large range of colours and for making colour gradients, where one colour seems to gradually change into another.

The important feature of such software is that the emphasis is artistic rather than functional and total control over colour is very important. For example, a CAD package traditionally offers a very few colours (perhaps six or eight) because the final diagram will probably be drawn on a pen-plotter. Illustration software, on the other hand, provides hundreds, or even thousands of colours, together with dozens of different fill-patterns and line thicknesses because the artist needs this sort of variety to create realistic and attractive drawings. This sort of software could be used for generating diagrams for textbooks, for advertisements, for illustrations for television programmes and a wide range of commercial art.

Business presentation software   Many of the early users of computer graphics had come from a scientific, mathematical or engineering background. It is not surprising, therefore, that such users programmed the computer to draw graphs. Once computer facilities became cheap enough for use in the business world it was a short step to using them for the analysis and presentation of business data also.

From these origins have emerged two types of graphing software - one for scientific use and the other for business. The emphasis in scientific graphing is on providing the widest possible range of graphs and charts, including sophisticated statistical analysis of the data and 3-D plots (see Plates 6 and 7). The emphasis in business graphics ('presentation') packages is much more on the attractive presentation of information (see Plate 8). For this reason many of the basic drawing features of illustration software are also found in presentation software. This means that graphs and charts can be supplemented with text, pictures and simple diagrams.

Presentation software is used to communicate information in a business context. The users of this type of software have probably not had any artistic training and will not feel able make sensible decisions about the use of colour, lay out and typefaces. These packages, therefore, usually offer a wide range of professionally-designed 'templates'. These are pre-designed samples where decisions about colour and style have already been made and only the data and titles have to be substituted for the dummy data. Another important feature is the 'slide show'. This the computerised equivalent of showing a series of photographic slides. Instead of using a projector, the computer shows the 'slides' on its own screen. This is quicker than the photographic process and has the bonus that the computer can also be used to generate dynamic transitional effects between slides (like fades) and can also incorporate animation and sound.

Desktop publishing The term desktop publishing (DTP - Plate 9) is, perhaps, self-explanatory. It can be thought of as a natural development of word processing but gives the user much greater, and much easier, control over the appearance of the final document. Once, quite separate from word processing software (WP), many DTP facilities are now commonly available as part of WP packages and this has meant that 'printed' documents can be produced by someone with no typographic or print training - and often the results look like it!

For the professional printer or typesetter, the technology offers a new way of practising traditional skills. This type of user will sometimes avoid using the term DTP and prefer to talk about 'electronic publishing' - to emphasise the distinction between the amateur and professional use of the technology. Another view of the subject is to see it as a special form of line-based graphics software, where the graphic objects which are to be manipulated are 'scalable fonts'. A font is the technical term used for a particular design of printed character. A scalable font is one which can be scaled up, or down, in size without sacrificing quality. Unlike drawing software, DTP offers the tools to lay out the graphic objects - the fonts - rather than for creating them.

Paint software This type of drawing software (see Plate 10) is designed to provide an artist with the freehand drawing and painting facilities normally offered by the use of paints and coloured pencils. The results depend very much on the artistic skill of the user rather than the computer's ability to automatically generate geometrical shapes. The key to enabling artists to express their creativity lies in the provision of a very wide range of colours and drawing media.

The facilities offered by paint brush packages overlap to some extent with line-based illustration software in that they provide a range of geometrical shapes. However, once the shapes are committed to the screen there are very few geometrical editing facilities which can be used on these shapes since they are stored as a collection of coloured dots (pixels). The editing methods that are available mostly depend on two techniques - changing the colours of sets of pixels, and copying blocks of pixels. An example of the first is the automatic filling of a shape with another colour or pattern. An example of the second is the creation of a mirror-image of an existing shape. The software also offers a range of artistic 'editing' effects like the facility to mix two colours at their boundaries to soften the hard edge.

Photographic retouching

This is a development of paint software, which is designed for manipulating photographs and other scanned images (see Plate 11). This involves scanning images into the computer so that they are stored as a series of coloured pixels, and then making changes to some of those pixels so as to alter the appearance of the picture. This both duplicates and extends the sort of tricks which photographers have traditionally performed on photographs during the printing and developing process to 'improve' the results or to produce interesting artistic effects.

Animation and 3-D

Animation

Using a computer to create animated images is a natural extension of the paint or drawing package. An animated image is only a series of slightly different images, displayed rapidly one after the other. The computer display, like a TV set, does this all the time, even when displaying a perfectly static image (see chapter 3). At the simplest level, animation software allows the artist to draw a series of slightly different images on the screen which are saved and then displayed rapidly in sequence (see Plate 12).

The computer can be used to automate many of the time-consuming, but routine, aspects of this process like filling in areas of colour or generating slightly different versions of an image. Other computer-generated effects include transitions, where one shape gradually changes into a completely different one ('morphing') and geometrical changes like rotation, zooming and panning. Animated images can be displayed on the computer, but more often they are transferred to video tape via a special piece of hardware (see chapter 3). This type of hardware can be designed to work the other way - by transferring video images to the computer and this has led to the development of software which can process images created by a video camera as well as computer-generated ones.

3-D images

All the images so far considered have been two-dimensional (2-D). Strictly speaking, all computer images are 2-D in that they are displayed on a flat screen. Some images, however, are designed to give the illusion of depth using the traditional techniques of the artist, like perspective and shading. Unlike the artist, who uses skill and experience to produce these effects the computer uses a series of calculations, based on the laws of physics. These calculations need a specification of the basic shape of the object, the colour and type of surfaces on the object, their positions in space, the type of illumination and the position of the observer. Based on all these factors, the computer calculates what the object should look like and can generate a highly realistic image, looking just like a photograph, of an object which 'exists' only as a specification in the computer. Plate 13(a) and (b) show two stages in this sequence. Plate 13c shows a more complicated 3-D image. The best 3-D software will also produce animated sequences by generating a series of slightly different images of the objects.

Multimedia   The term 'multimedia system' refers to a system which uses a variety of different media of communication. Micro computers have always had some sort of graphics capability, however crude, and have usually been equipped to produce some limited sounds. What the current fashion for, so-called, multimedia computers really reflects is a growing capacity to produce good-quality graphics, sufficient power and memory to handle digitised video and animation sequences and the addition of good-quality sound systems. The proper integration of these opens up the opportunity to develop software which communicates with the user in a much more exciting way than traditional text with the simple, limited graphics which are all that have been available until recently.

Computer games have long depended for their appeal on exciting, interactive graphics and sound. The impact of multimedia software is bringing that sort of imaginative approach into other areas of application, particularly training and education, reference works and hobbies. Plate 14 shows the opening screen of a multimedia encyclopedia which uses still images, video sequences, animation and sound to supplement the text. Multimedia, in fact, can be seen as an attempt to bring together all the graphics facilities discussed in this book, together with high-quality audio, in the belief that the result will be more than the sum of its parts.

Summary   1 Considerable changes have taken place in recent years in the field of computer graphics. This book describes the whole range of computer graphic applications which are currently available and will help readers choose and use suitable software and hardware to take advantage of these applications.

2 Graphical user interfaces have become the standard method of interaction with a computer. Computer graphics can help to make 'friendly', intuitive interfaces and are making a big contribution to

improving ease of use.

3 Computer drawings can be stored in two different ways -as lines and as dots ('pixels').

4 CAD (computer-aided design) was one of the first major applications of computer graphics. Though designed for engineers, CAD contains many general drawing features which are common to all computer-based drawing packages.

5 Many of these drawing facilities have been incorporated into general-purpose 'illustration software'.

6 The basic facilities of line-based drawing can also be used in other applications - particularly in software designed to produce graphs, charts and attractive text displays for use in business.

7 Computer graphics and line-drawing techniques have been used to extend the facilities of word processing software to the point where publications can be typeset and printed from a desktop computer ('desktop publishing').

8 Pixel-based drawing packages, called paint software, have been developed for the needs of creative artists who wish to use free-hand drawing methods.

9 Special versions of paint software, called photo-retouching packages, are now used to process photographs which have been scanned into the computer.

10 Computer images can be animated using software which helps the artist automate the production of many slightly different versions of the same picture.

11 Highly realistic images with a 3-D appearance can be created. A precise model of the object is stored in the computer and its appearance then calculated by tracing rays of light from imaginary light sources to the viewer's eye, via the processes of reflection and refraction.

12 A convergence of technologies has brought about multimedia systems in which graphics, animation, video and sound are combined to produce games, works of reference and training software.

1 Graphical user interfaces

Key points
- *developments in interface design*
- *styles of software interface*
- *graphical user interfaces (GUIs)*
- *icons, windows and menus*

What is a GUI? It has been argued that since computers left the research laboratory and became commercial products, there have been a whole series of limitations on their usefulness. Each of these limitations had the effect of restricting the practical usefulness of the current generation of computers. This, in turn, imposed limitations on the growth of computer usage and made computers less effective and less productive than they might have been. Whenever one of these limitations was removed by some new development in hardware or software, computers became much more productive for a while, prices effectively fell and further growth occurred until that growth, in turn, ran into the next limiting factor.

Limitations to growth
In the 1960s the limiting factors all related to the immaturity of the hardware which was still in an early stage of development. Memory was very restricted, processors slow, capital and running costs high and reliability unsatisfactory. By the 1970s large strides had taken place in hardware design. The development of solid-state electronics - at first discrete, followed by integrated, circuits - led to increased speed and reliability, larger memories and dropping costs. These developments led to a huge increase in the number of powerful, reliable and affordable machines and that led to an increase in the number of would-be users. The new limitation now became the dearth of users who had the technical skills needed to write the programs necessary to run a computer. The hardware bottleneck had been replaced by the first software bottleneck.

The software bottleneck

The solution to this problem was the development of high-level programming languages which distanced the programmer from the workings of the computer. Programming became an exercise in logic which required a familiarity with the computer language but did not require understanding of how the computer worked. Software could now be produced by non-technical people. In fact, for a time, using a computer became equated in the popular imagination with being a programmer. The use of these languages made it far easier to develop applications programs, like word processors and spreadsheets. These applications, in turn, could be used be people who had no knowledge of computers or even of programming techniques. The development of applications programs led to a further huge rise in the number of potential users (and owners) of computers. These developments were constantly fuelled by falling prices and increasing power, driven by continuing hardware innovation.

New users

It gradually became apparent, however, that this shift in the typical user, from technical to non-technical, was in turn creating a new bottleneck and another check on further growth. The software was still being written by technical people, as if for other technical people and the ordinary user was finding it too difficult to use. Only those who were prepared to invest considerable time in learning computer jargon and complicated procedures were likely to become computer-literate. During the 1980s and the early 1990s, therefore, attention has increasingly turned to the question of ease-of-use and the subject which has come to be called 'human-computer interaction' (HCI). The third bottleneck, therefore, was usability.

Interaction styles   Interaction with a computer, in the earliest days was a very indirect process - called batch-processing. It involved computer programs being entered, in batches, by specialised personnel so that the computer could process each in turn with minimal periods of costly inactivity. It was rather like a mass-production line in which it was important to keep the expensive machines constantly in use. Computer time was expensive and human beings had to wait their turn in order to guarantee maximum return from the investment. The user probably never even saw the computer, let alone operated it. The results of running the program might not be returned until the next day.

Interaction

With more powerful computers it became possible for them to 'time-share'. This meant that, running under a special piece of software, the computer shared its attention between a number of tasks simultaneously, with the result that each user felt that they had constant, sole access to the machine. It was no longer necessary for the user to be subservient to the machine. With the development of the modern CRT display to output results of the computer's activity, it became possible for users to operate the computer themselves in an interactive fashion. The computer responded rapidly to each input and the user could therefore engage in a continuing dialogue.

The command-line

At this stage, input was limited to a typewriter-style keyboard and a monochrome, text-only monitor. The result was that software used a style called the 'command-line interface' (CLI). This meant that instructions (commands) were entered on a single line of the screen, from the keyboard. The appropriate commands had to be learned, as had the exact syntax - the rules which governed the way the commands were used. Figure 1.1 shows a typical DOS command line (DOS is the disk operating system used on most IBM compatible computers). At one time it was not possible to make any kind of intelligent use of a computer without learning at least something of the CLI. This style of interface derived naturally from the style used in programming languages, and seemed perfectly natural to the programmers who wrote the software. To the non-technical user, however, this style of interface was often quite daunting and carried the unspoken message that 'to use a computer you must become a computer expert'.

Figure 1.1. Part of the definition of a typical command used in a command-line interface (CLI)- from Microsoft's MS-DOS operating system.

Copy Command (MS-DOS)

Function :

copies one or more files to the specified location.

Syntax :

Copy [/Y] [/-Y] [/A] [/B] source [/A] [/B] [+ source [/A I /B] [+ ...]] [destination [/A I/B]] [/V]

The current situation

Three developments have changed all that. First, technical improvements in displays, input devices and the processing power of the computer have made it possible to generate, at a reasonable cost, high-quality colour images in real-time. This has liberated the interaction style from the narrow confines of monochrome text. High quality, colour images of all kinds can be rapidly generated.

Second, creative thinking about what makes a system easy to learn, and use, have stimulated an enormous amount of interest in the processes of human-computer interaction. All manner of inventive interaction styles have been tried and much thought has gone into what makes a 'user-friendly' system. It is no longer felt necessary to shroud the whole process in mystery and obscure jargon.

Last, commercial competitive pressures to sell systems to the ordinary man and woman in the street have made it imperative to offer easy-to-learn software. For the computer to become a commodity item like a video recorder it has become essential that operating it must be made simple, non-threatening and even entertaining. A related commercial factor is the increase in the sophistication of software packages. There has been a process of adding more and more functions to software in order to stay ahead of the competition. This has produced the situation where, for example, any one of a dozen word processing packages will do all (in fact, more) than the ordinary user will ever want them to do. When this happens, software for many users no longer sells on its technical specification, which is more than adequate for any real task. What sells the software at this point is ease-of-use rather than obscure features which the user will never want.

Interface styles

The menu

The first step towards a better interface was the menu system. One of the main problems of the command style was that the user had to remember what commands were available - as well as remembering what they did. This was not helped by the fact that early software designers seemed to revel in unnecessary obscurity. The user might guess what the command COPY did, but how on earth could they be expected to guess what the command GREP (used in Unix) might do? The answer, of course, was to be very careful in choosing the names of commands so that their meaning could be guessed, or at least, easily remembered once explained. That still required the user to commit time to the learning process and if the software was used infrequently it was all too easy to forget them again. The idea of the menu was a disarmingly simple solution. Put all the commands or choices which are open to the user on the screen and let the user recognise and choose, instead of having to remember. Figure 1.2 shows a simple, imaginary, one-screen menu system. This sort of system also reduced the amount of typing, since choice could often be achieved by a single keystroke. This also meant an increase in speed. A third benefit was that reduced typing meant fewer typing errors, a big benefit for the amateur, one-finger typist which many users are.

Simple systems The beauty of this style of interface was that it could be implemented on a monochrome text-only display. At its simplest level a menu consists of a number of separate option lines of text on the screen, each with its reference number or letter. To choose an option, the user simply types the appropriate number or letter. The problem with this simple version of the system is that the user is restricted to a small number of commands. To offer more commands it is necessary to have more than one screen-full, and to provide the user with a simple method of finding their way to the right screen. The best way of doing this is to group commands together in some easily-understood fashion and to use the first screen menu to offer access to the other screens. It is also necessary to offer a way of returning from the secondary screens to the first screen. As monochrome text-only screens gave way to colour graphical systems it became possible to use more sophisticated

Figure 1.2. An elementary, text-based, menu system. The user makes a choice by typing a number from the keyboard and pressing the 'Return' or 'Enter' key.

> **'SimpleText'**
>
> **Choose one of the following :**
>
> **1. Create New Text File**
>
> **2. Edit Existing Text File**
>
> **3. Save Current File**
>
> **4. Print Current File**
>
> **5. Delete File**
>
> **6. Change Printer Set-Up**
>
> **7. Change Simple Text Defaults**
>
> **8. Exit**

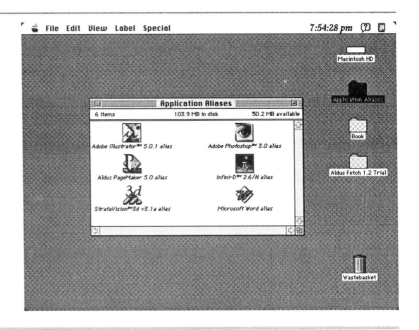

Figure 1.3. The Apple Macintosh graphical user interface (GUI).

menu systems which are described later.

Direct interaction

Graphical screens of steadily-improving quality opened up a whole new world of possibilities. It became feasible to think in terms of images instead of words. What has now become labelled the 'graphical user-interface'(GUI) was pioneered at the Xerox Company's Palo Alto Research Centre in the USA. Their ideas were successfully marketed on a big scale for the first time in the Apple Lisa and Macintosh computers. More recently, similar styles of interface have spread to other computer systems. The essence of the GUI is that words are replaced by pictures, wherever possible, and that actions are specified directly rather than indirectly. Figure 1.3 shows the Apple Mac desktop display with a 'window' open. This

Figure 1.4. Files and folder icons in the Macintosh GUI. The file icon represents a piece of paper, with the top right-hand corner turned down. The folder icon represents a cardboard folder with a name tab at the top left.

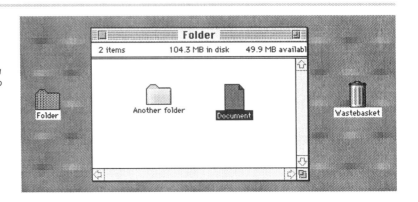

window (called 'Application Aliases') contains six small pictures, 'icons'). All windows look similar to this; their functions are discussed in more detail later on. This window sits on the 'desktop' which has five other, much simpler icons, sitting on it also.

Figure 1.5. Groups of icons, assembled into 'toolboxes' (taken from Aldus PageMaker, Adobe Illustrator and Adobe Photoshcp). A toolbox is a collection of software utilities, each of which can be activated by clicking the appropriate icon.

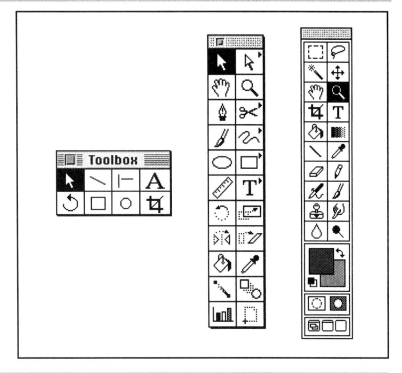

Icons Currently the limitations of the display and the restrictions on processing power mean that the pictures which are used can only be very simplified, stylised, representations of the objects - called icons. The principle, however, is that an object is represented by a picture rather than a word. In the Apple operating system (see Figure 1.4) a file - like a word processor document - is represented by a simple rectangle, with the corner 'folded'. This icon looks rather like a sheet of paper and has an obvious relationship to the object it represents. As in other operating environments, files are organised into groups. In conventional interfaces these groups are called 'sub-directories'. Here they are represented by a rectangular icon - oriented in landscape mode - with a tab at the top corner and called a 'folder'. The theory is that anyone familiar with a traditional office knows what a document or a cardboard folder looks like. Even if the user doesn't initially guess what the symbols represent they are very easy to remember, once their meaning has been explained.

Figure 1.5 shows another use for icons. Here, icons have been brought together to form three 'toolboxes' - taken from three different pieces of software. A toolbox is a collection of icons, each of which represents a tool - a useful utility which enables the user to perform a task. The magnifying glass is easily recognised; it is used to magnify the picture. The hand is used to move a picture or a block of text. The paint tin is used to 'pour' colour into an empty space. The scissors are used to cut off part of a picture. Other much-used icons are the watch (or egg-timer) to represent the passage of time and the wastebasket to represent the act of disposal.

The word used to represent this philosophy of interface design is 'metaphor'. A picture of an easily-recognised object represents some object or function in the computer. In this case, an 'office' metaphor is being used. The screen presents a desktop, of the sort which is found in an office. The desktop is covered with the sort of objects which are commonly found in offices (though, strictly speaking, the wastebasket is not usually kept there!).

Metaphors It is not only objects which are represented visually in the metaphor, but actions also. The designers try to find ways of representing familiar actions using icons. This needs a more natural interactive medium than a typewriter keyboard and the mouse was invented to allow the user to point at objects on the screen and to move them about. The user, with the aid of a pointing device like a mouse, manipulates the icons in a way that feels intuitive and doesn't have to be learned because the actions are already familiar. In every way the philosophy is : 'Don't make the user learn anything that is not strictly necessary. Use their existing knowledge and skills'.

Comparison with the CLI In a command-line interface, the user needs not only to learn the name of appropriate commands but, probably, quite a lot of jargon in order to understand the manual which has been written to explain those commands. Take the example of the simple act of getting rid of some information which the user has saved but no longer needs to keep - the equivalent, in a real office, of throwing away a piece of paper. The user must first learn that when computer information is saved on disc it is called 'a file'. They must learn that when files are given names, with the most popular make of business computer (the IBM-PC), there are very restrictive rules about how those names are created. They must learn that files are stored in a 'sub-directory', on a disc. They must learn how disc drives are named. Finally they must learn that the command for scrapping a file is called DEL and the syntax of that command is:

DEL c:\subdir\file.ext.

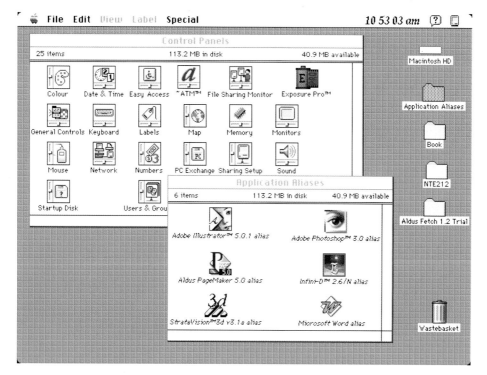

Plate 1. The Apple Macintosh graphical user interface (GUI).

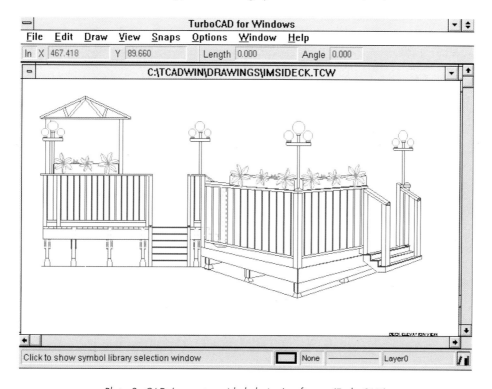

Plate 2. CAD (computer aided design) software (TurboCAD).

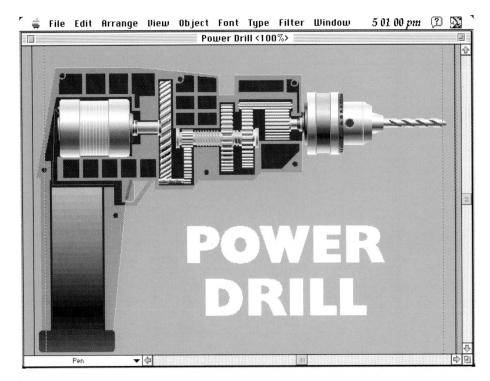

Plate 3. (a) Drawing of a drill created using vector software (Adobe illustrator).

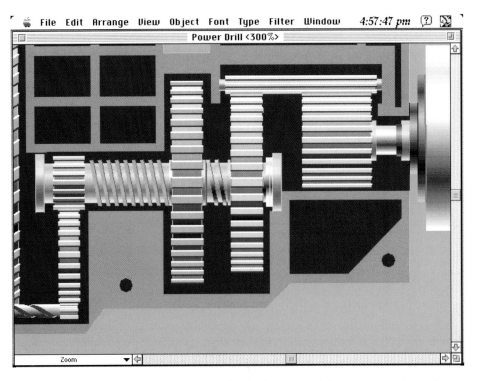

(b) Part of (a), magnified to show more detail. The quality of the image is unchanged.

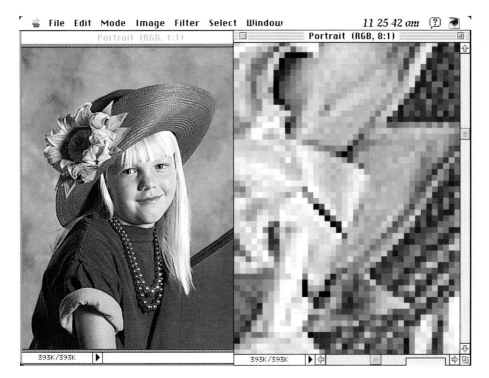

Plate 4. A scanned image (taken from Adobe Photoshop), with a small portion much magnified - showing the individual pixels.

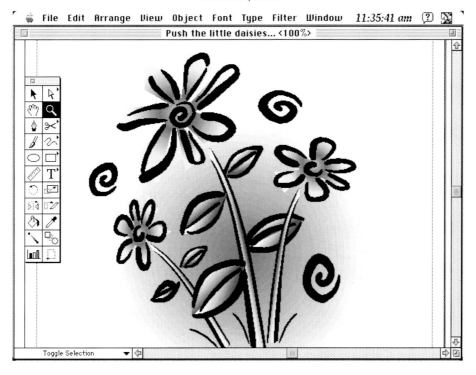

Plate 5. Illustration software (Adobe Illustrator).

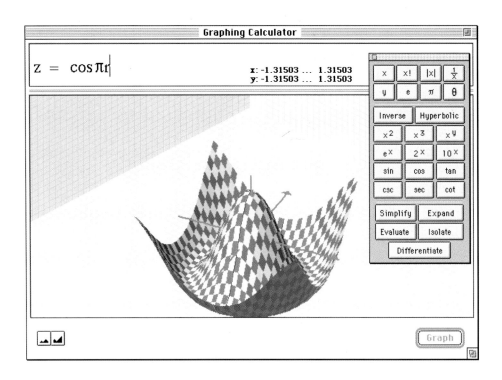

Plate 6. Scientific graphing software (provided with the Apple Power Mac) - a 3-D plot of a mathematical function.

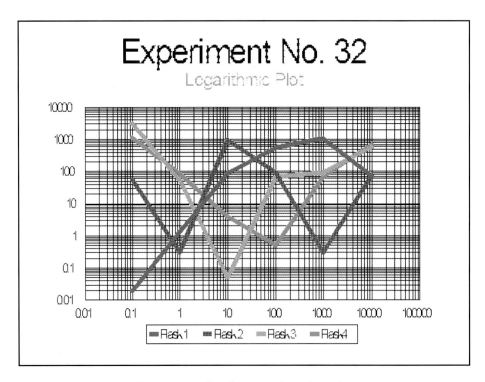

Plate 7. Scientific software - a logarithmic plot.

Sales figures (1993/4)

with details for north-east region

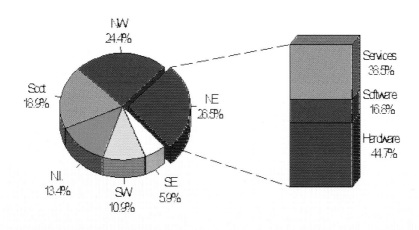

Plate 8. Business presentation software (Harvard Graphics).

Plate 9. Desktop publishing software (PageMaker).

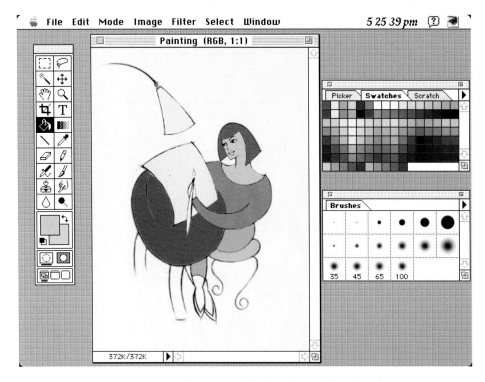

Plate 10. Painting software, used for sketching (Adobe Photoshop).

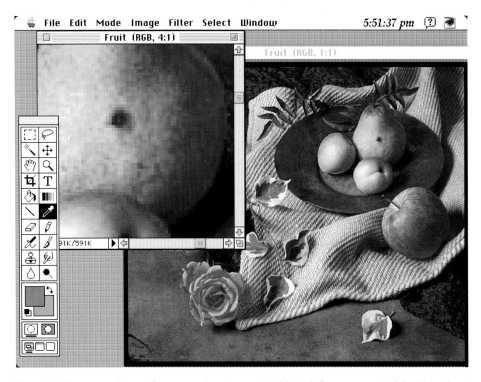

Plate 11. Photo-retouching software, used to 'remove' a blemish from a pear (Adobe Photoshop).

Plate 12. Six images from an animation sequence (taken from Animator Pro).

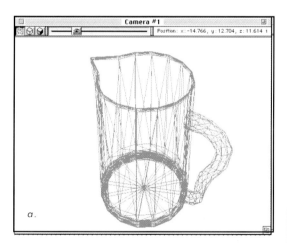

Plate 13. (a) A wire-frame image of a jug. (b) The rendered version of image (a). - both taken from Strata Vision 3d.

Plate 13. (c) A more complicated rendered image from Stata Vision 3d.

Plate 14. The opening screen of a multimedia encyclopedia (The Software Toolworks).

The Apple GUI In contrast, with the Apple Mac interface, the file is called a document (if it is a text file) and represented by an icon which looks like a document. It is kept in a 'folder' which looks like the sort of cardboard folder which is kept in a filing cabinet. It is deleted by simply dragging the icon of the document, out of its folder, over to the wastebasket (another icon). Using your hand to pick something up and take to the waste-bin is an act we all know how to do. Figure 1.6 a and b show a file being dragged to a wastebasket, and the state of the wastebasket afterwards.

Other metaphors The office metaphor is not the only one which can be used. Objects from many walks of life can be turned into icons. We are all familiar with the sliding volume controls used on stereo systems. In icon form, this can be used to change the value of any software variable such as contrast, colour or number of pages - as an alternative to typing in a numerical value from the keyboard. The mouse is used to drag the slide along a scale between the minimum and maximum values. A digital read-out can be used to display the result in numbers, also, if it is important to quantify the variable being changed. Figure 1.7 shows the metaphor of slider-bars applied to creating a colour from four components.

A watch icon with moving hands, or an hourglass icon with sand trickling through it, can both be used as metaphors of the passage of time. They mean: 'Please wait - this will take a little time'. A dial with a moving hand, or a moving line like the mercury in a thermometer, can be used to illustrate how far some activity has progressed and how long it is going to take to complete. Other metaphors include a palette of colours like a child's paint box into which

Figure 1.6 (a). A document icon is dragged towards the empty wastebasket. (b). As soon as the document icon is on top of the wastebasket icon the mouse button is released and the icon disappears 'into' it. This is indicated by the wastebasket bulging to show that it contains 'rubbish'. The file is not actually deleted from the disc until the wastebasket is emptied. Until then the 'rubbish' can be recovered, if necessary.

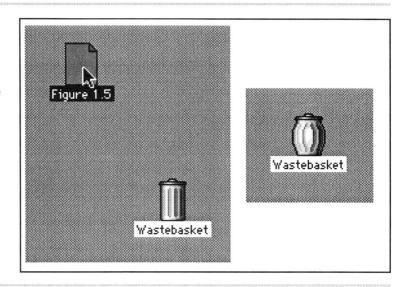

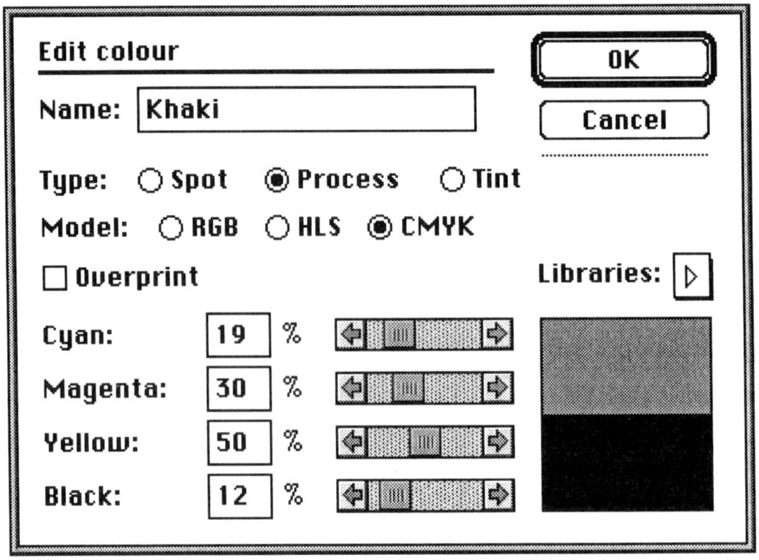

Figure 1.7. Four slider bars are used in this dialogue box (part of Aldus PageMaker) to specify a colour. Each bar can be dragged, independently of the others, to change one of the four components of the colour (cyan, magenta, yellow and black).

the user dips a paintbrush (by clicking with the mouse) or a selection of tools in a toolbox (see Figure 1.5), from which the user chooses an appropriate tool for a particular job.

Direct interaction   When the user drags a document icon to a wastebasket icon the activity is sometimes called 'direct interaction' because the user feels as if they are directly performing the task, and not operating a computer. When, in DTP software, the user drags a representation of a scanned photograph from one place on the page to another it feels very like performing the equivalent task of physically moving a real photograph. When 'balloon help' is used in the Macintosh operating environment the user simply points to an object on the screen and a cartoon-like speech bubble appears, which explains what the function of that object is. It is as if the computer is explaining something, as a person might when someone points to an object they are unfamiliar with.

No new 'computer skills' are needed. It is the first stage towards a form of 'virtual reality' where the user feels they are living in a real world. In fact, the computer is beginning to fade into the background. It is becoming the best of tools, one which is such a natural extension of the hand and eye that its existence is forgotten. The best tools are hardly noticed. Bad tools draw attention to themselves because they cause problems and frustration.

Windows
One of the major restrictions to the development of the GUI is the size and quality of the screen. The standard screen is about the

same size as an A4 sheet of paper. The standard quality, measured in resolution, is about 60-70 dots per inch. When compared with an office desk, in the office metaphor, it looks woefully inadequate. My office desk can hold about 20 A4 sheets of paper, without them overlapping each other, and many more if they overlap. The quality of the text on those sheets of paper is at least 300 dots per inch and in many cases much better. There is simply no comparison in the total information content of the two systems, and paper and desks are cheap! The major advantage of the computer system, of course, lies in the quantity of information which can be stored, the speed of retrieval and the capacity to process it in a vast range of ways. It would be nice, however, if the computer's ability to display in could be improved. That is where windowing software comes in.

Multiple windows
However big a desk, most of us end up with pieces of paper overlapping each other, so that we can see part of each sheet - just enough to recognise it and bring it to the top of the pile when needed. This is what a window in a GUI does. A window is a rectangular area of the display in which part of a document, or any other file, can be seen. Multiple windows can be created - just like sheets of paper - overlapping each other or placed side-by-side like tiles on a wall. Any window can be brought to the top of the pile instantly, simply by clicking the mouse on any part of it which can be seen. As a result some of the restrictions of small screens can be overcome. Figure 1.8 shows a number of windows overlapping each other.

Figure 1.8. Three overlapping windows in the Macintosh GUI. The 'active' window is always shown as being on top of the pile.

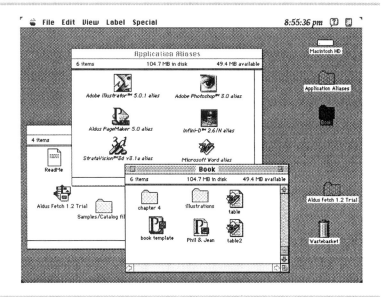

How to use windowing software

Scrolling windows

The first set of conventions which must be learned is how to handle windows. Windows have a number of standard components: a title bar at the top, scroll-bars at the side and bottom and minimise buttons. Figure 1.9 shows these components. In some systems the scroll bars will only be shown if they are needed - that is if the window is too small to show all of its contents. In the Apple Mac GUI the scroll bars are darkened if this is the case. In fact the name -window - suggests the fact that the view of a window's contents is often restricted. Frequently only part of it can be seen, just like someone looking out of a window on to the world outside. If other parts of the content are to be viewed in the window then it must be scrolled. Scrolling is very like the action of unrolling one end (and rolling up the other end) of a parchment scroll so that different parts of the text come into view. Unlike parchment scrolls, GUI windows can scroll in two dimensions.

Scrolling is done in one of three ways. One is by dragging at the small rectangular icon on the scroll-bar, which acts like the slider on a slide-bar. (If all the contents of the window are visible, these slider 'knobs' are not displayed). The position of the slider represents the position of the window with respect to the whole document. This is the quickest way of making large changes in position. The second way is by clicking on either side of the slider, which makes it scroll one screen at a time. The most sensitive way is by clicking on the arrows at either end of the bars, which scrolls it one line at a time.

Figure 1.9. A window has been reduced to such a size that some of its contents can no longer be seen. The scroll-bars can be used to move (scroll) the contents of the window so that different parts of it can be seen.

Closing and moving windows

Unlike a real window, a computer window can be moved and re-sized. It can be reduced in size by dragging at the bottom right-hand corner or, in some systems, by dragging at the sides of the window. Clicking on a button placed at the top right-hand corner of the window will reduce it to its original size (assuming it has been enlarged). Clicking on a button at the top left will close the window altogether - reducing it to an icon. To restore the window again, the icon must be double-clicked which will restore it to its original size and position. If the window is in an inconvenient position, it can be moved, by dragging it, using the title bar. Windows can be made to overlap by dragging one on top of another. If any portion of a window, which is covered, is still visible it can be brought to the top of the pile by a single click anywhere in that visible portion. Otherwise the covering windows must be dragged aside or a pop-up menu system used to select the window which is desired.

Menus

The same basic idea of the window has been applied to the menu to give it a new lease of life in the GUI. What had, in the text-only menu been a page of choices, is hidden in a menu title at the top of the screen. A row of these menu headings (called a menu bar) can be fitted along the top of the screen without taking up too much room. Some systems use a vertical menu bar down the side of the screen. When a choice is to be made from one of these menus, the user clicks the heading with the mouse and a small window pops down. Figure 1.10 shows one of the menu items, pulled down, and the user choosing the 'Open' option. In the Apple Mac GUI the menu only stays down as long as the mouse-button is held down. This is a pull-down menu. The menu is rather like a spring-back roller blind which can be pulled down when wanted but flies up again as soon as it is released. When a choice has been made from the menu it automatically disappears, leaving only the menu heading. Although it is usually described in these terms - as a roller blind - it can be seen that it illustrates the same philosophy as a window, being reduced to an icon and being restored when wanted. Menu choices can give rise to other menus (see Figure 1.11) and there is no reason why the process cannot be repeated many times but in practice it is usually considered too confusing and time-consuming to have more than about two sub-menus.

The WIMP system

The modern GUI usually uses all these graphical devices - direct interaction, icons, windows and menus. It is sometimes termed a

*Figure 1.10. A 'pull-down' menu in
the Macintosh GUI. The user is in the
act of choosing the 'Open' option
with the mouse and so its title is
displayed in 'reverse' or 'inverse'
video (the black and white parts
are reversed or inverted).*

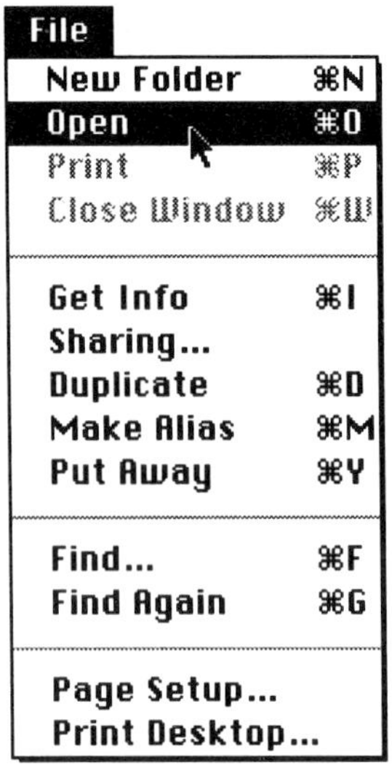

File	
New Folder	⌘N
Open	⌘O
Print	⌘P
Close Window	⌘W
Get Info	⌘I
Sharing...	
Duplicate	⌘D
Make Alias	⌘M
Put Away	⌘Y
Find...	⌘F
Find Again	⌘G
Page Setup...	
Print Desktop...	

WIMP system - Windows Icons Menus Pointer. Some people think that WIMP stands for Windows Icons Mouse Pull-down menus, but it is much the same! The important point is that the techniques of computer graphics are being used to improve the quality of computer interfaces and change the appearance of computer software. This use of computer graphics has led to the superficial assumption that improving the design of the human-computer interface and the use of graphics are one and the same thing. This clearly is not so. It is possible to design a poor interface which is brimming with every graphic gimmick in the book. It is equally possible to design a good interface for some applications which make no use of graphics. Nevertheless computer graphics offers an invaluable resource to the interface designer and I believe that future improvements - like more realistic images, video, sound and 3-D capabilities - will offer even more scope.

Software packages The pioneering work on GUIs was done by **Xerox** in their **Star** interface but the first commercially successful exploitation of this design was in the **Apple Macintosh** operating system interface - now called **System 7**. This software is an integral part of all Macintosh computers. A number of attempts have been made over the years to emulate the success of the Macintosh GUI for PC compatibles but all except **Windows (Microsoft)** or the two derivatives of Windows, have either disappeared or become minor players in the field.

Windows is currently a 'front-end' to the DOS operating system, and is therefore optional for users of PC compatibles in a way that System 7 is not. However, most PC compatibles are supplied with a copy of Windows and a high proportion of new software is designed to run under Windows, so for many users Windows has become obligatory. The time will come soon when the interface is fully integrated into DOS as it is in the Mac. The two Windows derivatives, referred to above, are the GUIs which are used by Microsoft in its other operating system **Windows-NT** and by IBM in its PC operating system **OS/2.**

Good GUIs, based on similar principles, have been developed by other computer manufacturers, for example those used in the **Acorn Archimedes**, **Commodore Amiga** and the **Next** work-station. The latter is an example of an excellent GUI-based operating system which has survived the demise of the original computer and is now being offered in a version for PC compatibles. Another link between microcomputers and work-stations and other more powerful systems is called **X.** This was designed to give a uniform GUI which would run on a wide range of computers and is widely used on Unix systems. A commercial version **DESQview/X** is available for PCs. Another approach -that of trying to improve Windows - has been followed by **Hewlett Packard**. Their **New Wave** runs in conjunction with Windows, adding extra facilities to it and presenting the user with an 'improved' interface.

Finally, Xerox, the pioneers have not run out of ideas. They have developed a number of 3-D style graphical interfaces including one based on a series of 'rooms' connected by doors. It remains to be seen if any of these ideas become a standard as their Star design has.

Figure 1.11. A secondary menu, being chosen from the primary menu, in Aldus PageMaker. The existence of a secondary menu is indicated by a small black triangle at the end of a line, pointing to the position where the second menu will appear.

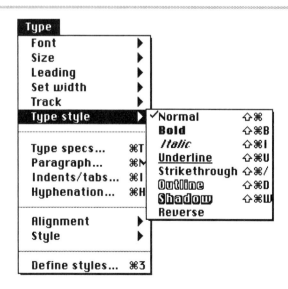

23

Summary

1 It has been proposed that growth in the use of computers has always been held back by one of a series of hardware and software problems, the latest of which has been the difficulty in devising easy-to-use interfaces.

2 There have been a number of different styles of software interface, which can be seen to relate to the historical stage of development at which they were devised.

3 The modern graphical user interface (GUI) was pioneered by the Xerox company in their Star interface - and then developed commercially in the Apple Mac computer.

4 One of the main advantages of the direct-interaction style of interface is that it helps users bring their existing skills to the problem of computer operation.

5 Computer graphics is of crucial importance in the modern GUI since it consists of a number of graphic objects which are manipulated in a standardised manner.

6 The most important graphic object in a GUI is the 'window'. It has been used in a variety of ways to solve the major problem of a severely-restricted working space on computer display systems.

7 A very important concept, used in the GUI, is the 'visual metaphor'. The first, but not the only example, is the Apple Mac office metaphor.

Basic theory

Key points
- *the importance of theory*
- *the basic terminology of computer graphics*
- *how text and graphics are stored in a computer*
- *image compression*

Why theory? This book is about the practice of computer graphics - what can be done and how to do it. It is, however, often valuable, even when tackling the most mundane of problems, to have some grasp of the underlying theory of what you are trying to do. Most of us are only motivated to grapple with abstract ideas when we can see the necessity for them - in the immediate context of a problem. For that reason, wherever possible, the concepts of the subject are developed in this book as the need arises.

However, some basic ideas are common to all areas of the subject and these are best introduced as soon as possible. That is the purpose of this chapter. Nevertheless, there will be some readers who would question whether any theory is needed for those who simply want to use the computer as a tool. For those, let it be said that there are four very good reasons why even the most pragmatic computer user will benefit from some understanding of the underlying ideas of the subject.

Ease-of-learning
First, it is much easier to learn (and relearn) to use any system if the user understands what is happening. Without an understanding of the underlying concepts of a piece of computer software or of a set of computer hardware, learning can only be by rote - 'first do this, then do that', and so on. If your memory is less than perfect then, when you forget how to do something, there is nothing for it but continual reference to the manual. If there is no mental 'model' of the system there is no way to work out a sensible approach to achieving a desired result. With understanding, on the other hand, and with a well designed, intuitive software interface,

learning a new system and, just as important, returning to it and relearning after a period of time, is far easier and much less discouraging.

Easier problem solving

Second, it makes problem solving much easier. This is closely related to the first point. Every computer user, however expert, has known the discouraging experience of running into problems which don't seem to be covered in the manual. The output from the printer doesn't look like the screen display or the help system 'explains' something using jargon which the user doesn't understand. Solving problems of this sort can sometimes be impossible without expert help and can waste an enormous amount of time if the user has no real understanding of the underlying principles of the subject.

Informed choice

Third, users are in a far better position to choose the right tools for a job - hardware and software - if they have a basic understanding of what is needed for a particular purpose. The user is much less likely to be seduced by the latest fashion and much more likely to buy the right tool for the purpose.

Keeping up-to-date

Fourth, users are better able to follow developments in what is a fast-changing field and less likely to be committed to computer systems which are obsolescent or to miss newly-emerging industry standards.

What sort of practical questions, then, might a user ask which can only be answered with some understanding of the principles of computer graphics? First, as in any subject, it is necessary to master the jargon:

- what is a pixel?
- what is a palette?
- what is a scalable font?
- what is a bit-mapped font?
- what is dithering?

Some of these questions only need a good glossary but others require more than definitions; they need the development of a set of ideas. When those ideas are grasped it becomes possible to move onto broader, more practical questions :

- why does it take so much longer for a printer to print a graphic than a page of Courier text?
- is there any way of speeding it up?
- what is the value of a large (and expensive) monitor?
- why is it so difficult to get a good colour printout of a computer graphic image?
- why does a laser-printer copy of a black and white image look so much better than the same image on the screen?

This chapter establishes a groundwork of ideas and definitions which will be used throughout the rest of the book.

Pixels and vectors
To begin it is necessary to discuss the way that images are stored in a computer. Most people will accept the idea that a computer can store and manipulate numbers, because they still think of computers as number-crunching machines, even though they have no idea how this is done in practice. It is much less obvious how a glorified pocket calculator could store and process images. How, for instance, does the picture get 'into' the computer and how is it stored in the memory or saved on a disc? The output process is less obviously a problem because we are so familiar with the basic technology - the computer monitor looks just like a television set. In fact the analogy is a little misleading because, unlike a computer system, a television set does not store or process the images it displays. It merely acts as a channel for them, as they are continuously picked up by the aerial.

Understanding how an image can be coded for storage in a computer makes it much easier to describe how images can then be displayed on a computer screen and printed on a computer printer. It also provides the basis for a discussion on the way that images can be created (rather than simply manipulated) by a computer.

There are in fact two fundamentally different ways of describing an image in a way that a computer can handle: as a series of lines or as a series of dots. The first is called a 'vector' description and the second a raster, or bit-mapped or dot-matrix description. In the introduction, vector images were also referred to as 'line-images'. Each of them has its own particular advantages and disadvantages and it is often necessary to use both. This usually involves converting an image from one description to the other (called 'scan-conversion' in one direction and 'tracing' in the other).

Vector images
The method that was first used to store images in computers was dictated, in part, by the very small amount of memory available for that purpose. Images were treated as a series of lines, some straight, some curved (see Figure 2.1). Because most of the lines

Figure 2.1. 'Vector' images (taken from Adobe Illustrator). They are defined, mathematically, as a set of straight lines and curves.

that were needed could be represented by relatively simple mathematical equations it was possible to store this information very economically. For example, to specify a straight line all that is needed is a knowledge of the positions of the two end-points of the line. For display purposes the line can then be reconstructed, knowing its geometrical properties. Similarly, for a circle all that is needed is a knowledge of its centre and its radius.

The display and printing devices used at the time were suitable only for this type of diagrammatic line image (for example, maps, engineering and architects' drawings and graphs). Modern computer graphics systems, which are capable of displaying and printing realistic photographic-quality images, needed the development of new technologies - a process which is still continuing.

The advantages of vectors
There were, however, two fundamental advantages to this approach, which still hold good today. One has been mentioned already: relatively small amounts of memory are needed to store such images. This is because most of the information is implicit in the equation which describes their shape. All circles are the same except for two small differences : their size (measured by the radius) and their position (measured by the location of the centre). All straight lines are the same, except for the positions of their two end points (or, to put it another way, the slope, the position of one end and the length). These individual differences can be coded and stored very economically.

The second advantage of vector images is that it is possible to manipulate them in the computer in a wide variety of ways without any loss of final image-quality. For example, in a line-drawing package, a well-defined shape can be stretched, enlarged or rotated

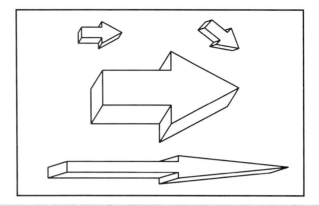

Figure 2.2. A vector image of an arrow - taken from Adobe Illustrator - has been copied three times, and each copy then edited. One has been rotated, another enlarged and a third stretched - all without any significant loss of quality.

to produce an image which is of the same high quality as the original (see Figure 2.2). In a desktop publishing package, so-called 'scalable' fonts can be manipulated in a similar way. Scalable fonts are fonts which are stored in the computer by means of a mathematical description of the shape of the lines which make up each letter. Individual characters, of any required size, are generated from that basic description when needed. As a result, each character, of whatever size, can be displayed at the maximum quality which the display is capable of. In contrast, the quality of pixel-based images of characters, or anything else, will suffer considerably when magnified - as described in the next section.

Pixel images   The alternative approach to storing an image is to define it as an array of dots or 'pixels' (picture-elements). This is the equivalent of placing a fine rectangular grid (like graph paper) over an image and then recording the contents of each cell in the grid. What is measured, depends on the type of image and the degree of sophistication employed in the recording process.

In the case of a two-tone monochrome image (for example a black

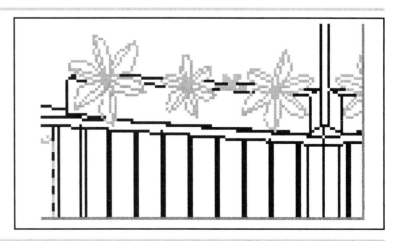

Figure 2.3. A portion of a bit-mapped image (part of Plate 2, taken from IMSI TurboCAD) which has been enlarged. The individual pixels are plainly visible.

and white line-drawing, like a newspaper cartoon) all that is recorded is whether the cell is predominantly black or white (see Figure 2.3). The phrase 'predominantly black or white' has to be used because in many cases the cell will cover a region where there is both black and white, and the cell has to be counted as one or the other.

This process inevitably leads to a reduction in the quality of the image since some of the fine detail of the original picture has been lost. If, for example, the cell was mainly black the small amount of white is effectively lost by this process. This degradation of the image in the 'sampling' process can be reduced by making the cells smaller and, as a consequence, increasing their number. This means that there will be less chance of cells being a mixture of black and white. It also means that when they are, less information is thrown away. This type of degradation of the image will disappear only when the cell is no larger than the smallest detail in the original image. An image which is stored as a very large number of pixels - which contains a large amount of detail - is said to be a high-resolution image. The term 'resolution', derived from the word resolve, is used to indicate the capacity of the system to store or reveal fine details.

Halftones
In the case of a halftone monochrome image (like a black and white photograph) it is the grey-level in each cell which is measured (effectively, the amount of white light reflected from the surface, if

Figure 2.4 (a). A photograph which has been scanned to produce a grey-level bit-mapped image. (b) The enlarged view of the central portion shows the pixels very clearly. The original image appears in the Software Toolworks Multimedia Encyclopedia (see chapter 8).

a   b

the original is a print) - see Figure 2.4 a and b. In the case of a coloured image it is the colour in each cell which is measured (see Plate 6). In both cases more memory is needed to store the image because bigger numbers are needed. This is because there are more possibilities. In the first example, the only possibilities were 'black' or 'white'. In the second example there might be, say, 16 possibilities, corresponding to 16 different values of grey (so-called 'grey-levels') which can be measured in a cell. In the third case there could be thousands of possibilities corresponding to thousands of different colours. The more possibilities there are, the larger the range of numbers which is needed to code for them, and the more memory is needed.

Whichever way it is done, the advantage of this type of process is that it matches the predominant modern imaging technology - television - very conveniently. Television systems create and display images by a process of scanning. This involves the regular sampling of the original image by means of a large number of closely-packed parallel lines, which encodes the information electrically. This data is then transmitted to a receiver which reconstitutes the image by reversing the process. Pixel-based images simply take this process one step further by splitting up the scan lines into separate dots (the pixels). A computer therefore can store an image as a set of pixel values - a sequence of numbers representing the colours or grey-level values of each dot.

Storage and display Given that there are two ways of storing images - vector and pixel - it is necessary to discuss the connection between each of them and the display systems. There are in fact four variables to consider: the two image-coding methods and the two hardware-determined computer processes, storage and display. Images cannot only be stored in two different ways, they can be displayed in two different ways also. This means that in principle there must be four possible combinations of storage and display:

- vector storage and vector display
- pixel storage and pixel display
- vector storage and pixel display
- pixel storage and vector display

Early systems
The first combination was the first to be used in the pioneering days of computer graphics, but is now obsolete. Vector storage was used because of the small amounts of computer memory available. Images were also displayed as vectors on modified oscilloscopes in which the lines were drawn directly on the screen. This system

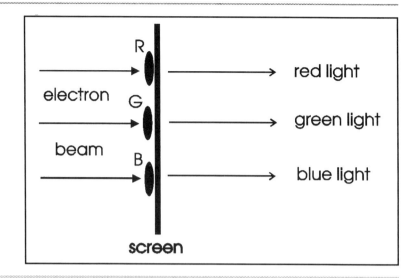

was capable of producing very high-quality line images and has been used extensively for engineering CAD (computer-aided design). Some systems may still be in use.

Raster systems

The second and third combinations have now become the standard methods, both using raster-scan monitors, based on television technology, in which the scan-lines are divided into a fixed number of pixels (as briefly described in an earlier section). The raster technique is explained in more detail in the next chapter. For the purposes of this discussion it is enough to say that raster lines are a series of closely-packed horizontal lines which are used to create an image. A raster-scan monitor creates these lines by sweeping an electron beam rapidly across the face of a television tube. As the beam is turned on and off it creates dots (pixels) on the screen. The picture is the sum total of all these dots.

Pixel storage is used when the images are, in large part, created by the user by hand, using a mouse or graphic tablet (as in a Paintbrush package) or scanned from an original drawing or photograph using some type of document scanner. Vector storage is used when images are created by the computer from graphics 'primitives' - basic shapes like rectangles and circles (as in drawing packages) - or using scalable fonts (as in desktop publishing packages).

Vector software

In this, third, case (vector storage and pixel display) a conversion process is required every time an image is retrieved from memory for display on the screen (or, for that matter, printed on most printers). This conversion from a vector to a scan-based, pixel, display is called scan-conversion. Some of the delay involved in the updating of certain complex images is caused by the time involved in this process. The reverse process - converting from a pixel-based image to a vector description - is also possible. Some drawing packages offer a tracing facility in which each of the separate lines in a scanned pixel-based image is fitted to a mathematical formula and then stored in vector form.

The fourth possibility - pixel storage and vector display - has never been implemented. This theoretical possibility of storing an image as a bit-map and displaying it on a vector-display should not, therefore, be confused with the process of tracing bit-mapped images in order to convert them into vector images. Both these forms of image are now displayed on raster systems. Vector hardware displays are, in any case, obsolete. They were specialised devices which were developed before the cheap, large-scale memory, on which pixel images depend, became available.

Colours and grey-levels So far we have looked at the basic process of coding an image so that it can be stored in a computer system. It is essential, however, than we can also see the image and for this a display device is needed. It is important also to be able to produce a 'hard' copy (a copy printed on paper). The next chapter provides a review of the basic principles and characteristics of these devices. Here it is necessary only to examine a few basic principles involved in these processes, particularly in the context of the way that colour and grey-levels are handled.

Emissive and reflective images There are two different ways of producing images - one is based on the generation (or emission) of light and is used in most television sets and computer displays. The other is based on the absorption and reflection of light and forms the basis of printed images.

Emissive images
In the case of a conventional computer monitor, which in most essentials works like a television set, an internal high-energy electron beam is fired at, and absorbed in, a special phosphor which then emits light (see Figure 2.5a). In the case of the flat-panel displays used in portable computers the details are different - the light is generated in conventional fashion at the back of the panel and then selectively transmitted through liquid crystals. Sometimes the back light is replaced by reflected ambient light. In the case of gas-plasma displays the light is generated by tiny cells of glowing fluorescent gas. In all of these methods, however, it is possible to alter the brightness of a pixel by arranging to generate or transmit more

or less light at that point on the image. The individual pixels, in other words, can be set to any one of a number of different intensities rather like an electric light fitted with a dimmer switch. This is used to produce a range of grey-levels in a monochrome image or a range of colours in a coloured image.

Absorptive images
In the case of printed images the principles are quite different. Most printing processes involve putting large numbers of tiny dots of coloured ink on the paper. These dots do not emit light. They act as preferential absorbers of the room lighting in which they are viewed (see Figure 2.5b). This light normally contains within it a full spectrum of colour components. This means that the perceived colour

Figure 2.5 (b). White light (the 'ambient' light or normal illumination provided by sunlight or artificial light) is partially absorbed and reflected from the three primary coloured inks.

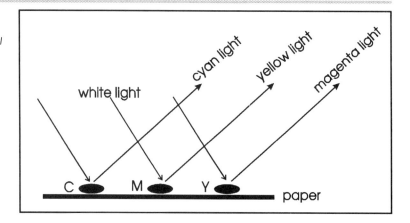

of the ink is actually the colour of the light which enters the eye of the viewer after being absorbed and reflected by those inks. In this process some of the original colour components of the white light are absorbed and lost. This is said to be a subtractive process because the inks selectively remove certain wavelengths from light, which originally had all possible (visible) wavelengths.

For example, red ink is a substance which absorbs the non-red components of white light (the blue end of the colour spectrum). It follows from this that the perceived colour of a printed image is highly dependent on the illumination of the image. Lighting engineers go to great lengths to try to create artificial lights which have the same colour qualities as natural (sun) light but do not always succeed. The colour of clothes, for example, can look very different in the artificial lighting of a shop when compared with their appearance in natural daylight. Also, as every artist knows, the quality of daylight itself varies.

Figure 2.6. Additive and subtractive colour mixing. When the three primary colours are added, the result is white (w). When they are subtracted the result is black (k). The symbol 'k' is used for black so as not to be confused with blue, which uses the symbol 'b'.

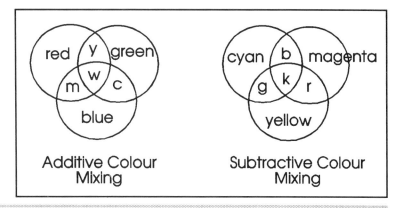

Additive Colour Mixing   Subtractive Colour Mixing

Illumination

Another simple consequence of these fundamental differences in the mechanism of image production is that printed images look better when well illuminated but the reverse is generally true of images on a computer monitor or television. In the first case it is the illumination which makes the whole process possible - you can't see a printed image in the dark. In the second case, bright illumination tends to degrade the image by flooding it with extraneous light which reduces the inherent contrast of the image and often adds unwanted reflections.

Primary colours The human eye can distinguish colours because the retina contains three different types of colour receptor, sensitive to three different ranges of wavelength. These correspond to the primary colours red, green and blue. All colour printing and display devices also use a minimum of three primary colours but the mixing process is different, depending on whether the devices are emissive or absorptive. In the case of emissive devices like a computer monitor the primary colours are red, green and blue, emitted by three different types of phosphor and the colour mixing process is additive (see Figure 2.6). The resultant colour, seen by the eye, is achieved by the addition of the three primary colours. Equal amounts of all three primaries produce white light. The absence of all the primaries produces no light to enter the eye and the result is black. Equal amounts of any two primaries produce colours which are usually labelled cyan, magenta and yellow, the secondary colours. Cyan is the result of adding green and blue, magenta the addition of red and blue and yellow, the addition of red and green.

Printing inks

In printing systems, where the colours are produced by the absorption of light, the primary colours are cyan, magenta and yellow; the secondaries are red, green and blue (see Figure 2.6). When all three primaries are present then all light is absorbed in the inks and in principle the eye sees black (the absence of any light). In practice with most inks the result is a muddy brown and to obtain a good quality printed black needs a fourth, proper black ink to be used. To achieve white, no inks are used so that the white paper shows through. Other colours are produced by mixtures of primaries.

Dithering Inks do not actually generate light and so it is not possible to control the intensity of colour coming from the component parts of a printed image in the same way that is used in monitors or televisions. The only control available lies in either the distribution or type of inks placed on the paper. It would, in principle, be possible to control the brightness of a primary colour in different parts of an image by the use of many different inks. For example, it should be possible to use 20 different types of yellow ink to produce 20 different shades of yellow - from a pale pastel shade to a bright saturated colour. In practice, however, many printing technologies use another method, which requires only one type of ink for each primary colour and produces its effect by varying the distribution of the ink on the paper. A small number of yellow dots on a white background looks, to the eye, like a very pale yellow. A large number of yellow dots, occupying the same area, looks to the eye like a strong, saturated yellow. The technique depends on the eye not seeing the individual dots but only the overall result of what are, in effect, a mixture of yellow and white dots.

Figure 2.7. Dithering. The top row of the figure shows pixels which are based on 4 basic printing elements. This system provides 5 possible grey-levels. The next two rows show a selection of 9-element pixels. There are clearly many more possible gray-levels but the pixels are much larger.

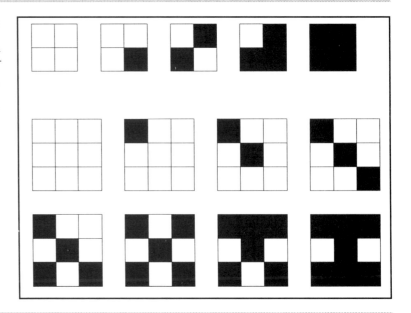

Dot-density

If the dots of ink which are placed on the paper are so small that the individual dot cannot be seen by the naked eye then it is possible to use groups of dots as pixels. The density of these dots (the number per unit area) determines the overall colour seen by the eye at that point (see Figure 2.7). This principle, called dithering, is used in most computer printers and often in displays as well. A more complicated version is used in traditional printing processes as well. The difference is that, in computer printers, the size of the dots is usually fixed both in size and position whereas in other printing techniques the size as well as the density is variable.

Now, a pixel was defined, in an earlier section as the smallest unit of a picture - a picture element. Clearly this definition now needs to be further refined since the basic dots produced by printers and displays are being used, in groups, to produce colour effects as well as spatial information. Spatial information is information about the structure of an image - what are the component parts of an image and where they are in space. If the image is made up of only two tones (say, black and white) like a line-drawing or a basic printed document then the dots contain only spatial information. They are either there or they are not (on or off). They show us where each component part of the image is but can have one of two available colour values. There is no true colour information. In a colour, or grey-level image, however, the dots are also being used to provide tonal or colour variations by the density of the dots.

Dots or pixels ?

The question that arises is: 'Should these dots be referred to as pixels?' It would seem not. In imaging theory, a pixel is the fundamental unit of spatial information and there is an assumption that such a pixel can have any one of a wide range of colours. From the point of the hardware designer the coloured dots which are produced by many output devices, like printers, can be grouped together and each group is treated as a pixel. In a monochrome screen a dot and a pixel are identical because it is possible to alter the intensity of the electron beam to make that dot vary its brightness - to change its grey-level. In a colour screen it needs three phosphor dots to make one coloured pixel, even thought the brightness of each dot can be varied. In a colour printer it make take many coloured dots to provide one pixel. In other words, different devices use different methods to achieve coloured or grey-level pixels, many of which involve the use of dot-density techniques.

Colours or detail?

The number of dots needed to make a coloured pixel depends on the number of colours required. It might take many dots to make one pixel. If a large number of different colours are required then that will need many different combinations of the three (or four) primary colours which are available. For example, in a printer, if two dots are grouped together to make one pixel then there are a very limited number of possible combinations which can be made from the three available primary colours: cyan and magenta, cyan and yellow, magenta and yellow; cyan with cyan, magenta with magenta, yellow with yellow. This adds up to only six possibilities - assuming that the order of the colours does not matter (for example, cyan with yellow is the same as yellow with cyan). In this example, there are in fact more possibilities. If a dot is not placed on the paper at all, then the colour of the paper - white - acts as a dot of another colour. Treated in this way, the example actually becomes a three-colour system with more combinations (such as cyan and white).

The only way of providing many more resultant colours is to group a larger number of basic dots together to make each pixel. Since the total number of dots in the image will be a constant (a feature of the hardware design) then there will be fewer pixels in the image, which in turn means that the image will contain less spatial information - less detail. Some computer printers offer a number of printing modes so that the user can decide to have more colours (and less detail) or more detail (and fewer colours). This is one of the classic 'trade-offs' of computer graphics.

Figure 2.8. An enlarged view of a bitmapped font. This is the 'system font' of the IBM-PC computer. The grid of perpendicular lines shows exactly how the characters are defined, pixel-by-pixel but is not seen in normal use.

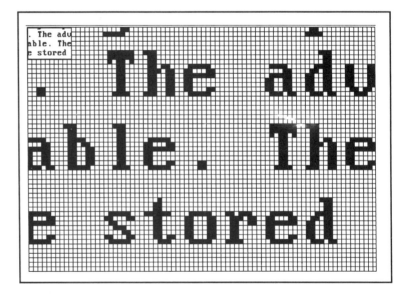

Figure 2.9 (a). A more normal view of a bitmapped font, without the grid lines. The individual pixels are much less obvious than in Figure 2.8 but it can be seen that such fonts cannot be scaled up without losing quality.

The earliest, an
users is as a wo
alent of a typew
ayed, but on the
tional typewrite

The text-only mode

The earliest computers did not have the luxury of graphics or even of interactive displays. It was not possible to obtain an immediate response of the sort we now take for granted. Entry and output of data was by teletype terminals which were a form of on-line electric typewriter. Even when television-style monitors were introduced so that rapid response from the computer became possible, only text displays were available. This meant that the screen 'echoed' the text which was being typed (to allow the user to confirm that no mistakes were being made) and also displayed any messages generated by the computer program, again as text. The exact shape of the text characters was determined by a set of patterns stored permanently in the computer so that only one font could be used - again like a typewriter. This is sometimes called the 'system font'.

The system font

In such a system, the shape of each letter is defined as a set of pixels in a standard-sized rectangle (see Figures 2.8 and 2.9a) and was given a simple code (called an ASCII code, where ASCII means the 'American Standard Code for Information Interchange'). The ASCII code is simply an integer between 0 and 255, which can be stored in one byte of computer memory. Each number corresponds to one letter of the alphabet or other printing character, like a punctuation mark. This is a very economic way of storing the 'image' of the set of characters which made up the display. If a screen consists of, say 25 lines of up to 80 characters per line, then a maximum of 25 x 80 = 2000 characters per screen is possible. The characters in the 'character set' include not only upper and lower case letters but also numbers, spaces between letters, punctuation marks and mathematical symbols. Screen displays need to be constantly refreshed, otherwise the image fades away very quickly, and so information about what is to be displayed is stored in a portion of computer memory called the 'refresh buffer'.

This type of display needs only one byte of memory per character, to store the ASCII code for each letter on the screen. The exact pattern of pixels which makes up each letter is called up from the permanent memory (ROM) where it is stored, each time it is needed. ROM is 'read-only memory', a form of integrated circuit in which information is permanently stored during the manufacturing process. It cannot be changed by the user. This is a good way of using limited memory resources because only 2000 bytes of refresh buffer are required.

Colour text systems
The first microcomputers used a system like this but there was soon a demand for both colour displays and simple graphics. Colour displays need two extra components - a colour monitor and some way of storing information about the colour of each individual character on the screen. The simplest way of storing the extra information is to allocate an extra byte for each character - the second one being used to store the colour information. This doubles the size of the refresh buffer to 4000 bytes.

The extended character set
True graphics needs a more radical change but a simple improvement can be provided by extending the character set to offer simple graphic symbols in addition to the conventional characters. The basic character set is the full set of symbols available for normal text activities. Since there are only 26 letters in the western-style alphabet the character set is not large. Even allowing for upper-case and lower-case versions of each letter (giving 52 characters), a range of punctuation marks and common mathematical symbols, the total can still be less than 100. Allocating one byte per character allows for any one of 256 different ASCII code numbers to be stored for each character position and so there is scope for the addition of a good range of graphic symbols.

Examples of commonly-used graphic symbols are small representations of playing-card symbols (club, diamond, spade, heart), arrows, printers' symbols like ®, ©, ¶, § and 'bullets' (e.g. •). A common addition is a range of rectangular and curved corners which together with horizontal and vertical lines can be used to create box shapes. It should be emphasised that though very attractive displays can be created using these facilities they should not be confused with `true graphics'. Each symbol is of a standard size (the same size as the alphabetical characters) and can be placed only in one of the 80 x 25 fixed positions on the screen. Nevertheless this system is still used very effectively on many modern microcomputers (for example the IBM-PC compatible systems). These words are being typed using a word processor which operates in this 'text-only' mode, and a number of apparently-graphic, mouse-driven, windowing interfaces also use this mode very effectively.

True graphics mode   In time there came a demand for 'true graphics', which meant a system in which every pixel on the screen could be independently controlled. This allows for any imaginable graphic display to be created, within the limit of the total number of pixels available (see Figure 2.9b). Such a system - usually called a bit-mapped display - requires that a separate code for every pixel is stored in the refresh buffer, not simply a code for every pre-defined character, and this requires much more memory. For example, the commonest screen mode (called a VGA, or Video Graphics Array) uses 640 x 480 pixels and allocates half a byte for each pixel to provide a range of 16 colours. Thus, the refresh buffer needs 640 x 480 x 0.5 bytes = 153,600 bytes - as opposed to the 4000 bytes a colour text system needs. This is nearly a 40-fold increase. The earliest systems did not offer either as many pixels or as many colours. For example, the first system used by IBM-PC compatibles (called the CGA system) provided 320 x 200 with four colours which was much less demanding. Even this, though, needed 320 x 200 x 1/4 bytes = 16,000 bytes of refresh buffer, a fourfold increase on the text-only system.

Early systems
Most of the microcomputers developed in the late 1970s and early

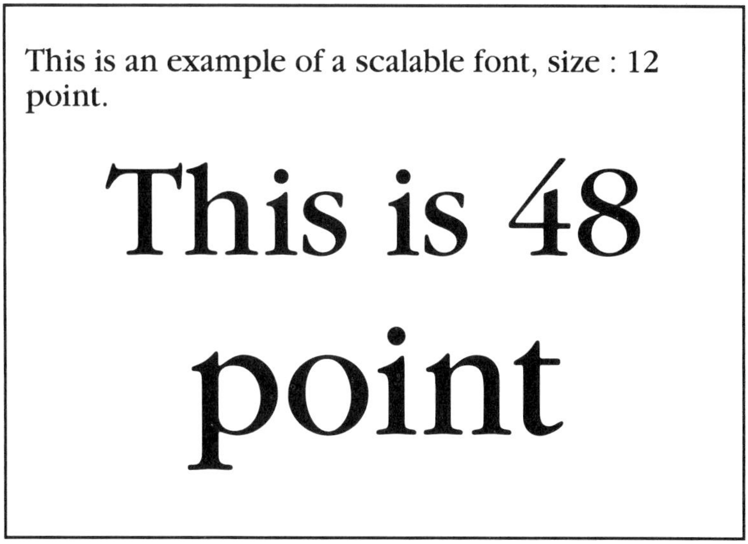

Figure 2.9 (b). With a true graphics mode, where every pixel on the screen is under independent control, it is possible to use scalable fonts which are of a high quality at any magnification.

This is an example of a scalable font, size : 12 point.

This is 48

point

1980s were provided with both a text-only mode of operation and one or more true-graphics modes. One important exception to this rule was the Apple Macintosh, which was designed from the outset as a computer for graphics applications and uses a bit-mapped graphics display for all its operations - though for some years it had no colour capability.

The reason that other computers were provided with both modes of operation was purely commercial. A graphics display is just as capable of displaying text as a text-only display. Text characters are simply treated as one form of graphic object. The only advantage of a text-only mode is that it is more economical. Many applications still do not need graphics or colour - basic word processing is an obvious example. For this the cheapest level of computer, fitted with a monochrome monitor, can run text-based applications software which makes modest demands on both memory and speed. Having said this, the current trend is for developers to produce software which needs colour graphics, very powerful processors and huge amounts of memory and hard-disc space, but with a modular system it should be possible to specify a computer with whatever is required and a text-only system is still a perfectly valid option.

Colour graphics

Reference was made in an earlier section to the fact that in text-only mode, colour information is stored using an extra byte of memory for each character. One byte stores the ASCII code which determines indirectly the position of all the pixels which make up the character in a rectangular block. The other byte, called the attribute byte, stores the colour information relating to that character. In the IBM-PC, four bits determine the colour of the character itself (the foreground), three bits control the colour of the background and a final, eighth bit determines whether or not the character is still or flashing on and off. This is an economical system, which with the sacrifice of only 2000 bytes enables any character on the screen to be in one of 256 different colour states. The source of the economy, both in the colour coding and the character coding, is the fact that each character occupies 9 x 14 = 126 pixels (see Figure 2.9a) and yet can be treated as a single entity.

One-bit-per-pixel

In true graphics mode, life is more complicated and memory-consuming, for here there is a requirement that every pixel shall be controlled independently of every other. The minimum condition is that each pixel should have one bit of memory associated with it which would mean that every pixel would be in one of two possible colour states. These two states are usually black or white but could be any two colours. This is a 'one-bit-per-pixel' system. It means, for example, that a character-sized block of pixels needs 126 bits (as compared with the eight bits used for the ASCII code, in a monochrome text-only system) but it would mean that the programmer would have total control on the state of those bits. It would be possible, for example, to create any character which was desired and not be restricted to the 256 preprogrammed members of the normal 'system font'.

More bits-per-pixel

To move beyond two colours needs more memory. For example, two-bits-per-pixel offer four possible states per pixel which means four different colours. Three-bits-per-pixel could support eight colours, four-bits-per-pixel offers 16 colours. Full professional level colour systems offer 24-bits-per-pixel (that is eight pixels per primary colour) which will support 16.8 million colours! Very few users have found the need for more than that. Systems which claim 32-bits -per-pixel often do not offer more colours; the extra bits normally store other types of graphic information.

Colour palettes   It doesn't follow that all the colours which a computer hardware system can produce will necessarily be available to the user at any one time (or indeed will be wanted). The limiting factor which determines the maximum number of colours which a system can produce is the number of intensity levels which can be generated for each primary colour. In the case of a colour monitor, this corresponds to the number of brightness levels (grey-levels) to which the colour spots on the viewing screen can be set. The factor which determines how many colours can be used at one time, however, is the size of the refresh-buffer and its associated circuitry because this is where the colour codes must be stored. The greater the number of colours which are to be coded the larger these numbers will be and the more memory space will be required, as explained in the previous section.

Some simple calculations

For example, if the number of intensity levels for each colour spot (red, green and blue) is four then, since they are independent of each other, this means that the number of colours that can be generated is $4 \times 4 \times 4 = 64$. Now, if there is sufficient memory available in the refresh-buffer to assign $4 + 4 + 4 = 12$ bits for each pixel on the screen, then all these 64 colours will in fact be constantly available to the user. The cost is having a refresh-buffer with 1.5 bytes (12 bits) per pixel. The alternative is to restrict the user to a smaller sub-set of the total number of possible colours. This sub-set is called a 'palette'. Some writers use the term for the sub-set itself, which

Figure 2.10. A colour look-up-table. Each colour in the table has its own colour code which corresponds to three particular values of red, green and blue intensities. The first entry in the table corresponds to white (maximum intensities of red, green and blue). Code 7 corresponds to black. Code 2 corresponds to a grey (equal intensities of red, green and blue which are less than the maximum of 255).

Colour Code	Red	Green	Blue
0	255	255	255
1	127	127	127
2	63	63	63
3	255	255	0
4	255	0	255
5	0	255	255
6	63	63	0
7	0	0	0

seems to me a logical use of the term. For a conventional artist, a palette is a board with a small set of specially mixed colours. Others, however, use the term to mean the total number of colours, from which the subset is chosen. Either way, there must be a way of choosing which particular subset is available for a particular graphic. This is done by means of a coding system called a 'look-up table' (LUT) - see Figure 2.10. The table consists of a list of colour codes which are to be used in the refresh-buffer. If, in the example already discussed, only eight of the colours were to be useable then the colour codes would be in the range 0-7 and would need three bits-per-pixel (since 3 bits can exist in eight different possible states). Each of these entries in the table would signify three particular values of intensity (one for red, one for green, one for blue) and each intensity could have one of four different values. By changing these values, a different colour LUT is created and a different subset of colours is available. This means that a large number of palettes could be created - each with its own LUT. However, only eight of the 64 colours would be present in each palette and only one palette available at any one time

Printing colour images

It has already been pointed out that there is a very big difference between the way that coloured images are displayed on a monitor and the way that they are printed on paper. One is an emissive process and the other absorptive. One uses colour addition and the other colour subtraction. These differences cause big problems of colour matching when printers are used to make hard-copies of a screen design. At the simplest level, when printing is to be done on a relatively cheap printer like an ink-jet, it is usually accepted that the result will only be an approximation to the screen colours.

If more professional results are required then the files will be sent to a print bureau for output on more expensive equipment and this requires some method of relating the colours chosen by the user with the output of the machine.

Variations in the monitor

One difficulty is caused by the simple fact that screens can be adjusted by the user, just like a TV set. The screen has controls to adjust the brightness and contrast. Changing these settings makes an enormous difference to the appearance of the colours displayed. The ambient light conditions - the light shining on the screen from room lighting or natural lighting - also make a big difference. The printer does not have brightness or contrast controls but even if it did, how would it be possible to ensure that the colours the printer produced would match exactly the colours the screen produced?

One solution that has been developed involves providing the user with a calibration device. This is a piece of hardware - a special light meter - which is placed against the screen and which measures the colours produced by it in an objective fashion. This means that the user can then adjust the screen controls in order to produce standard colours which will match those produced by the printer, and will also match the colour of the paper.

The big problem with this type of solution is that no printer can produce the same quality of colour which is created by an emissive device like a computer screen.

Colour cards

For this reason a more satisfactory solution is to try to standardise the colours produced by the printer and to offer a way of matching these to the output of the computer, regardless of the way that they will look on the screen.

This is how it works. A large number of standard colours are chosen and given codes to identify them. The printer manufacturers ensure that their printers can produce those colours. Printed samples of those colours are made available to the computer users, on small rectangles of card. The software designers ensure that the colour codes can be chosen from within their software applications. The user then knows that when a colour code is chosen and used in the application, the printer will produce a colour which looks like the sample provided on the card, even though it may look quite different on the screen.

In other words, it is accepted that the system is no longer WYSIWYG (What You See Is What You Get) - at least as far as the screen is concerned. You only get what you see on the printed sample card. These standardised colours (or pre-mixed inks) are called 'spot-colours'. The simplest form of professional colour printing uses only black and a few spot-colours. The next higher level of complexity involves process colours.

Process colours

This approach to defining colours involves specifying the percentages of primary colours - cyan, magenta, yellow and black. The advantage of this system is that, in principle, any colour can be created by a suitable combination of the primaries, whereas there is bound to be a limit on the number of spot colours that can be offered - typically about 1000. The disadvantage is that the dithering process used to create process colours cannot create such a strong, vibrant colour as a spot colour. The answer, in the most complex form of professional printing, is to use a mixture of the two processes. Spot colours are particularly suitable for such items as text or solid blocks of colour, where no variation of shade is required. Process colours are essential where many shades are required as in colour photographs.

Whichever method is used, suitable files must be sent to a printer which contains the colour specifications required. The colour separations are created by the software and the resultant files sent to the printer. These are four or more separate files, one for each of the primary process colours plus one for each spot colour, if any. The printer knows that one file contains all the details which are to be printed in cyan, another for magenta, another for yellow, another for black and others for the named spot colours. Using these files separate films are then made for the printing process. The nearest to an industry standard for printing colour is called **Pantone** though there are other systems (for example **Focoltone**, **Trumatch** and **ANPA**). The normal user is not required to buy any special software to use a system like Pantone. The applications software (for example the desktop publishing package or paint software) will have built-in facilities which enable the user to choose Pantone colours. To make proper use of the facility, however, it is necessary to buy a set of colour cards in order to see what the printed result should look like. It is not enough to rely on the appearance of the colour on the screen, for reasons explained earlier.

Summary

1 It is important to discuss some basic theory of computer graphics, even in a book which is primarily concerned with the practical application of computer graphics.

2 Computer images are defined in two different ways : as a set of lines ('vectors') or as a rectangular array of dots ('pixels').

3 All modern systems now display images as a set of pixels ('raster-displays') but some software stores images as vectors and some as

pixels. Each method has its advantages. As a result it is often necessary to convert images from one form to the other.

4 Colour and grey-level information is stored in a computer using an extended version of the technique used for simple black and white ('1-bit') images.

5 Images which are displayed on TV systems and computer monitors are called 'emissive' images; they actually emit light. Printed images are called 'reflective' images. They work by selectively absorbing and re-emitting light.

6 Emissive images use three primary colours - red, green and blue - which produce secondary colours by addition. Absorptive images use three primaries - cyan, magenta and yellow - which produce their secondaries by subtraction.

7 Secondary colour effects (and grey-level images) are normally produced by a process called 'dithering'. The process involves placing large numbers of tiny coloured dots in close proximity so that the eye detects an average effect but does not see the individual dots.

8 The consequence of this technique is that if a very large number of colours is required the image will lose some of its fine detail because the collections of dots will be larger in size.

9 Early computers used text-only displays which were economical in their use of memory. Text-only modes are still common but cannot produce detailed graphic images.

10 Modern computers offer 'true' graphic, bit-mapped displays which require much more memory and faster processing capacity but produce high-resolution colour images.

11 It is difficult to compare the colour of images displayed on emissive display devices with those which result when printed on paper. Systems have to be devised to standardise colour printing to ensure that printing processes produce predictable results.

Graphics hardware

Key points
- *why it is necessary to understand computer hardware*
- *parts of the computer which are critical to graphics*
- *choosing a suitable display for a particular task*
- *choosing from a wide range of printers and input devices*

Introduction The purpose of this chapter is to provide a brief review of the computer hardware which is necessary for graphics work. It is natural that the question should spring to mind - 'Why should an ordinary user need to know anything at all about hardware?' It has not seemed necessary to explain how a floppy disc drive actually stores information on the magnetic surface of the disc - it is sufficient to know that it does, and how to use it. However, though the user may not be interested in how the 'machinery' works it is important when buying or upgrading computer equipment to choose wisely, particularly those parts like displays and printers which are vital for graphics work. It can also be helpful when things go wrong - or seem to be going wrong - to have some understanding of basic hardware principles for this can sometimes help in solving the problem.

Problems with file sizes
For example, it is not uncommon for the new user to scan a picture, try to save it on a blank floppy disc and find that there is not enough space. Does this mean that something is wrong with the computer, or the scanner? After all, it is possible to fit dozens of word processor files on a floppy disc. In fact there is nothing at all surprising about this situation - as long as you have some idea about how a scanner creates images and how much room they take up. The general theory which would enable the user to do a quick calculation of the size of such a file has been covered in chapter 2. This chapter contains an outline of some of the important principles which are hardware-related. Though much technical detail is omitted, this chapter should be sufficient to help the reader to

choose the right equipment for a particular task and use it in a confident manner.

The computer itself Advertisers sometimes describe their computers as 'graphics workstations'. This might seem to imply that a special computer is needed for graphics applications work. In fact, since modern microcomputers are modular systems, it is more a question of choosing the component parts with care to ensure the computer is suitable for graphics applications. This does not apply only to the obvious graphics peripherals, like screens and printers. The specification of the main computer system is also important. Four broad areas need to be considered: disc storage, internal memory, processing power and the internal bus. All of them relate to the fact that graphic files are much larger than text files and so much larger quantities of information have to be stored and processed - sometimes very quickly.

It does not follow that all graphics files are large or will cause problems. The size of a graphic file depends on four factors: the type of file (is it a bit-map or a vector graphic?), the amount of detail in it, the number of colours and the type of file compression used in its storage. It can be helpful to do a few simple calculations to get an idea of the numbers involved. A screen of text in an ordinary word processor, such as I am using to type these words uses 1 byte of screen memory for each character. This amounts to about 2000 bytes altogether because the screen can hold about 2000 characters. If I were using a graphics package to draw a picture in 256 colours and using the 800 by 600 pixel mode, the screen display would need nearly 500,000 bytes, more than 100 times as much as the text display. This is because the 256 colour codes require that each pixel in the display has one byte of memory and there are 480,000 pixels altogether. This would be significantly smaller, when saved as a file, because compression methods are always used but it might still be about 100,000 bytes.

Scanned images
The problem becomes far worse when the images have been obtained by scanning because the scanner works at a minimum of 300 dots per inch (dpi), as compared with 60-70 dpi for screen images, so an A4 image (8.3 x 11.7 inches) will generate nearly 9 million pixels! All this has important consequences for the disc capacity of the machine. These images must be stored on discs and even with modern file compression methods they can take up an enormous amount of room. Many large scanned colour images simply won't fit on a normal floppy disc and even a hard disc can be filled very quickly. Increasingly, graphics software is being distributed

on CD-ROMs which have a capacity of about 600 Mbytes, largely because the clip-art images and fonts provided with them occupy so much space.

Processing images
The same basic principle applies to holding the images in memory, and the problem is being compounded by the growth in size of the applications software itself. The extra problem with internal memory is that if the application involves processing the image (as in photographic retouching software) then extra space will be needed to store at least part of a new, processed image, as well as the original. In addition, the image will probably have to be handled in un-compressed form which takes up more room than the disc version.

Processing power
Processing all this picture information will slow down even the most powerful computer, so it is important to have access to the most processing power available. In fact the special needs of graphics operations are now widely recognised and special graphics co-processors are increasingly used to take the work off the central processor (see a later section on video cards). It may therefore be more cost effective to invest in a special graphics card than in the latest central processor but, either way, handling large image files can slow down all but the fastest computer. All this information has to be moved around inside the computer from the central processor to disc drives, memory and the display. It travels along a 'data bus' (an information pathway) which in many computers is simply too slow because the development of faster processors has rendered the design obsolete. This then causes bottleneck problems like those which would result if fast-moving traffic from a three-lane motorway was suddenly transferred to a narrow country lane. This means that for many graphics applications a computer with a modernl high-specification data bus will be needed.

The display   All modern computers can be fitted with a range of different displays and it is difficult sometimes to know which would be the best buy since, unless money is no object, there is no single monitor which is equally good for all graphics applications. The main variables which need to be considered are:

- the size and shape of the screen
- its resolution
- the number of colours (or grey-levels) it can display
- the video card

Screen size and shape

Computer monitors, like television sets, are made in a number of standard sizes - the size quoted being a diagonal measurement of the screen. The normal shape also derives from television sets, being a rectangle which is wider than its height. The ratio of its width to its height is called its 'aspect ratio' and is normally about 4:3, again like a TV set. This shape was chosen initially for TV sets as being similar to cinema screens - before the wide screens were introduced - but is not always suitable, particularly for graphics applications like word processing and DTP.

Aspect ratios Computer images are frequently printed on paper and standard European paper sizes like A4 (8.27 by 11.69 inches) have an aspect ratio which is not very different from that of the screen. The actual size of the paper is in fact only a little larger than a 14 inch screen. Unfortunately the screen is often the wrong way round.

Printed pages are usually oriented in 'portrait' mode (like a portrait painting, with the longer dimension vertical) and screens are oriented in 'landscape' mode (like a landscape painting with the longer dimension horizontal). This means that a standard 14 inch monitor can only represent a little over half of an A4 sheet of paper in portrait orientation at the normal magnification (life-size). The only way of displaying the whole sheet is to reduce the magnification of the image to about 1/2 of the normal and see much less detail.

The alternative is to stay with a full-size image of part of the sheet of paper and to use the software to scroll the image horizontally and vertically, which can be a tedious process.

Large monitors To solve this problem many Apple Macintosh computers - especially those which are being used for desktop publishing - are equipped with special A4 portrait monitors, the size and orientation of an A4 sheet of paper, in portrait mode. Similar screens can be obtained for IBM-PCs also. Unfortunately this is unhelpful when the user wishes to work with documents printed in landscape mode but an ingenious solution has been provided by one manufacturer who makes monitors which can be rotated between the two orientations, so providing the best of both worlds, but at a price. An increasingly popular alternative is the use of larger high-resolution monitors with the normal aspect ratio. Typical sizes are 17, 19 and 21 inches. These can usually produce satisfactory images in either orientation. An alternative is the A3 screen (the size of two A4 pages, in portrait mode, side-by-side) and these provide the best, though most expensive, solution for DTP work.

Resolution

The resolution of a screen is a measurement of the amount of detail which it can display, usually expressed by the number of pixels. In a VGA monitor (which is the basic standard for IBM-PC systems) the image is made up from 640 by 480 pixels. A system similar to VGA is also used as the standard display in Apple Macs.

The increasing importance of graphics and the demand for better quality images has led to growing popularity of higher resolution standards such as 800 x 600, 1024 x 768 and 1280 x 1024 pixels. This has, in turn, had consequences for the size of the screen. A good 14 inch monitor could be used to display some of these higher resolution standards but the user would not obtain the full benefit because the details would be too small to see. For example, a horizontal line of 1024 pixels on a 14 inch monitor occupies about 10 inches (since the 14 inch measurement corresponds to the diagonal) so that each pixel is only 1/100 inch wide. This means that much of the detail in an image would be too small for the unaided human eye. The user would need a magnifying glass to get any advantage from the increased detail being displayed. The only practical answer is to use a larger monitor, with more pixels, so that more detail can be both displayed and seen.

Comparison with printers   The importance of getting the highest possible resolution screen is evident when a comparison is made with printing devices. Modern printers like laser printers and inkjets lay down dots on the paper at a minimum spacing of 300 dots per inch (dpi). Many, more modern, laser printers operate at 600 dpi and some at 1200 dpi. A 14 inch monitor operating in VGA mode, on the other hand, displays only 640 pixels in a line of about 10 inches - about 64 dpi. It can be seen that there is a considerable mismatch between the resolution of display systems when compared with printing hardware. It follows that the screen simply cannot show all the detail which could be printed on paper if the image is displayed at normal magnification, i.e. the same size as the final product.

The only answer is the process called 'zooming' - using the software to show magnified portions of the final image so that much more of the detail which will be seen on the printed page can also be seen on the screen. A common computer acronym - WYSIWYG meaning 'What You See Is What You Get' - is never strictly true. It should be 'What You See Is A Good, Low-Resolution, Approximation To What You Get' - at least if you work at normal magnification and are looking at the whole image.

Scrolling One of the drawbacks to zooming in on an image, to see this extra detail, is that only a small part of the final product can now be seen, as with a magnifying glass, and the software must provide a means of 'scrolling' or moving the magnified region to see other parts of the page. It can be seen, then, that there is a lot of scope for improvements in screen resolution and there is no sign of them catching up with printing processes, but large screens can be a big help. There is a wide variation in the quality and price of monitors and it should not be assumed that a large monitor will necessarily operate satisfactorily at high resolution. In fact, in my experience, the cheapest of the 17 inch monitors can only be used satisfactorily for long periods at the standard resolution of 640 x 480, or 800 x 600 pixels because of problems of flicker.

Colour
Colour monitors are, of course, more expensive than monochrome but a 14 inch colour screen is usually supplied as standard with a modern microcomputer and where a monochrome screen is available as an alternative the difference in price is quite small. In fact, a 14 inch colour monitor does not cost much more than an equivalent size colour television but larger screen sizes (17, 19 and 21 inch) are much more expensive than their TV equivalents (by a factor of between two and five times). A high-quality 21 inch colour monitor can cost two or three times as much as the rest of the computer system. This often means that a choice has to be made between a larger monochrome monitor or a smaller colour one, and the correct decision will depend very much on the applications for which the system is designed.

Desktop publishing and any other task which involves the overall design and layout of a publication which is bigger than A4 in size - for example, the two opposed pages of a magazine - needs a very large screen (such as A3). If the final result will be printed in black and white then size is far more important than colour. On the other hand, painting, some forms of drawing and photo-retouching are examples where colour is an essential part of the process and a colour screen, even a small one, is vital. Here a compromise may have to be made and the largest colour screen which is affordable should be chosen. Fortunately the growing importance of colour graphics has led to a rapidly growing market for the larger colour screens and prices have dropped significantly in recent years though the prices of 17 inch screens (a good compromise) vary enormously.

The video card

It is important to realise that a display system consists of two parts: the screen itself and the electronics which drive the screen. In the case of the IBM-PC compatible computer, the electronics (sometimes called the video card or graphics board) take the form of a separate circuit board which is plugged in to the computer and which can therefore be easily replaced if updating is required. In the Apple Mac the electronics are an integral part of the computer, though a special extra board is necessary for some of the larger screens. In either case it is important that the two components should be properly matched. It is not uncommon for computers to be sold, for example, with a video card which is capable of generating very high resolution images - but not with the cheap monitor which is supplied ! The final quality of the image on the screen and the speed with which it is displayed depend just as much on the video card as on the screen.

Accelerators

The important practical factor for the user is speed. A system which displays a very large number of colours must be able to handle the correspondingly large amount of picture information which must flow from the computer to the monitor. This inevitably adds to the cost of the video card. Many are sold as 'accelerator' devices, emphasising that the special graphics microprocessors which are fitted to them are needed to handle the information flow. Without them the screen will take an unacceptably long time to react to changes in the image, both because of the time taken to calculate what the image should look like and because of the time taken for this information to flow to the display. To get the best out of modern video cards, however, it is necessary to buy a computer with a modern, fast internal bus, capable of feeding the vital graphic data to and from the central processor and disc drives, at an appropriate rate.

Printers   The images produced by a display device are transient - they disappear when the power is turned off. They can be saved on a disc, like any other computer-generated file, and displayed at will but this takes time and requires the use of an appropriate computer and screen. There is, therefore, a big demand for paper copies of computer-generated images and there probably always will be until computers and their display devices become as light and cheap as pieces of paper. Until recently most printed copies of computer images were a very poor substitute. Early printers - like the dot-matrix printer and the daisywheel printer were really only suitable for monochrome (usually black) text. Even when higher quality printers like the laser printer and the ink-jet printer became affordable, colour was still either extremely expensive or of poor quality. In recent years the quality and price of colour printers have improved enormously and good quality colour images are at last becoming possible for most users. There are many different technologies involved in printers and the technical details are of little interest to most users but it is worthwhile understanding a number of basic principles.

Vector versus raster

There is only one type of printer which produces images by a vector technique. The principle of the pen-plotter is the simplest imaginable - it draws lines on paper by a process which mimics the behaviour of an artist. A mechanical arm lowers a pen on to the surface of the paper and then moves it across the paper by a combination of movements in two perpendicular directions. It has widespread application for producing line-drawings such as engineering drawings, maps and graphs. This type of device was the ideal partner of early graphics systems which used vector display devices to produce line images and is still used where those types of image are important.

All other printers create images by putting tiny dots of ink on to the paper. These dots are laid down in regular rows (a raster) which form a two-dimensional rectangular array or matrix. This has given its name to one of the earliest such devices - the dot-matrix (impact) printer - but in fact all printers except the pen-plotter could reasonably be called dot-matrix or raster devices.

Dot-matrix printers

The dot-matrix printer can be thought of as a modified typewriter in the sense that the paper is wrapped round a roller which is periodically rotated by an amount equivalent to the distance between two lines of text. Ink is transferred to the paper from a fabric or paper-like ribbon. Unlike a typewriter, where the printing mechanism is stationary and the paper and roller move, the dot-matrix printer has a small printer head which moves across the width of the paper parallel to the axis of the drum. The head contains one or more rows of tiny metal pins arranged in vertical columns. Ink is transferred to the paper when tiny electromagnetically-operated hammers hit selected pins, which then press the ribbon on to the paper leaving dots of ink behind.

Colour ribbons Simple colour images can be also be obtained, as in a typewriter, by the use of a special ribbon which has stripes of three primary colours running parallel with the length of the ribbon. The colours are selected by a simple mechanical device which moves the ribbon up and down to bring the correct colour into alignment with the print head.

This type of printer, particularly in its original form with a nine-pin print head, is suitable only for basic draft text applications. Though it is cheap, which makes it particularly attractive for domestic use, it is also noisy and is a low-resolution device by modern standards. It would not now be considered suitable for any professional applications, particularly graphics. In its modern form with a 24-pin or 48-pin print head it is still widely used as a replacement for the typewriter for business correspondence and as a lower-quality alternative to the laser printer with lower running costs. It could also be used as a cheap drafting device for some graphics applications, like DTP. The final output would go to a higher-quality printer.

Thermal printers

A development of the dot-matrix printer which is of more interest in graphics, the thermal wax printer, is a dot-matrix device which transfers ink to the paper by melting it rather than by the impact of moving pins. One reason that the colour impact printer is unsatisfactory is that the impact process only removes a small quantity of ink from the ribbon. While this means that the ribbon can be used over and over again (it is a 'multi-strike' ribbon) it also means that the colour effect on the paper looks rather feeble. The thermal wax printer, on the other hand, uses a 'single-strike' ribbon. The special waxy ink melts and comes completely off the ribbon, leaving a much more vivid coloured dot on the paper.

Primary colours All colour printing processes involve the use of at least three primary colours which are usually laid down, one colour at a time. In the case of a typewriter or an impact dot-matrix printer, the dots are laid down in horizontal stripes across the paper, the width of the stripes being equal to the height of the printer head. The head crosses the paper three times, one for each primary colour, before the paper is advanced ready for the next stripe. In many modern colour printers, however, all the dots of one particular primary colour (cyan for instance) are deposited on the paper first, before the ribbon is wound on to the next stripe to allow the next colour to be added. In many designs this means that each separate stripe is as large as the sheet of paper. Whatever the geometry chosen by the designer of the printer the use of a single-strike ribbon involves wasting a lot of waxy ink because a section of the ribbon, once used, cannot be used again. Of course there will often be a considerable amount of unused ink left in each of the three (or four) coloured stripes when a sheet of paper is printed. Unfortunately there is no way of ensuring that when the next page is printed that there will be patches of ink left on the ribbon everywhere they are needed for that page and so it is necessary to wind on the ribbon and use a new set of stripes. This makes these thermal printers expensive on consumables.

Dye-sublimation printers

A recent development in colour printers, the dye-sublimation printer, has much in common with the thermal wax printer in that it too involves heating ink on a ribbon and transferring it to paper. The enormous improvement in the quality of the final product of this type of device, however, is due to a radically different way of transferring the ink. This, in turn, produces a different way of making intermediate shades. All colour printers other than the dye-sublimation printer use dithering effects, as described in chapter 2. Dots of primary colours are placed side by side so that the eye sees the combined effect rather than the different primary-coloured dots, which are too small for the naked eye to detect. Unfortunately it also means that to obtain a large number of intermediate shades, spatial resolution must be sacrificed because a large number of primary dots must be used to produce a pixel.

Sublimation The dye-sublimation printer, however, uses special inks which, instead of melting into a blob of liquid ink, turn directly from a solid into a vapour (a process called sublimation). The amount of vapour from each of the three primary colours can be controlled by the heating process and the vapours themselves mix in the fibres of the paper to form single dots of intermediate colours. This means that dithering is not needed and huge numbers of shades of colour can be made without loss of resolution. The result looks more like a colour photograph than a normal computer printer output and the technique is often said to produce 'photographic quality' images.

Of course, the spatial resolution of 300 dpi cannot compare with the crystal size of photographic emulsions. For colour halftone images like photographs the dye-sublimation printer is the best available system. Of course, not all computer output requires halftone images with thousands of shades of colour. A pie chart may only need half a dozen shades, in solid blocks of saturated colour or in hatched patterns and for this sort of application a thermal wax printer may be just as suitable as a more expensive dye-sublimation device.

Ink-jet printers

These devices place tiny dots of ink on the paper by spraying thousands of micro-droplets from tiny jets. Early designs used a single jet and 'steered' the ink spray to the correct position by means of electrostatic fields. Modern designs use a small printer head, containing up to 60 separate, independently controlled jets. The head moves across the paper in the same manner as a dot-matrix printer. Problems with the ink drying in the tiny jets have been overcome - partly by the development of more suitable inks, and partly by the use of disposable jets. The jets and the ink reservoir are combined into a single small unit which is replaced when the ink runs out. Occasionally one or more of the jets does get blocked but the printers are usually fitted with a mechanism which is designed to force ink through to unblock it.

Monochrome inkjet printers are proving to be serious rivals to the laser printer. They are usually much cheaper to buy (half the price or less) and the output quality, with suitable paper, can look very similar. The consumable costs work out higher however because of the cost of the combined reservoir and ink-jet nozzles which are discarded when the ink runs out.

Wicking   The proviso about suitable paper is a reflection on the basic printing process, which involves squirting liquid ink onto paper and waiting for it to dry. Although modern inks are designed to dry very quickly they still have time to spread away from the original point of impact and produce tiny unwanted extra lines on the paper. This process is called 'wicking' because the paper acts like the wick of an old-fashioned oil lamp which relies on a liquid seeping through the material of the wick.

The effect can be seen most clearly in blotting paper which is designed to encourage this process and so mop up excess liquid. Suitable paper for ink-jet printers is designed to minimise this effect, usually by means of appropriate coatings applied to the paper. Another way of minimising wicking, however, is used in some colour ink-jets. This involves the use of special inks which are solid at room temperature and must be melted before being used in the printer. These 'phase-change' printers squirt hot melted ink onto the paper and the ink then cools on impact, turning back into its solid state before it has chance to migrate through the paper away from the impact point.

Laser printers

The laser printer is based on the same electrostatic technology used in photocopiers. The image, in the form of thousands of pixels, is transferred to a photoconductive drum by means of a laser. The laser produces a focused spot of light which can be turned on and off to produce an 'image' in the form of electrostatic pixels on the drum. In order to produce a line of pixels across the whole of the drum's length the laser beam is mechanically scanned by means of a rapidly rotating multifaceted mirror. This produces scan-lines (a raster) and the drum itself also rotates (as in the photocopier) so as to lay down many lines of pixels. Because the toner is a dry powder which does not soak into the paper, and because the laser beam can be focused to an exceedingly small spot, the resolution of the laser printer is potentially better than an ink jet.

Basic laser printers have a minimum resolution of 300 dpi and 600 dpi printers are becoming common. Some ink jets are rated at 360 dpi but it doesn't follow that the results will necessarily be as good or better than a laser printer. The size of the dot is just as important as the number of dots per inch. If the dots are too large they will simply overlap each other and a large number of dots per inch does not guarantee high resolution.

Colour laser printers are now becoming increasingly common and their prices are dropping but are still much more expensive than ink-jets and colour thermal devices. Some use three drums, each one applying one of the three primaries to the paper. Some use a single drum three times, to apply the coloured toners in turn to a secondary belt, which then transfers the composite image to the paper.

Photo-typesetters

These devices resemble laser printers except in the way that the final image is formed. The major limiting factor of a laser printer is not the size of the focused laser, which can be made extremely small, but the size of the toner particles and the precision of the basic process of charging a drum, attracting particles to it and transferring those particles to paper. In a photo-typesetter the laser beam is used to expose a photographic emulsion directly - the emulsion then being developed chemically like any other photograph. The obvious disadvantage is that the results are not obtained as quickly or as conveniently. The advantage is that photographic emulsions have very small crystals which gives them very high resolution. Images with 1200 dpi, 2400 dpi and even better are possible. This technique is the favoured method for high quality printed work. Because the printers are expensive to buy and most potential users do not want to get involved in photographic processing, special bureau services are available to which computer-generated images can be sent on a disc, the results being returned quickly by post.

Photographic recording

Another technique, which is particularly appropriate for the production of colour transparencies and prints, involves photographing the image displayed on the computer monitor. Normal colour monitors are not suitable for high-quality results because of the triads of colour phosphor dots which can be seen quite clearly in an enlarged photograph. For this reason special photographic recorders use high-resolution monochrome screens which do not have phosphor dots and produce the colour image by multiple exposures through colour filters.

The device consists of a light-tight box containing the monitor, the camera and a revolving wheel with three primary-coloured transparent filters. The monitor is connected to the computer via electronic circuits which can separate out each of the primary coloured components of the image. When the red portions of the image are displayed on the black and white monitor (as white, of course) they are photographed through a red filter onto colour film. The other two components (the green and the blue) are then added to the film in the same way by photographing them through red and green filters, respectively, but without advancing the film. By this means high-resolution images of up to 4000 lines can be captured on to film and transparencies or prints produced. Again, specialist bureaus exist to which images on disc can be sent and the photographic output returned.

Video output and input

Increasing interest in computer animation and the use of computer software for the creation of title sequences has led to the demand for equipment which would enable computer-generated sequences of images to be transferred to video tape. Similarly, there is a demand for images which have been captured by TV cameras and stored on video tape to be digitised and transferred to the computer. These developments have been spurred on by the interest in multimedia systems and the result is that specialist hardware to perform these operations, which have been available for a long time, have now become affordable systems. They can take the form of a single plug-in card which then acts as an interface between the computer, the normal analogue TV and video systems. Some true multimedia computers already have the necessary electronics built-in to their main boards.

Input devices　The most important input devices for graphics use are pointing devices - means by which the user can choose from menus, drag objects and draw on the screen. One helpful way of classifying the various technologies for performing these operations distinguishes between direct and indirect devices.

Direct devices

Direct devices enable the user to point directly at the screen. This approach has a number of obvious advantages. To point to something directly is the natural way of choosing it. To draw directly on the surface where the image appears is the way we have all learnt from our earliest days. Some users do find using an indirect device, like a mouse, difficult to get used to, partly because the action of drawing or pointing is completely separated from the object being drawn on, or pointed at. Direct systems do have two disadvantages however. Because computer screens are normally set up vertically, it can be tiring to spend a long time holding the arm up in that position. The other problem is that sometimes the arm obscures the vision by covering parts of the screen. The first problem can be solved by installing the screen at a more suitable angle - almost horizontal - and by embedding it into the desk.

The light pen   The earliest direct pointing device was the light-pen. This is a pen-like stylus, which is connected to the computer by means of a cable. It has a light-sensitive tip which picks up the momentary brightening of the screen as the raster pattern is regularly refreshed. The computer is able to calculate where on the screen the pen is being held by measuring the time taken from the beginning of the raster scan to the instant when the pen picks up the increase in light intensity. This system has traditionally been used in computer-aided design systems but has mostly given way to the graphic tablet (see later in the chapter).

The touch-screen   An alternative, direct, device does not require the user to use a pen or any other pointing device - except the finger. A special touch-sensitive transparent layer is attached to the front of the screen. The user simply touches the screen and one of a variety of different methods is used to locate where the finger is. Some systems use strain gauges to detect the pressure of the finger on the screen. Some use an array of narrow, invisible light beams and detectors. However they work, the major advantage of this approach is the absence of the pen. In fact, in many applications, no keyboard is required either.

Touch screens are normally used in association with menu-driven software (see chapter 1). This type of software is particularly suitable where the user is accessing information in an environment where a keyboard would be unsuitable. One example is a public-access information system, perhaps in a department store or at a tourist centre. Another example is a stock-dealing room where the users are using telephones, making notes on pads and moving from one screen to another. A third environment might be a school, with young children who have not yet acquired keyboard skills. The touch-screen is ideal in any situation where the only interaction that is needed is to choose from a list of options to retrieve information.

Indirect devices

The best-known example of this category is the mouse. First used commercially with the Apple Mac graphical interface, it consists of a small plastic box, which is sometimes mounted on small wheels, and is rolled along over the desk. The majority of mice use an electromechanical system to detect movement relative to the desk or mouse pad. The movements of a ball, which protrudes from the base of the mouse, are transmitted by friction to two small rollers, mounted at right-angles to each other. These detect the two components of movement of the ball - right/left and up/down - and convert them to electrical signals using a rotating disc system. Some expensive systems use a mouse based on optical principles, which has no moving parts. It relies on a special lined mouse pad and uses optical sensors in the mouse to detect movement over the lines.

The roller ball   A development of the mouse - the roller ball - is really an inverted mouse. It is operated by the user rolling the ball by hand and has the advantage that it does not require as much clear desk space as a normal mouse. The mouse, in either form, has become the commonest of all input devices - the only one, other than the keyboard, which is likely to be provided with a computer as standard equipment. Mass production has resulted in it being a very cheap device; in fact it is effectively free to the purchaser. For this reason it is also the input device which all modern software will support.

The graphic tablet   The main alternative to the mouse is the graphic tablet. This is very much more expensive and occupies much more room on the desk. It consists of a special tablet -a large flat plastic surface - and a pen-like device which is used to draw on the tablet. The pen is connected to the computer with a cable, like the mouse, although cordless models are available, which communicate via infrared beams to a detector in the computer.

There are a number of advantages to the graphic tablet which make it preferable for many users. The pen, sometimes called a stylus, is a more natural drawing tool than a box on wheels (the mouse). In fact some mouse manufacturers have tried to address this perceived advantage of the tablet by providing a mouse shaped like a pen. Another advantage is that menus and icons can be placed on the tablet, instead of the screen, thereby releasing precious space on the screen for drawing. These menus take the form of a sheet of paper or thin card, stuck on top of the tablet because the stylus does not have to make contact with the tablet for its presence to be detected by the electronic system embedded in it. Sometimes tablets are provided with specialist design software and the menus are printed on the tablet permanently. Another advantage lies in the size of the tablet, which is often bigger than the screen. This means that the artist can draw on a larger area than would be possible using a direct method.

The digitising tablet   The facility to place sheets of paper on the tablet means that the system can be used to trace existing pictures. An extension of this method, the digitising tablet, has been developed to input very precise graphic information like data from maps and detailed diagrams. The pen-like stylus is replaced with something much more like a mouse - sometimes called a puck because of its resemblance to a hockey puck. The distinguishing feature of the puck is an attachment for lining up its position very precisely. It takes the form of a small sheet of transparent plastic with cross-hairs printed on it. When the cross-hairs are lined up precisely with a point on the map, a button on the puck is clicked and that position is automatically entered into the computer.

Scanners

A document scanner is a device for inputting digitised versions of existing pictures, like photographs, maps or other documents. It looks very like a desktop photocopier. The document is either fed into a slot or placed upside down on a glass sheet in the top of the scanner. An intense source of light, in the form of a fluorescent strip, slowly scans the length of the document. Accompanying the scanning light is a rod-like component which contains digitising elements. This measures the light and dark regions of the paper by detecting the amount of light reflected from the paper. This gradually produces an analysis of the whole document at up to 300 dpi. The simplest systems simply record the information in binary form - black or white - but most scanners now can also detect a number of grey-levels. Some scanners are designed to scan colour images also, using a system of colour filters. The net result of all this a large graphics file, as described at the beginning of the chapter.

Hand-held scanners   There are also hand-held scanners which are much cheaper, and quite adequate for scanning small images. They are usually 4 inches wide and are rolled across the image, rather than having the light source scanned across the stationary document. Some of them are supplied with software which will 'stitch' together a large image which has been scanned in parallel 4 inch strips. For occasional use, therefore, a hand-held scanner can substitute for the much more expensive A4 document scanner.

OCR One very useful application of document scanners is called optical character recognition (OCR). A special piece of software is used to analyse the scanned images of printed characters and recognise what they are. This can be used to turn typed and printed material into word-processor files, which can then be edited and reprinted in new forms. Apart from these obvious advantages the file size for a set of ASCII codes is enormously reduced, when compared with a 300 dpi image.

The digital camera This is a recent development which is becoming increasingly important as a rapid way of producing digitised pictures. It looks like an ordinary 35 mm camera but the normal film back is replaced with a two-dimensional array of electronic elements which are light sensitive. These CCDs (charge-coupled devices) are manufactured as a small chip onto which the image is focused, instead of onto film as in a normal camera. They measure the light intensity at each point in the array and so produce a digitised image instantly, which is then stored on a small floppy disc.

Film digitisers The film industry has become very interested in digitising images because of the application to computer-generated special effects. Highly-specialised versions of the document scanner have been developed to deal with the transparent photographic images used in films. These make it possible to digitise a whole series of frames from a film so that the computer can be used to modify them to produce the effect that is desired. These are then displayed on a special computer monitor and re-photographed using a cine-camera. Simpler versions of this type of technology are applied to digitising 35 mm transparencies.

There are other ways of digitising existing images, using a video camera as the source of the image. The analogue picture signal is then fed to a 'frame-grabber' which converts the signal to a stream of digital information. This has ben referred to already in the section on Video output and input.

Current hardware　　*The computer system*

The most important factors are :

- processor power and speed
- memory size
- hard-disc size
- the internal bus.

The general rule for processors is to buy the fastest and most powerful you can afford. Because of rapid changes in computer specification it is wisest to buy for the future, so for an IBM-PC compatible a 486 processor should be a minimum for serious graphics work and a Pentium preferable. For the Apple Mac, the new Power-Mac series should be the aim. However, for some applications, the lower-level technology - Intel 386 and Motorola 68040, respectively - provide a very respectable basis and are not to be despised if economy is the key.

Memory size is important for GUIs and for processing images, particularly in photo-retouching. Most computing work can be speeded by increasing the RAM since it reduces the time wasted by shuffling data back-and-forward between RAM and hard-disc. For a PC compatible, 4 Mbytes is an absolute minimum, 8 Mbytes preferable and 12-16 Mbytes better. Apple Macs require rather less memory since more of the operating graphic system is held in ROM but similar figures should be aimed at.

Hard-disc size is important, simply for storing graphic files but increasingly all applications software occupy large amounts of disc space. A minimum size might be about 350 Mbytes but 500-700 Mbytes is preferable.

There are a number of internal buses available for the PC compatible. The original AT-bus (often now called the ISA or Industry Standard Architecture) is now obsolete though millions of existing machines use it. It is restricted to moving data 16 bits at a time and at a clock speed of 8 MHz. Since all new machines have 32-bit processors and run at speed of 33-100 MHz the bus is clearly a major bottleneck. The choices are between EISA (an extended version of ISA), VESA's VL bus or PCI. Many computers offer two different buses on the same machine so that the customer has more choice of interface cards (which must be designed to fit one or other of the systems). Apple Mac owners have never had to worry about such matters since Apple have always used their own NuBus system. However Apple are committed to using the PCI bus system in the future. Any of these new faster bus systems will make a big difference to graphics work, when compared with the traditional ISA bus.

Monitors

There are many monitor manufacturers but very few companies make the most important component - the tube - and so many products, with different badges, will have identical tubes inside. There are two competing technologies for making colour tubes. The standard method uses a shadow mask with circular holes and phosphor dots arranged in a triangular pattern. The alternative technology was devised by Sony and is called the Trinitron. This uses a mask made up from parallel wires and phosphor dots arranged in stripes. The Trinitron mask absorbs less of the electron beam and so is capable of producing brighter colours. One by-product of the design is that the fine horizontal stabilising wires which hold the mask steady can be visible in the final image. Most users seem not to notice, or mind about this. The standard size of tubes has been 14 inches but there is a definite movement now to 15 inch tubes. Larger monitors, with 16-17 inch tubes, are preferable for graphics work and 19, 21 and 23 inch tubes are even better for graphics but are very expensive. Some graphics work - for example some DTP - does not need colour output and for this work a monochrome screen is preferable, since for any particular budget a much larger screen can be bought. For example, a 17 inch colour monitor might cost as much as a 21 inch grey-scale monochrome monitor.

Video cards

Video cards can vary in price by a factor of ten. The difference between the two ends of the price spectrum are:

- resolution
- number of colours
- speed
- special facilities.

The cheapest cards will provide the standard graphics mode (S-VGA) for IBM-PC compatibles with the current minimum number of colours (256) and no 'acceleration'. More expensive cards will offer higher resolution (above 800 x 600), more colours (up to 16.8 million) and faster processing of the graphic data.

Most of these more expensive cards are sold as 'accelerator' cards because they use an on-board microprocessor to speed up the work. Specialist cards will contain built-in facilities for speeding up certain types of graphic work - for example, 'Windows accelerators' process the clipping operations associated with windows and 3-D cards speed up the calculations associated with rendering 3-D images.

Printers

Dot-matrix printers are only useful as cheap 'proofing' devices and are not much used in graphics work. They are, however, cheap to buy and cheap to run.

Monochrome ink-jet printers can produce excellent results. They offer 300-360 dpi and with the right paper look just as good as a 300 dpi laser printer. They are cheaper to buy than a laser printer but their consumable costs can be higher because of the short life of the ink cartridges.

Monochrome laser printers come in a wide range of prices depending on the resolution (300 or 600 dpi), number of pages per minute (4-16ppm), on-board memory and number of installed fonts. The expensive ones are intended for heavy-duty, multiple-user situations on networks. Toner cartridges cost up to four times as much as an ink-jet cartridge but last much longer. More expensive professional-level laser printers are available which print at 1200 and 1600 dpi and even greater resolutions.

Colour inkjets are the cheapest way of obtaining acceptable-quality colour. If the output requires solid blocks of vibrant primary colours a thermal printer may be preferable to an inkjet though the consumable costs are much higher. For best quality colour photographic images a dye-sublimation printer is needed. Colour laser printers are still very expensive but coming down in price all the time.

Summary

1 The ordinary user needs to know something about computer hardware, in order to choose graphics peripherals wisely and to use them properly.

2 The central processor of the computer and its internal bus system are required to handle exceptionally large amounts of computer data, generated and processed in graphics work, and so it is important to have a suitable basic system if work is not to intolerably slow.

3 There are four characteristics of the computer display which are important in graphics work. These are : the screen size, its shape, the number of colours and grey-levels it can handle and the video board which feeds information to it.

4 There are a wide range of printers and plotters which are available to produce 'hard-copy' - copies of the computer image on paper. Each has its own characteristics and many, though not all, are suitable for one or other graphics application.

5 Printers are not the only suitable graphics output devices. Images are increasingly being transferred to video tape.

6 Hand-held graphics input devices are of two types - direct devices for drawing directly on the computer screen, and indirect

devices in which the drawing instrument is used on another surface.

7 There is a wide range of input devices and it is important to know how they are used and which device might be most suitable for a particular application.

8 Document scanners and other, video-based, techniques are available for digitising existing drawings or text and provide an alternative way of inputting graphics information.

Desktop publishing

Key points
- *the relationship between word processing and desktop publishing (DTP)*
- *using a GUI*
- *laying out a printed page using a DTP package*
- *problems associated with colour*

What is DTP?　DTP can be thought of as a natural development of word processing - the earliest, and still the most important, application of the personal computer for most users. At its simplest the computer is used as the electronic equivalent of a typewriter. The text which is typed on the keyboard is immediately displayed, but on the computer monitor rather than on paper. The advantages over a traditional typewriter are considerable. The text is held temporarily in memory (though it can be stored permanently on magnetic disc when necessary) and need only be printed when all the editing and corrections have been made. Typing mistakes can be corrected, text can be edited and reordered - all without the need for any unnecessary retyping. Text can be saved and reused in a another context. Nothing need ever be typed twice and mistakes in the final product can, in principle, be completely eliminated in a way that cannot be guaranteed by mechanical typewriting where all keystrokes are immediately translated into the final printed product. Modern word processors have added to these basic features additional aids such as spell-checkers and even grammar and style checkers.

The final product
The limiting feature of the basic word processor was the appearance of the final printed text. The first printers to be used were impact dot-matrix devices which were of poor quality compared with a modern typewriter. The development of the daisywheel printer and the single-strike ribbon, however, ensured that results

71

as good as an electric typewriter could be achieved but only in a limited number of typewriter-style fonts and with only the same control over layout that a typewriter provides. What the word processor could not do was to rival professional printing processes. DTP - the use of personal computers for typesetting and page layout - had to wait for two hardware developments which took place in the 1980s. These were high-resolution bitmapped graphic screens (together with computers powerful enough to handle the amount of data implied by such displays) and high-resolution printers.

The first affordable system was the Apple Macintosh which was designed as a graphics-oriented personal computer with a graphics-based user interface, together with a 300 dpi laser printer and appropriate software. This combination made it possible for the user to concentrate on the layout and appearance of the final page - which could be displayed on the screen - and to produce an end product which was an acceptable approximation to a professionally printed document. Figure 4.1 (and Plate 9) show a screen-shot of **Aldus PageMaker** running on an Apple Mac.

Working with imported files
Most DTP software was initially designed to work in combination with word processors and graphics software by taking text and graphics files produced by such software and combining the results into a suitable document. For example, the text-editing facilities which were built in to DTP packages were originally quite elementary because it was assumed that all work in typing in the text and correcting it, using such features as spell-checkers, would

Figure 4.1. Screen-shot of DTP software (Aldus PageMaker), running on a Macintosh.

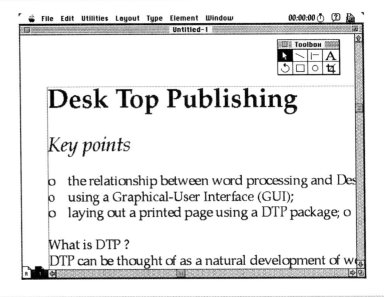

Figure 4.2. The 'pasteboard' facility
in PageMaker. In this view the page
is empty but a text-frame and a
graphic are on the pasteboard,
ready to be dragged into place on
the page.

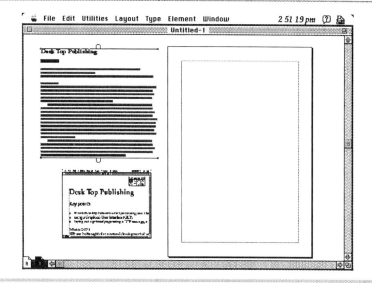

be done using a word processor. There was good logic in this. Word processors used text-only mode which could display the text as fast as the typist could type it. DTP packages were designed to display the precise appearance of the text which was a much slower process and the computers of the day could not be expected to produce instant updating of the screen as the text was typed in. It would not, in any case, have made economic sense to use the more expensive facilities of a DTP computer simply for entering text.

All this has since changed and any modern computer can offer the WYSIWYG features of DTP. As a result modern DTP software usually offers a wide range of word processing features such as spell-checkers, and search and replace editing, so that DTP software can be used for the text entry if desired. This has been true for some time with DTP packages designed to run on powerful workstations and mini computers and is increasingly true of micro-based software.

Types of DTP   At first sight DTP packages can look very much alike but more detailed investigation shows that although they inevitably have many features in common they are often aimed at different types of user and different end-products. Some packages are best described as 'page-oriented' or 'design-oriented'. Early versions of **PageMaker (Aldus)** and **Quark XPress (Quark Computers)** fell into this category. For example PageMaker (see Figure 4.2) features a 'clipboard' - a large space, like a drawing board- on which the page is placed. Graphics and text can be arranged around the edge of the page on the clipboard, then dragged onto the page, moved around until a suitable position has been found, and then 'pasted' into place. This approach is intended to appeal to design-oriented

73

users and is ideal for the production of single pages such as post-ers, advertisements or short magazine articles. The emphasis here is flexibility in manipulating the text and graphics and to enable a trained artist or typographer to achieve the desired design.

Long documents

In contrast, **Ventura Publisher (Corel)** is a good example of a DTP package which from the start was intended for the production of large documents. Here the emphasis is on the ability to handle a large number of pages, to create indexes automatically and to be able to reformat documents without the user's intervention.   In practice, many of these distinctions have diminished as later ver-sions of each piece of software have adopted features originally introduced in their rivals. Where significant differences still remain they will be discussed later in the chapter.

The interface   DTP software was amongst the first to use a graphic interface of the sort introduced with the Apple Macintosh. The two important features are the WYSIWYG display and the direct interaction style. Traditional word processing software of the sort I am using to write this book displays the text in text-only mode using the 'system font' - that is, the style of characters which are built-in to the hardware of the computer. This font may bear very little resemblance to the font used by the printer. DTP software, on the other hand, will al-ways display the shape of characters which will be used in the fi-nal document. The general principle is that the screen should al-ways look as near as possible to the end product ('What You See Is What You Get').

Printer codes

Just as important, however, is the way that the user is able to inter-

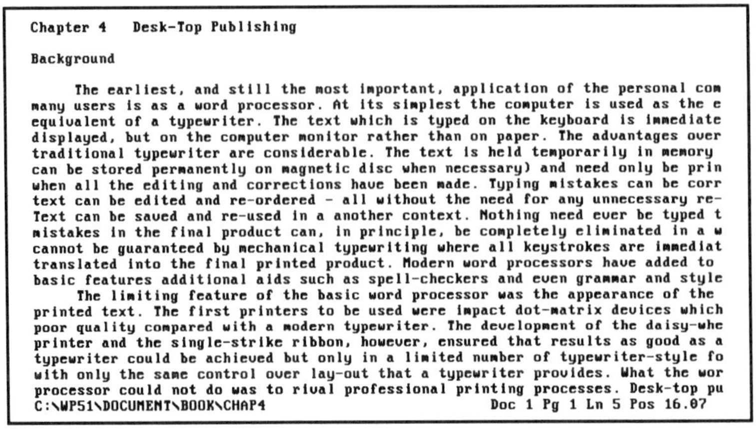

Figure 4.3. A screen-shot of a text-based word processor (Word-Perfect 5.1, DOS version). The screen gives very little indication of the appearance of the printed document because it uses the system font of the computer which may look very different from the printed font.

```
Chapter 4    Desk-Top Publishing

Background

     The earliest, and still the most important, application of the personal com
many users is as a word processor. At its simplest the computer is used as the e
equivalent of a typewriter. The text which is typed on the keyboard is immediate
displayed, but on the computer monitor rather than on paper. The advantages over
traditional typewriter are considerable. The text is held temporarily in memory
can be stored permanently on magnetic disc when necessary) and need only be prin
when all the editing and corrections have been made. Typing mistakes can be corr
text can be edited and re-ordered - all without the need for any unnecessary re-
Text can be saved and re-used in a another context. Nothing need ever be typed t
mistakes in the final product can, in principle, be completely eliminated in a w
cannot be guaranteed by mechanical typewriting where all keystrokes are immediat
translated into the final printed product. Modern word processors have added to
basic features additional aids such as spell-checkers and even grammar and style
     The limiting feature of the basic word processor was the appearance of the
printed text. The first printers to be used were impact dot-matrix devices which
poor quality compared with a modern typewriter. The development of the daisy-whe
printer and the single-strike ribbon, however, ensured that results as good as a
typewriter could be achieved but only in a limited number of typewriter-style fo
with only the same control over lay-out that a typewriter provides. What the wor
processor could not do was to rival professional printing processes. Desk-top pu
C:\WP51\DOCUMENT\BOOK\CHAP4                        Doc 1 Pg 1 Ln 5 Pos 16.07
```

*Figure 4.4. The same screen as
Figure 4.3 except that the printer
codes (which are normally hidden)
have been revealed. The codes
give clues as to the final appearance of the printed page.*

```
Chapter 4   Desk-Top Publishing

C:\WP51\DOCUMENT\BOOK\CHAP4                           Doc 1 Pg 1 Ln 1 Pos 14.33
{     ▲     ▲    ▲     ▲    ▲    ▲    ▲    ▲     ▲    ▲    ▲    ▲ ]  ▲    ▲    ▲
[Font:CG Times 12pt][BOLD]Chapter 4[bold]    [BOLD]Desk-Top Publishing[bold][HRt]

[HRt]
[BOLD]Background[HRt]
[bold][HRt]
[Tab]The earliest, and still the most important, application of the personal com
puter for[SRt]
many users is as a word processor. At its simplest the computer is used as the e
lectronic[SRt]
equivalent of a [ITALC]typewriter[italc]. The text which is typed on the keyboar
d is immediately[SRt]
displayed, but on the [UND]computer monitor[und] rather than on paper. The advan
tages over a[SRt]
traditional typewriter are considerable. The text is held temporarily in memory
(though it[SRt]
can be stored permanently on magnetic disc when necessary) and need only be prin
ted[SRt]
when all the editing and corrections have been made. Typing mistakes can be corr
ected,[SRt]

Press Reveal Codes to restore screen
```

act with the image of the document. Traditional word processors give instructions to the printer by means of printer codes. These are codes which are embedded in the document, though not usually directly visible to the user, and which have some effect on the way that the printer will produce the final document. For example, a particular code will make the printer print all the text which follows it in bold - until another code cancels the instruction. These codes will be inserted by the user by the use of key strokes such as a combination of the Control key together with the `B' key or by a particular function key. The only clue to the user that the document will look any different as a result of the code might be that the text which is affected could be displayed on the screen in a different colour or that some representation of the code might be displayed, embedded in the text.

Figures 4.3 - 4.5 show how this works for one widely-used word processor - WordPerfect 5.1. Figure 4.3 shows the normal screen. No attempt is made to show the precise appearance of the characters as they will be printed. The only concession to realism is that the number of characters on a screen line is the same as the number that will be printed on a line on the paper. Because, in this case, the chosen font is Times Roman 12 point, more than 80 characters will fit on a printed line. This means that there is not enough room to fit them all on the screen and so it must be scrolled sideways to read the ends of the lines. Figure 4.4 illustrates another mode of use in which the screen shows the, normally-hidden, printer codes. This gives extra information about the final appearance of the page - for example, which words will be in bold or underlined and where the lines will end. The codes are shown in square brackets. In this figure, [HRt] means 'Hard Return' (the Enter key has been pressed by the user to end a paragraph). [SRt] means 'Soft Return' (the soft-

Figure 4.5. The same screen as in Figures 4.3 and 4.4, except that now it is in 'preview' mode. This mode shows the appearance of the final document, but does not allow any editing to be done.

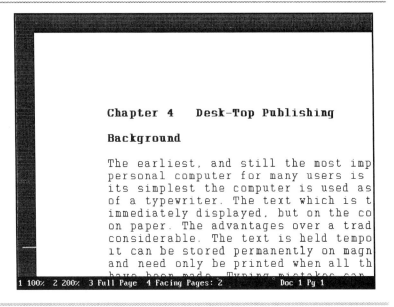

ware has terminated the line because no more characters can fit on. [BOLD] switches the printer to print in bold and [bold] switches it off again. [ITALC] and [italc] do the same for italics. In this display all the characters can be seen without scrolling. Figure 4.5 illustrates a screen in which the final appearance of the page is shown ('Page Preview' mode). No editing can be done in this mode, however.

Direct interaction

The concept of direct interaction is based on the idea that the user should be able to interact with the document in a more natural way. For example, a section of text might be made bold by the perfectly natural process of pointing to it on the screen, using the mouse, followed by the selection of the 'Bold' feature from a menu of options. The result is that the text is then displayed in bold on the display, just as it will appear in the final document. The principle of direct interaction will become clearer as other examples of DTP operations are introduced.

How to do DTP : Stage 1 Most DTP packages use a very similar approach to laying out a document. Before a document (sometimes called a 'Publication') is created, the screen is blank, apart from the menu system. The first stage involves defining what size and shape of page is wanted. This is done by choosing the New Document option from the file menu and this pops up a selection window (called a 'dialogue box') - see Figure 4.6. The main choices to be made are:

- page size orientation of the pages ('landscape' or 'portrait');
- the width of the margins;
- the number of newspaper-style columns (if any);
- single or double-sided pages.

The reason for the last choice is that some designs make a distinction between left-hand pages and right-hand ones. One obvious difference is that the page numbers may be in different positions and the headers may be different (as in this book).

Page display
The result of making these selections is that the software creates an image of the empty page on the screen, with the size of the margins and columns shown by guidelines.

The page is displayed either life size, magnified or reduced, as the user chooses. Until screens are the same size and resolution as the printed page it is necessary to be able to view the page in all these ways and usually between six and eight different magnification values are available. Figure 4.7 shows the choices which are available in PageMaker. The choice is made from a menu, which is itself an option in another menu, and both menus are shown pulled down. 'Fit in window' sets the magnification factor so as to fit the page completely inside the window which is being used to display the document. 'Show pasteboard' is the view shown in figure 4.2; the page is considerably reduced so as to show the space around it. 'Actual size' represents the page and its contents at exactly the same size that it will be printed. '25% size', '50% size' and '75% size' are reduced views - smaller than life-size. '200% size' and '400% size' are enlarged views. In figure 4.7, the screen is set at 200% magnification, as shown by the tick against that option.

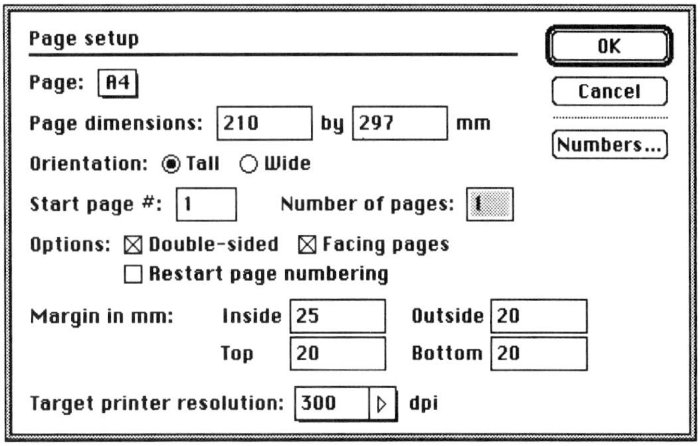

Figure 4.6. The 'Page setup' dialogue box in PageMaker. The basic decisions about page size and shape and the width of the margins are made using this box.

Page setup   OK

Page: A4   Cancel

Page dimensions: 210 by 297 mm   Numbers...

Orientation: ⦿ Tall ◯ Wide

Start page #: 1   Number of pages: 1

Options: ☒ Double-sided ☒ Facing pages
☐ Restart page numbering

Margin in mm: Inside 25   Outside 20
Top 20   Bottom 20

Target printer resolution: 300 ▷ dpi

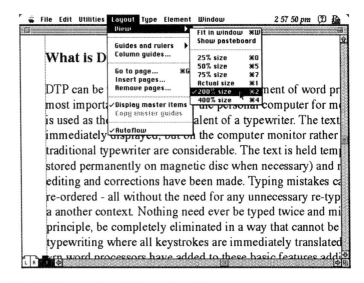

Figure 4.7. The document in PageMaker can be viewed at one of eight different 'zoom' levels (magnification values). Here a zoom level of 200% is being chosen from the 'View' menu.

Even a very simple DTP package should show a bare minimum of three views. One is a normal ('actual') size - where, with most monitors, only part of the page can be seen. This helps the user judge the size of the typeface and its readability. A second is a reduced size. In this, the whole page can be seen on the screen, though the text is probably not readable, but it helps the user judge the overall appearance of the page. The third is an enlarged size. Here only a few lines of text can be seen but it helps the user check on fine details.

Master pages
Master pages provide an important aid to laying out the document which should be used right from the start. In PageMaker the master page is represented by icons at the bottom left-hand corner of the page. They are labelled L and R (if double-sided pages are being used). To the right are page icons (labelled 1,2,3, etc). Clicking on one of these icons takes the user to a display of that particular page. The master page is used to display recurring items such as page headers and footers, page numbers or graphics like the horizontal lines used at the top of these pages. Anything placed on a master page will appear on all the following pages in addition to the material which is unique to that page. PageMaker only provides two master pages - one for right-hand pages and one for left. This is a minimum but it is more useful to have the freedom to create a larger number (as in Quark XPress which allows over 100) to cope with changes of style that might occur in the middle of a document. Magazines, for example, often adopt three styles with one, two and three columns, respectively, for different types of material.

How to do DTP : Stage 2 The next stage involves placing imported text and graphics on the page. At this point two different philosophies have been adopted. Some DTP software (like **Ventura Publisher**) requires the user to draw a rectangular 'frame' (a boundary or box) on the screen where the text or graphic is to go. This involves selecting the appropriate frame-drawing icon and then using the mouse to click and drag a box on the screen. If more than one frame is drawn then one can be selected by clicking on it with the mouse pointer. Its status is then indicated by means of tiny black squares at the corner of the frame which shows that it is currently the 'active' or selected frame. Using an appropriate menu choice, an existing text or graphic file is then chosen and this will be imported and placed into the active frame. Figure 4.8 shows a frame containing text.

'Roller blinds'
PageMaker also uses frames to control the position of text, but does not require the user to draw them. They are created automatically when text is placed (see later). The frame is designed to look like a roller-blind which is why there are small semicircular handle symbols at the top and bottom. If the bottom handle is pulled up, using the mouse, the frame gets smaller, like a blind being rolled up, and less of the text can then be seen. The fact that some of the text is not now being shown is indicated by a small triangle symbol in the bottom handle of the blind. When text continues on to another page or column this is signified by a '+' symbol in the bottom handle of the first blind and the top handle of the second frame. When a frame is selected, small black squares - described above - can be seen at the four corners of the blind.

Figure 4.8. Text is placed in a frame (called a 'roller-blind' in PageMaker). The frame is visible only when the pointer icon is chosen from the toolbox, and when the frame is selected - by clicking on it.

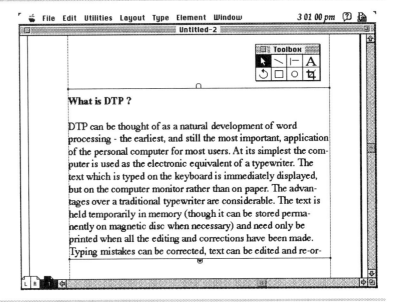

79

Importing files

Imported text files can be simple ASCII files which contain only the text characters and little else, or they can be word-processor files, complete with the embedded printer commands used by that particular word processor. Modern DTP packages have import filters for a range of word processors which recognise at least some of these printer commands and translate them into a form which the DTP software recognises. This will result in the text which has been emboldened or italicised in the word processor retaining those features in the final DTP product. Similarly the software will accept a number of different types of graphic files created in a range of graphic software, and saved in one of the widely-used formats. The DTP package will translate them into the form used by the DTP software.

Once the text or graphic is placed in its frame then any changes to its position are made by using the mouse to drag or re-size the frame, the contents of the frame following it like an object in a box.

The PageMaker method

The alternative to creating a frame and placing text in it, is used in **PageMaker** and is often claimed to be simpler and more natural than the 'frame-oriented' approach used in **Ventura**. The user is not required to draw any frames, simply to select the file from a menu and 'place' it by clicking the mouse on the screen where the text or graphic is to go.

The apparent contrast between the two approaches is not as important as it seems. The software still needs to 'know' exactly where the text is to go, not merely where it should start. This detailed information is supplied indirectly by the original choice of page margins and the number and width of columns. The text will flow from its starting point until it meets a boundary (either a right-hand margin or a column boundary) and then begin a new line, using a left-hand boundary as the starting point. Thus the frame does exist implicitly and is initially set by the choice of margins and column boundaries (for the sides) and by the mouse click which determines the top of the frame.

Once placed, the boundaries of the frame are shown on the screen in the appropriate mode and can be moved or re-sized in the way already described.

Autoflow

PageMaker has an 'autoflow' feature which ensures that when text is placed it flows into the column guides and creates as many new pages as are needed. Its page-oriented approach still shows however if changes are then needed. If text has been placed on the document without columns there is no automatic way of automatically reformatting it into columns, as in Ventura.

Graphics are placed in the same way as text. In the frame-oriented approach, a frame is drawn and selected and the graphic chosen from a menu. It is then appears in the frame, scaled in size so as to fit the frame. In the PageMaker approach, the graphic is chosen from a menu and 'placed' by clicking the mouse. The graphic then appears in a default size and must be dragged into the size required.

How to do DTP : Stage 3   *Fonts*

The next stage involves defining the exact appearance of the text and graphics. The most obvious factor which contributes to the appearance of the text is the choice of fonts. The word font (or fount) is a typographer's term which indicates the precise appearance of the printed characters. The exact shapes of a family of letters, and other characters, are the outcome of skilled design and are given names such as 'Times', 'Helvetica' and 'Palatino'. Traditional designs which use delicate details at the extremities of the character (called 'serifs') are termed serif typefaces.

Simpler, modern styles like Helvetica which have no serifs are termed sans-serif. Each named family will have subtle variations - such as bold versions (thicker, darker-looking characters) and italic (sloping) forms. Some typefaces may have more than one bold design (called bold and extra-bold or black and extra-black). These are usually used for large headings in newspapers and magazines. There can also be special narrow versions of a typeface, again for use in headings, where tall eye-catching letters are needed which do not take up too much space on the line. Figure 4.9 shows 12

Figure 4.9. A few samples of typefaces, including the well-known 'Times' and 'Helvetica' and a narrow version of Helvetica.

Antiqua Ultra
Cooper Black
Helvetica
New York
Sans Black Condensed
Windsor

Broadway
Brush Script
Helvetica Narrow
Palton Light
Times
Zapf Chancery

fonts. One is a very commonly used serif font ('Times'). Two show different versions of the sans-serif typeface 'Helvetica' - the normal one and a narrow version. Some of the others are more decorative fonts, which are suitable for posters, in large sizes perhaps, but would not be very readable in large quantities and in small font sizes.

As a general rule, a large version of a character will not be simply a scaled-up version of the small one. The proportions will need to be subtly changed as the size changes and this is all part of the typographer's skill in designing the character set. The term font is usually used to distinguish a particular size and type of a named typeface (e.g. Times bold, 12 point) but it is also used more generally for the whole family. The term 'point', used here, is a typographer's unit of measurement for the height of the character.

Choosing fonts

Because DTP software is WYSIWYG, whenever text is placed on a document it must have a font assigned to it. This is a default font, selected by the user as part of a set of general 'preferences'. To change the font assigned to a particular portion of text, the text must first be selected using the mouse and the named typeface and size then chosen from a menu. There is a menu option which will allow the user to select all the text, when that is required, but there will also be mouse operations to choose smaller blocks of text when that is needed. The most flexible method is to click and drag the mouse over the text which is then displayed in reverse (black and white exchanged) to indicate which parts of the text have been selected. A widely-used convention allows the choice of a single word, with a double click on that word and a paragraph with a triple-click.

Graphics

Another basic feature of the layout is the way that graphics are combined with text. This is usually a simple matter of placing the text first and then placing graphics on top of the text in the required position. In frame-based software, a frame must be drawn first. In PageMaker-style software, the graphic is simply placed on top of the text. Once the 'text wrap' option is chosen from the menu, the text then automatically 'wraps round' the graphic image leaving a small amount of clearance all the way round, like a margin.

Figure 4.10 shows an example of this. The small black squares at the corners of the graphic show that it is selected and can be moved, for example. The dotted line illustrate how much 'standoff' has been allowed - that is, how much clearance there is between the graphic and the text. If the graphic is not rectangular there is a way

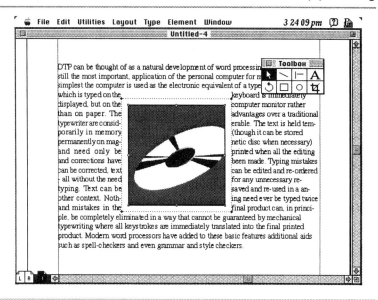

Figure 4.10. A graphic, placed in the middle of a block of text. The 'text wrap' facility has been used to ensure that the text flows round the edges of the graphic, leaving a small margin.

of adapting the text to the shape of the graphic, if desired. This often means some detailed adjustments by the user, using the mouse to adjust the ends of each line of text, or reshaping the effective boundary of the graphic.

Anchors

There will also be some simple method of attaching some explanatory text to the graphic (its caption) which will then move with the graphic if it becomes necessary to change its position on the page. It will also be possible to 'anchor' the graphic to a particular word in the body of the text so that if extra text is added earlier in the document, which pushes that text on to another page, the graphic will move with the text it illustrates. In PageMaker this is done by adding the text as an 'in-line' graphic. This means placing the text when in text mode (see later for a discussion of modes), in which case it is placed at the current position of the text cursor. It then behaves as if it were a text character.

How to do DTP : Stage 4 Having created a document and placed the text and graphics in place there are many fine details which can then be adjusted. For example, the font is not the only aspect of the text which needs to be under the user's control. Other important matters include the alignment, the line spacing and the character spacing. One alignment option is 'aligned left' or 'left-justified' (like a typewriter) - with the left end of the lines matching up, but with right ends left ragged. Another is 'fully-justified' or just 'justified' (lined up at both ends, as in most printed books). Another is 'centred' (often used in headings). Another is 'aligned right' (the complement to aligned left). Another is 'force justified' in which the text is forced to match both ends of the line even when there is not enough text to fit the line at normal word spacing. This is a special form of justification which is sometimes applied to headings. Figure 4.11 shows four of these alignment types : left, right, centred and justified. These (and all the following controls) are set by selecting the text and then choosing the control option from a menu.

Leading

Control over line spacing (called 'leading' by printers) can be applied to the normal lines of text to make more or less text fit on to a page or to make the text look more or less 'dense'. Figure 4.12 shows the same paragraph set with two different values of leading. In both cases the text has size 14 point. The top paragraph is set with the lines very close together, with 14 point leading. In the bottom paragraph the lines are much further apart - 21 point leading. Spacing between paragraphs can also be set. There are a number of different approaches to indicating to the reader where a new paragraph begins. One method relies on the indentation of the text at the beginning of the new paragraph. Another uses a larger first letter - a 'drop cap'. A third way is to add a little extra space between the last line of the old paragraph and the first line of the next (except where the new paragraph appears at the top of the page). This extra space can be automatically added.

Figure 4.11. Four example of text alignment : left aligned (ragged end), right aligned (ragged beginning), centred, and fully justified (aligned at both ends).

DTP can be thought of as a natural development of word processing - the earliest, and still the most important, application of the personal computer for most users.

DTP can be thought of as a natural development of word processing the earliest, and still the most important, application of the personal computer for most users.

DTP can be thought of as a natural development word processing - and still the most important, application of the personal computer for most users.

DTP can be thought of as a natural development of word processing - the earliest, and still the most important, application of the personal computer for most users.

Figure 4.12. Two copies of the same
piece of text but set with very
different values of 'leading' (line
spacing).

DTP can be thought of as a natural development of word processing - the earliest, and still the most important, application of the personal computer for most users. At its simplest the computer is used as the electronic equivalent of a typewriter.

DTP can be thought of as a natural development of word processing - the earliest, and still the most important, application of the personal computer for most users. At its simplest the computer is used as the electronic equivalent of a typewriter.

Figure 4.12. Two copies of the same piece of text but set with very different values of 'leading' (line spacing).

Character spacing

Spacing between characters is a more subtle matter. Printed fonts are proportionally spaced - that is, each letter has its own width depending on its shape. This is unlike typewriter fonts, in which all letters must be given the same space because of the nature of the machine. Here the paper is advanced by the same amount for each key press, so the letters must have the same width. Each proportionally spaced font will have its recommended inter-character spacing but the user may always chose to squeeze the letters a little closer or pull them further apart (called tighter or looser 'tracking'). Again, this affects the sense of how dense - closely packed - the text is on the page. Figure 4.13 shows a proportionally-spaced font and a mono-spaced font. The letters are the same size - 28 point. Note the amount of space allowed for a narrow character like i in the top example. In fact 15 characters in the top line occupy only the same space as about 10 in the third line. Note also how the designer of the mono-spaced font has artificially widened

Figure 4.13. Two different fonts - one proportionally spaced and the other mono-spaced. The first is more compact and easier to read than the second.

Proportionally spaced font : milk
```
Monospaced
font: milk
```

Figure 4.14. Examples of pairs of letters which have been 'kerned'. They have been moved closer together because their shapes are complementary.

WA Wo Av
To   VA Po

the letter i to make it appear as wide as all the other letters.

Another aspect of inter-letter spacing concerns the spacing between certain pairs of characters whose shape is complementary and in which the standard spacing does not look quite right. This effect is most noticeable when large character sizes are used, as in headlines. Combinations such as W followed by A, where the slope of the final stroke of the W and the first stroke of the A naturally fit together, are best dealt with by 'kerning' (see Figure 4.14). This means bringing them closer together than they would be if some standard inter-letter spacing were used. The result is that letters are not required to occupy their own rectangles in space in such a way that they do not overlap. In the case of, for example, the pair WA, if a vertical line is drawn at the end of the first character it will cut through the second. The two letters are overlapping each other's space.

Automatic kerning of a variety of these character pairs is a standard feature of DTP software but manual adjustments should also be possible, for the user who is not happy with these settings. It should also be possible to turn kerning off for the smaller characters to speed up the process of laying out the text.

Hyphenation
The whole question of inter-word and inter-character spacing becomes more complicated if the text is justified. More space must be added to a line to ensure that the end of the line corresponds with the margin or column marker. This can create a very uneven effect, particularly if the text is set in narrow columns when it may result in very large spaces between words. The worst cases are caused by long words. If, for example, a ten-character word cannot be fitted on to a line and is moved to the next line it automatically creates ten spaces on the first line. These will be placed somewhere in the middle of the line to produce a justified setting. The only way to avoid these large white spaces is to split long words at the end of a line, separating the two parts with hyphens. DTP software can au-

Figure 4.15. A typographer's 'orphan'. The figure shows the bottom of the page of a book. The sentence beginning 'Nothing need ...' is the beginning of a new paragraph and occurs at the bottom of the page, just above the footer and page number. It should be moved to the top of the next page.

The limiting feature of the basic word processor was the appearance of the final printed text. The first printers to be used were impact dot-matrix devices which were of poor quality compared with a modern typewriter. Typing mistakes can be corrected, text can be edited and reordered - all without the need for any unnecessary retyping. Text can be saved and reused in a another context.

Nothing need ever be typed twice and mistakes

Using Computer Graphics   21

tomatically hyphenate words with the aid of a special dictionary but this can sometimes result in hyphens at the end of two, three or even four consecutive lines. To avoid this it should be possible to specify the maximum number of end-line hyphens which are acceptable.

Other layout features
DTP provides many other tools to control the layout of text and the general appearance of a document:

Widows and orphans are 'stray' lines of text which occur when a new paragraph begins very close to the bottom of a page or ends very close to the beginning of one. A widow is defined as one or more lines at the end of a paragraph which occur at the top of a new page or column. An orphan is one or more lines at the beginning of a paragraph which occur at the end of a page or column. Figure 4.15 shows an orphan. Both widows and orphans can look unsightly and DTP software can avoid them by making small adjustments to the interline spacing, which over the length of a page will expand or contract the text to avoid the problem.

Unless all pages consist of solid blocks of text, with no special inter-paragraph spacing and no headings of a larger size, then the text on two opposing pages will not necessarily line up at the bottom. To solve this problem, a form of vertical justification is needed, in which small extra spaces are introduced between lines to cause them to match up. A similar effect is produced when text is set in

Figure 4.16. Unbalanced columns. There is not enough text to fill both columns so the amount in the first, needs to be reduced to bring the two into balance.

DTP can be thought of as a natural development of word processing - the earliest, and still the most important, application of the personal computer for most users. At its simplest the computer is used as the electronic equivalent of a typewriter. The text which is typed on the keyboard is immediately displayed, but on the computer monitor rather than on paper. The advantages over a traditional typewriter are considerable. In memory (though it can be stored permanently on magnetic disc when necessary) and need only be printed when all the editing and corrections have been made. Typing mistakes can be corrected, text can be edited and reordered - all without the need for any unnecessary retyping. Text can be saved and re-used in a another context. Nothing need ever be typed twice and mistakes in the final product can, in principle, be completely eliminated in a way that cannot be guaranteed by mechanical typewriting where all keystrokes are immediately translated into the final printed product.

columns which, at the end of an article will probably not match either, since one column may be full and the other not (see Figure 4.16). This needs a special 'column balance' feature to even them up and produce a neater effect.

How to do DTP : Stage 5 Having total control over the appearance of text can be a mixed blessing, because the more controls which are available to the user, the longer it takes to define and apply these controls. There are two answers to this problem: sensible defaults and automation. The use of defaults in all software simply recognises the fact that having control doesn't mean that the user always wants (or knows how) to use it. If sensible default values for such things as interline spacing and pair-kerning values are specified, then the amateur user and the user who is in a hurry can produce good results with little effort or experience. The expert user can still retain control.

Automation
Automation provides ways of letting the computer do the hard, repetitive work. One of the most useful forms of this is the 'paragraph tag' (sometimes, confusingly, called a 'style sheet' which can mean something else, or a 'style'). A paragraph tag is a description which can be attached to a paragraph and which carries with it the values of all the many typographic controls which can affect that paragraph. For example, if a particular paragraph has been set in 12 point Helvetica, justified, with 14 point leading and 1 inch indent, then these and any other settings can become a tag. The tag is given a name - perhaps, 'body text', to mean that these are the values which will be used for most of the body of the text in the document. Once all these values have been set, for one particular para-

graph, then any other paragraph which should look the same can be 'tagged' with the same settings. To do this, the paragraph is chosen and the appropriate tag name selected from a menu, a process which is much faster than individually resetting all these values for each paragraph. Figure 4.17 shows two paragraphs which have been tagged with two different styles. A list of available styles is seen in the 'Style Palette' which is a floating menu. A number of pre-defined styles may be provided with the software but these can be edited and added to as required.

Other forms of automation

Automatic page numbering can be achieved in PageMaker by placing a special symbol on the master page. As a result all the normal pages are then numbered automatically, in sequence. The same principal can be applied to the numbering of chapters, subsections of chapters and diagrams. This feature is particularly useful when editing the text causes material to be moved from one part of a document to another, since the numbering process will be automatically reset to take account of the changes. Indexes and tables of contents (TOC) can be generated automatically. Since the software can hardly be expected to 'know' which words are to be featured in the index, the author must go through the text and mark each appearance of each word which is to feature in the index, but after that the process of listing those words alphabetically and recording the pages they appear on, is automatic. The same sort of process can be used to generate a list of contents.

Figure 4.17. Paragraph (or style) tags in PageMaker. The second paragraph in this figure has been selected (it is in inverse video) and a style -'body text' - is being chosen from the style palette.

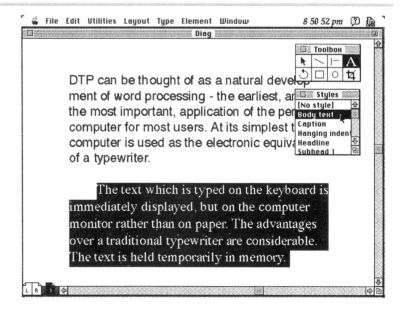

Aids to layout   The use of DTP usually implies a concern for the appearance of the final document and this in turn should involve thought about the overall design of the page. Page designs are often based on a series of columns - not necessarily of equal width - together with invisible horizontal boundaries which effectively divide the page into a grid pattern. This basic design concept lends itself to a huge variety of different page styles and DTP software offers a number of aids to the process of laying out the basic elements. These aids include rulers, guides and templates.

Rulers

Rulers are what the name implies - a representation of rulers by the side of the page, whose 'zero-points' can be moved to coincide with any convenient point, such as the edge of the page or the margins. Figure 4.18 shows a screen with the rulers displayed at the top and along the left side. In the top left corner there is a small icon which represents the intersection of the rulers. It takes the form of two crossing, dotted lines. This zero-point of the two rulers can be dragged into a suitable position; the screen-shot shows it being moved. The dotted lines illustrate the rulers in transition and help the user to line them up precisely with the edges of a page or a diagram. When the mouse button is released these dotted lines disappear and the rulers jump to their new position. After that, positioning of objects is aided by the fact that equivalent dotted lines appear on the rulers, corresponding to the position of the mouse cursor.

Figure 4.18. The figure shows the two rulers in PageMaker. They run along the top, and down the left side, of the screen. The zero-point of the two rulers can be moved to any convenient position using the mouse. The crossed lines in the figure show the location of the zero-point as it is being dragged into a new position.

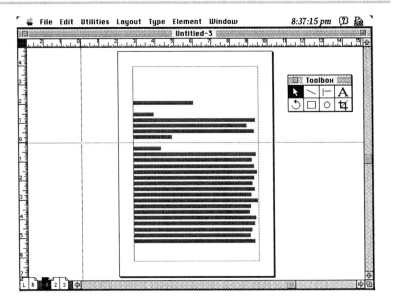

Guides and templates

Guides are non-printing lines which can be dragged into place over the page as an aid to lining up components of the design, such as blocks of text or pictures. Templates are whole page designs - for a wide range of types of document -provided by professional designers, which the amateur can adopt simply by replacing sample text and images with their own. Templates can also be designed and saved by the user and provide a valuable way of imposing a 'company-style' on documents produced by a variety of users.

Modes   Much, early, computer software used the concept of different operating states (referred to as 'modes') - partly to overcome limitations in the input hardware, particularly in the area of keyboards, but sometimes as a chosen design feature. For example, in early text editors, pressing a particular key (say `I') signified that the software should go into `Insert' mode. This meant that all further keystrokes should be interpreted as text characters to be inserted into a text file. Another keystroke (which could not be any of the normal text keys, for obvious reasons) signified that text insertion was finished and that any further keystrokes should be translated as commands - to save the file to disc, for example. This was called `Command' mode. Modal software is software which interprets the same event in different ways - depending on the mode it happened to be in. This can be a source of endless confusion and mistakes for the inexpert user.

Mode-less interfaces

One view of good interface design, adopted by the developers of what became the Apple Mac interface, is that software should be mode-less wherever possible. The same actions should not result in different results on different occasions. The purpose of mode-based designs, however, is to enable a limited number of input facilities (the limited number of keys on the keyboard, for example) to serve a large number of purposes. The SHIFT key on the typewriter serves this purpose, enabling lower-case and upper-case letters to be typed with the same character key. Graphic interfaces also have a limited number of input possibilities. Even if there were no limit to the input options which the designer could invent there is a limit to the number that the hapless user can remember! So there can be a very good logic to using the same input or command technique to perform different functions - as long as these functions are sufficiently similar to make logical sense.

For example, in DTP software, it may be necessary to select a block of text for two different sorts of activities. If a block of text is to be selected so that its position on the page can be changed - as

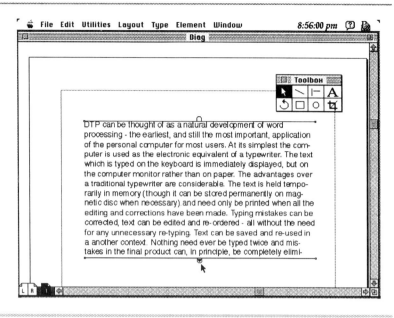

Figure 4.19. A block of text has been selected in 'frame-mode' (with the pointer tool) so that it can be moved or its shape changed. Compare this with Figure 4.17 - also taken from PageMaker - where a paragraph has been selected in 'text-mode' (with the text tool).

described earlier - then, in some software, a 'frame mode' must be used. If, on the other hand, some text is to be selected so that its font or alignment is to be changed, or a word deleted, then a 'text mode' must be used. The selection method may be identical - usually, clicking on the block. It is the mode which determines the end result of the operation.

In Figure 4.17 a paragraph has been selected in order that its font can be changed. The selected paragraph appears in inverse video. This means that the black characters are shown in white and the white page is shown in black. Notice that this operation has been done after clicking the Text icon (the letter A in the toolbox). In some software it would be said that the text-mode had been selected, in order to perform a text operation. In Figure 4.19 it can be seen that a Selection icon had been chosen (the arrow icon in the toolbox). In this case the frame is not big enough to display all the text and this is signalled by the small triangle at the bottom of the 'roller-blind' - next to the mouse cursor.

This mode could be called a frame-mode - one in which frames can be manipulated. The reason for devising different modes, then, is to allow the same basic action to produce different results. The user does not have to learn two different actions to produce the same basic effect, but does have to learn to select the correct mode.

'Tools'

In some software, PageMaker for example, this distinction is described differently. It is said that a different `tool' must be chosen to achieve the two different results rather than a different mode being selected. In Figure 4.19 the selection tool has been chosen from the Toolbox. In Figure 4.17 the text tool has been chosen. This terminology may, in fact, be more accessible to the user since the idea of a mode is rather abstract but everyone knows what a tool is. The operation is, however, the same - the user clicks the appropriate icon. The use of the term tool emphasises the idea that to achieve a different effect, a different means must be used. The idea of the mode suggests that the computer must be put into a different operational state.

Software philosophy   There are two different issues in DTP design philosophy. One relates to the question of single or multiple authorship. Some DTP packages are designed to produce multi-author documents like technical manuals. These must operate on a network in such a way that more than one author can work on the document at the same time without confusion arising as to what the latest state of the document is and who has rights to change what. It should also be possible to cross-reference between the work of the different authors.

The other variable concerns the question of how all-embracing the package is. Some software aims to provide everything that is needed, which includes word-processor features like convenient text editing, search-and-replace and a good range of drawing facilities. Others are based on the premise that text will be imported from a word processor and illustrations from a graphics package.

The problem with this latter approach is how to make changes to the text, for example, after a lot of work has been done in the DTP package. It is clearly desirable to be able to reverse the process, and export the text back to the word processor for further editing without losing the layout work already done. Some DTP systems are designed to make this possible. The layout instructions which have been added in the DTP software take the form of non-printing codes, embedded in the text. When the text is then viewed using a word processor, the codes are seen (usually enclosed in brackets).

Some users actually prefer doing some of the layout work, that would normally be done in the DTP package, using a word processor. It is done by simply adding the necessary codes as the text is typed. In some cases it can be much quicker to add codes, perhaps using a simple macro, in a word processor, than by mouse clicking, using the graphical interface of a DTP package. Even if this is not possible it will normally be possible to export the text from the DTP package in the format of a common word processor. If the

Figure 4.20 (a). A screen shot of PageMaker, with Adobe Type Manager turned off. The large typeface characters are of very poor quality.

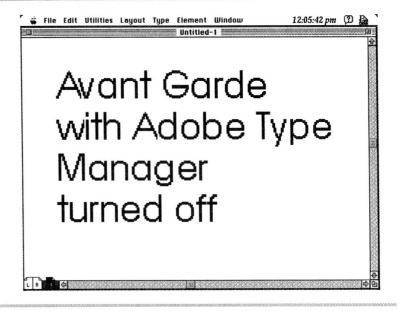

DTP lay out has been saved as a template, the modified text can then be laid out in the same style without losing much of the original work.

Page description languages (PDLs)

DTP can only hope to rival professional printing if a wide range of suitable fonts are available. Early printers, like the dot-matrix printer, provided very few fonts, being limited by the poor resolution afforded by a nine-pin dot-matrix system. The laser printer, with 300 dpi resolution offered the opportunity of many more, and higher-quality, fonts. One initial problem was the amount of memory needed for the font descriptions, since each size of each character needed its own unique description (its bit-map) and bold and italic versions of the characters counted as separate descriptions. The answer to this problem has been 'scalable' fonts and the PDL.

Postscript
A PDL is a programming language which can be used to describe the precise appearance of a printed page. When the first, relatively low-priced DTP system was assembled using the Apple Mac, Aldus PageMaker and a laser printer, an important component was the PDL called **Postscript (Adobe)** which rapidly became the standard for DTP. Using Postscript the DTP software could send a description of the page to be output to any printer which was equipped to handle Postscript code. The code contains a description which is independent of the detailed characteristics of any particular printer.

This means that the appearance of the page will be the same whether it is printed on a 300 dpi laser printer or a 2400 dpi photo-typesetter. The only difference will be the resolution of the output. For this to be possible the fonts which are available using Postscript are scalable (introduced in chapter 2). Scalable fonts are vector descriptions of the basic letter shapes which can be scaled up and down to generate bit-mapped character descriptions of any size required. The software takes account of any desirable subtle changes to the shape of the letter which are needed when it is magnified or reduced. Because this scaling process takes place in the printer, as the PDL code is interpreted, it can generate a bit-map at the best resolution the printer is capable of.

Postscript emulation
Postscript printers are more expensive than ordinary printers because of the cost of the license for the Postscript interpreter software, which usually resides in the printer, to handle the Postscript code being down-loaded from the computer. There are, therefore, a number of 'Postscript emulators' offered by other companies which will accept Postscript output and create a bit-map for printing on a non-Postscript printer, even a dot-matrix printer. Two examples of this are: **GoScript Plus (Graphic Sciences)** and **Freedom of the Press (Ctrl-Alt-Deli)**. The main rivals to Postscript are **TrueType (Apple and Microsoft)** and **PCL - Printer Control Language (Hewlett Packard)**.

Figure 4.20 (b). The same screen as Figure 4.20 (a), except that Adobe Type Manager has been turned on.

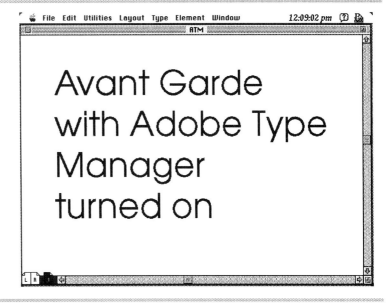

One of the advantages of a PDL is that the professional user can produce 'proof' copies on a relatively cheap printer and then send the file to a professional printer or print bureau, knowing that the output will be identical in form but of higher quality. One of the restrictions on the first version of Postscript, as used on the Mac, was that it was only a 'page-description' language. Although Display-Postscript could have been used to create 'screen-fonts' suited to the much lower resolution of the monitor the Mac already had its own software, called Quickdraw, to draw graphics on the screen. Later, when the Mac operating system was updated to System 7, Apple produced its own system called **TrueType**.

TrueType

After being introduced on the Apple Mac, Postscript moved quickly to PC compatibles also but they didn't have the equivalent of Quickdraw and so initially a limited number of bitmapped versions of the fonts had to be used for screen display. More recently Microsoft have introduced TrueType into 'Windows' version 3 and as a result Macs and PCs use both of the two main rival scalable font systems.

Because of the problem of displaying fonts accurately on the screen a number of 'font managers' have been developed, mainly for use with Windows on PC compatibles. The most widely used of these are **Type Manager (Adobe)** which is available for the Mac also, **Facelift (Bitstream)** and **Intellifont (Hewlett Packard)**. Figure 20 (a) and (b) shows two screen dumps of large fonts, with and without the benefit of Adobe Type manager.

A basic Postscript printer is equipped with 35 standard fonts but an estimated 20,000 Postscript fonts and 2000 TrueType fonts are available from a variety of companies. Quite a large range of share-ware TrueType fonts are also available. Increasingly, graphics packages are supplied with a range of fonts - usually TrueType. CorelDraw! 5 (see the illustration applications software section of chapter 5) is an extreme example of this trend; it provides 740 TrueType fonts.

Not all fonts are of a high standard, especially the 'free' ones. Sometimes when the characters are enlarged and printed, major imperfections can be clearly seen though they will probably not show up when at a smaller size.

Professional typographers and printers increasingly buy fonts on a CD-ROM, sometimes in a 'locked' form. In this case the disc is sold for a few pounds though it may contain over 1000 fonts. Only when a particular font is actually needed does the user pay for it and receive a code which can then be used to unlock that particular font and down-load it onto the computer.

Colour

The first, and simplest DTP, was designed for output to monochrome laser printers but the addition of colour facilities to DTP software has followed the recent improvements in colour printers. Another factor is the way that hardware-independent PDLs have led to the growth in print bureaus, offering high-quality monochrome and colour printing facilities. If the DTP file is to be printed on a local colour printer, then the only problem is the perennial one that colour on a monitor tends to look so different from that on a printer. For best results, and for large volume printing, it is necessary to use the services of a professional printer. In this case a local printer is used to produce 'proofs' (for checking and correction) after which colour separations are produced for sending to a print bureau, as briefly outlined in chapter 2.

Comparison of DTP packages

PACKAGE	COMPUTER	COMMENTS
PageMaker (Aldus)	PC & Mac	First DTP software (1985); easier to use and cheaper than Quark; has built-in editor and long document features; excellent all-round performer.
Quark XPress (Quark Computers)	PC & Mac	Main rival to PageMaker; better typographic control; 127 master pages; wide range of XTensions (software add-ons); firmly established with designers and typographers; more structured in its approach than PageMaker.
FrameMaker (Frame Inc)	PC, Mac & Unix	Powerful drawing system; equation editor; frames within frames; good long document facilities; used for technical documents; needs 8 Mbytes.
3B2 Diamond (Advent Desktop)	PC, Mac & Unix	Very fast and expensive; cut-down version available; uses its own GUI; can mix pages in portrait & landscape views; for professionals only.
Interleaf (Interleaf)	PC & minis.	Can be used across a range of computer types and across networks

Ventura (Corel)	PC	Much cheaper than PageMaker & Quark; frame oriented; comes with scanner software, database publisher,large quantity of clip art & 600 fonts (on CD-Rom); excellent value for money.
Publisher (Microsoft)	PC	Budget price; good help & tutorials; spell-checker & thesaurus; 35 fonts
Pressworks (GST)	PC	Budget price; frame-based; derives from Timeworks; spell-checker & thesaurus; good value.
PageMaker Classic (Aldus)	PC	Earlier version of PageMaker sold at budget price.

Summary   1 Desktop publishing (DTP) can be thought of as a natural development of word processing, with certain important differences. With the availability of very powerful microcomputers many of these differences are beginning to disappear.

2 There are a number of different types of DTP software. The traditional distinction has been between those which are oriented to the production of long documents as compared with those which are more page and design-oriented. There are also specialised versions of DTP for handling database information and very technical documents.

3 The graphical-user interface (GUI) was first used on the Apple Macintosh and first widely used for DTP.

4 There are a number of basic DTP techniques, using the GUI, for specifying the general appearance of a printed page.

5 DTP also offers a wide range of fine controls which can be used to affect the detailed layout of blocks of text and graphics in documents.

6 It is important to understand the concept of operating modes (sometimes called 'tools') which are used to classify the very wide range of controls available to the user.

7 In many DTP packages there are features which enable the production of long documents to be automated.

8 There are problems of price associated with professional-quality printing and colour which usually require access to a professional bureau service where expensive equipment can be accessed.

5

Vector drawing

Key points
- *vector drawing and editing techniques*
- *Computer-Aided Design (CAD) software*
- *Illustration Software*
- *Business Presentation Software*

What is vector drawing? In chapter 2, a distinction was made between vector and pixel-based drawing software. Vector drawing packages take many forms but all of them have a core of common facilities and use a very similar approach to the task of drawing pictures. All of them store the images in the form of generalised descriptions of individual shapes. This means that parts of the picture can be redrawn and edited easily. They can also be viewed at different magnifications without loss of quality and printed on high-resolution printers to produce better results than are apparent on a monitor. DTP software is a specialised type of vector drawing package in which the majority of images are of scalable fonts. The first part of this chapter describes all the basic drawing methods which are used in vector drawing packages. The techniques are similar whatever software is used, though the illustrations are taken from two particular packages - **Adobe Illustrator** and **Corel Draw!**. Later sections concentrate on the special features which distinguish one type of software from another - CAD, Illustration software and Business Presentation software!.

How to use vector drawing software The heart of a vector drawing package is its facility to produce, automatically, a range of basic geometrical shapes - straight lines, curved lines, rectangles, circles, ellipses, arcs and polygons, for example. In most packages, the user chooses which shape is to be drawn by clicking an icon (or selecting from a menu) and then using the mouse to indicate where the object is to be placed and how large it is to be. Figure 5.1 shows a screen containing a range of simple geometrical shapes and a 'floating' toolbox which consists of icons which represent drawing tools. Some packages use a row

Figure 5.1. A screen-shot of a vector-drawing package (Adobe Illustrator), with a variety of geometrical shapes chosen from the toolbox.

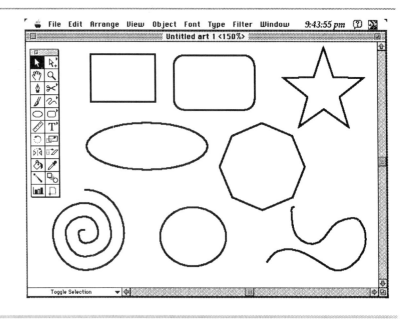

of icons along the top of the screen (often called an icon bar) - placed immediately below the menu bar. Often the icons duplicate the facilities of one of the items in the menu bar. Not all the icons are for drawing operations. Some are for activities like modifying an existing shape or magnifying the image. Some icons give rise to other icons - these are the ones with a small triangle pointing to the right. This is the same principle which is frequently used with multiple menus (see chapter 1).

Placing objects

The method used to specify where the object is to be placed depends on the particular piece of software. Most objects need two points - for example the two ends of a line or the centre and a radius for a circle. The most obvious way of designating the points is to click the mouse twice, once for each point -the software then draws the object in the appropriate size and position. An alternative way of placing the object on the screen uses a 'rubber-band' display (or 'marquee'). In this method the user clicks on the screen - as before - to indicate one end of the line or corner of the rectangle, but then drags the mouse across the screen to the second point. 'Dragging' means moving the mouse while the mouse-button still held down; clicking normally implies a single click of the button which is immediately released. In this case the button is not released, so as to enable the rubber-band line(s) to be dragged across to the end position. When the mouse is dragged a dotted line (or rectangle, where appropriate) is displayed on the screen, joining the two points. The purpose of the marquee line or rectangle is to show clearly where the final shape is to appear. It is as if one end of a rubber-band is anchored by the first click of the mouse but the other end is stretched. When the correct position has been reached and the mouse-button released it, also, is fixed. This method has the advantage of showing clearly where the object is at any stage allowing the user to exercise judgement about its final position.

The marquee   For a straight line the two ends of the rubber-band line correspond to the ends of the final line to be drawn on the screen. In the case of a rectangular marquee, the two points correspond to diagonally-opposite corners of the rectangle. The top of Figure 5.2 shows an ellipse being drawn using a rectangular marquee (the dotted line). The mouse cursor (shaped like an arrow) shows that the dragging action is not complete. When the mouse button is released, the elliptical shape is fixed, the marquee disappears and the mouse cursor is freed for other purposes. When a circle or ellipse is being drawn there is an alternative marquee method, used by some software. In this case the first point corresponds to the centre of the circle, not the corner of the rectangle. When the mouse is then dragged, the rectangular marquee grows out from that central point.

There are, in principle, two alternatives to the marquee method. One is simply to require the user to draw the object, as suggested at the beginning of this section, and rely on editing techniques to change it if it is the wrong size or position. The other is for the software to draw the object in some standard size at a position in-

Figure 5.2. Two methods of showing where a shape is to be drawn. One is a dotted-line 'marquee'. The other uses small black squares at the corners of the marquee. (Screen-shot taken from Adobe Illustrator).

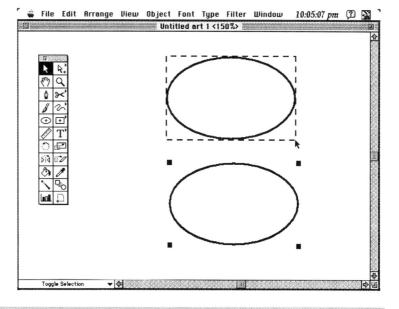

dicated by a single click and, again, rely on editing techniques to drag it into the desired size and position. Both of these have been used but the marquee method is more normal.

Selecting objects

It is inevitable that, whatever basic methods are used, the user will want to make changes to the drawing at some stage. In vector software, each element or object which is drawn is treated as a separate part of the drawing and can be changed at will. The computer actually keeps a list of all the component parts of the drawing as it is being created. If then the user wishes to remove, say, a line from the drawing, the computer erases the screen completely and uses the list of parts to redraw it from scratch, exactly as before, except omitting the chosen line. This might seem an unnecessarily complicated way of doing things but it is an effective way of disentangling a large number of lines and shapes which probably overlap each other. Any other way of removing a line would probably remove parts of other components - just like rubbing out lines with a rubber.

Choosing an object From the user's point of view, the first stage in an editing process is to choose which of the many elements is to be changed. It is normally done by simply clicking on the object with the mouse. More than one element can be chosen by holding down a designated key and clicking on each object in turn. If the key is not held down then choosing a second object, after one has already been selected, usually deselects the first. The appearance of the object will then change in some way to confirm that it has been selected, just as in DTP software. Either its colour will change or it will be shown with small black squares at its periphery. Figure 5.2 shows the two conventional methods for indicating that an object has been selected. The top ellipse shows the marquee method - the same method which is used in drawing the shape. The bottom ellipse indicates selection by the use of small black squares.

Usually a shape will stay selected until action is taken to deselect it, such as clicking it a second time, clicking on another object or clicking on a blank space. Sometimes the software finds it difficult to be sure which object the user intends to select - particularly when a number of objects have been drawn in the same space. The best way of coping with this is that if the wrong object has been selected, then all the objects in that region will be selected in turn as the user continues to click the mouse. When the correct one has been reached, the user stops clicking and performs the editing process.

Editing objects   *Moving and re-sizing*
Once selected, common editing functions can normally be done very directly, using simple mouse actions. To move an object, a dragging technique is used. It usually requires the user to point to somewhere in the middle of the shape and then move the mouse whilst holding down the button, as already described in the last section.

Re-sizing is done in a similar way, except by dragging at a corner or side. It has already been said that a common convention in graphics software is that, when the object is selected, small black squares are displayed at the corners of the shape (or if it doesn't have corners, at the corners of a marquee). These are usually referred to as 'handles'. Other handles may appear halfway along the sides of the object, or its marquee. In some software designs, if the object is dragged using one of its corner handles, then it changes size while maintaining its aspect ratio - the ratio of one side to the other.

This means that an object can be made larger or smaller, without any distortion in its overall shape. If a side handle is dragged then it changes shape, but only in that dimension. Dragging at a handle on the right, for example, will stretch it horizontally but not vertically. Some systems, however, do not use this convention and dragging at the corner can change the aspect ratio of the shape. To prevent this happening, a key (often the Shift key) must be held down while the shape is dragged.

'Nouns and verbs'
Some changes, like copying the object, will require the selection of an appropriate menu item or keystroke. However, the object must be selected first, after which the appropriate editing action is chosen. This is sometimes called a 'noun-verb' approach to editing, using the analogy of language and the parts of speech. The object is the noun, which is chosen first. The verb is the action which is to affect the object. While this has become the standard sequence, it is clearly possible to imagine the reverse method - the action is chosen first, then the object to which it will apply.

The advantage of the conventional method is that it is common for the user to want to perform a series of editing actions on an object. It is convenient to be able to select the object, which then stays selected until the user chooses otherwise, and to choose each editing action in turn. The 'verb-noun' sequence would involve constant re-selection of the object.

Deselecting objects

Some software designers have chosen a convention which, while it uses the 'noun-verb' sequence, causes the object to be automatically de-selected after each editing operation. This can be very irritating when multiple editing is needed though it does avoid mistakes with inexperienced users who have failed to understand the normal convention and find themselves editing the wrong object. These sort of differences of approach can cause a lot of trouble when users move from one piece of software to another. As a result it has become recognised that one of the key aims of good software-interface design is consistency, both within a package and between different systems.

Another example of such differences is the question of what happens when one object is selected and then the user clicks on a second. In some systems both are selected. Probably the better approach is for the second to be selected and for the first to be deselected. If the user wants both to be selected a designated key on the keyboard, such as the 'Ctrl' key, should be held down when the second object is clicked. Another way of selecting more than one object is to choose an appropriate icon and then draw a marquee shape round the objects. Standard editing facilities which are performed, in the way so far described, include: deletion, moving, resizing, skewing, copying, rotating and producing a mirror image.

Aligning objects

Sometimes a number of objects are drawn which then need to be lined up, as if against an invisible ruler drawn on the screen. It can be done using an editing feature called 'align'. The objects are all selected and then one of four types of alignment is selected: right, left, top or bottom. If, for example, left align is chosen, all except the first selected object will move in a horizontal direction until their left-edges line up. Some software allows special non-printing lines to be drawn, or dragged onto, the screen to assist this purpose. Another, similar approach uses a grid - a non-printing rectangular array of lines. The grid is used either so that the user can line objects up 'by eye' or, more precisely, by means of a 'snapping' facility (see next section).

Reversing an operation

One of the most useful of all editing features is 'Undo'. Undo allows the user to make mistakes, experiment or have a change of mind. When selected, undo will reverse the last change to the diagram - so a deleted object will be reinstated or a change of colour reversed. A good undo facility will allow a whole series of actions to be reversed. Some only allow the last action to be changed.

Mouse-cursors

Because of the variety of editing functions which are available, the user can sometimes be confused as to which one has actually been chosen. A useful way of reducing mistakes is for the software to give the user a clue by means of special screen cursor shapes. For example, when the editing action is 'move', the screen cursor changes from the normal arrow shape to a four arrow symbol (as in Figure 5.3) or the shape of a human hand, showing that the object can now be dragged into a new position.

Grouping objects

While it is often useful for the component parts of the picture to be treated as separate objects there comes a time when it is more convenient for the total picture (or a significant part of it) to be behave as a single entity. This can be done by using the 'group' facility. All the components which are to be grouped are simultaneously selected, and after the command 'group', will then behave as one. The whole picture can then be moved, re-sized or copied in one operation. If changes to individual components are needed at a later stage then the process can be reversed by 'un-grouping'.

The basic geometrical shapes which can be created by the software - rectangles, circles, curved and straight lines, for example - are sometimes called 'graphics primitives' and might seem, in them-

Figure 5.3. A shape being dragged. The normal mouse-cursor (usually a simple arrow shape) changes into a 4-headed arrow shape to indicate the type of operation being carried out. The dotted-line marquee shows the outline of the object's position as it is moved. (Screen-shot taken from CorelDRAW!).

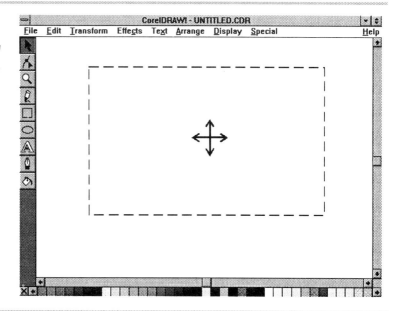

Figure 5.4. Rulers at the edge of the picture can be used to position objects more precisely. The zero-points of the rulers can be dragged to any suitable position. (Screen-shot taken from Adobe Illustrator).

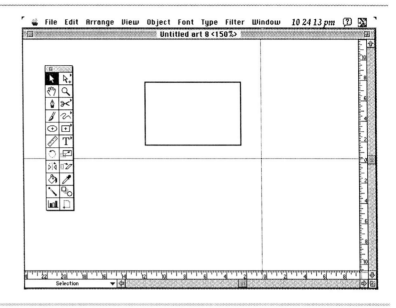

selves, very limited. Complex diagrams, however, are assembled by bringing together many such primitives and by varying their attributes (see later).

Useful drawing aids
The two most important aids to the drawing process are rulers and grids. Using a menu selection, two rulers (one horizontal and one vertical), using any suitable units, can be placed by the side of the drawing - see Figure 5.4. Usually their zero points can be moved to any chosen position to make measurements easier. To relate the rulers to objects in the drawing a special extension to the mouse-cursor can be used. When the cursor is moved over the drawing, two perpendicular dotted lines, intersecting at the mouse cursor, slide up and down the rulers, indicating accurately the position of the cursor. An additional help, shown in Figure 5.5, is a display of these measurements - here shown in a floating window. The figures is this case are X: 2.528 inches and Y: 0.88 inches, where X represents the horizontal distance and Y the vertical distance, measured from the edge of the picture. An alternative is to display them in a fixed box at the top or bottom of the screen.

The grid
A grid is a rectangular array of points or lines which can be displayed on the screen to aid the positioning and lining up of objects - see Figure 5.6. Since the separation of points, or the intersection of the lines, on the grid can usually be chosen by the user it is possible to place objects with considerable precision and it is easy to produce diagrams with great accuracy. The facility to change the

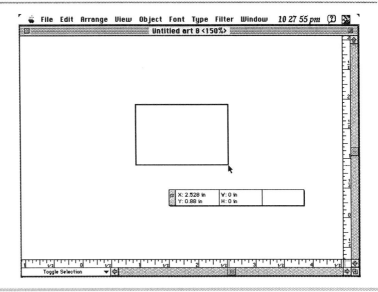

Figure 5.5. A movable window (sometimes called a floating palette)in Adobe Illustrator. It is used to provide a digital read-out of such quantities as the position of the cursor or the position and size of a selected object.

line spacing is particularly important when 'zoom' is used. Some software packages have a system in which the number of lines or points which is displayed depends on the magnification being used. This automatically copes with the problem of overcrowding of the lines at low magnification (and vice versa) but can be confusing if the user does not realise what is happening.

Snapping
A very valuable extension of the grid facility is 'grid-snap'. It means that drawing operations can be deliberately restricted if the user wishes. With snap set to 'on', drawing can only take place starting and finishing at a grid point. When the cursor is moved it is pulled,

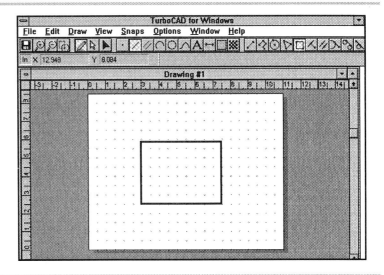

Figure 5.6. A grid is displayed on the screen in IMSI TurboCAD to help with the positioning of objects. This process can be speeded up by making the objects 'snap' to the grid.

as if by magnetism, to the nearest grid point. It makes certain drawing operations - like placing objects at regular intervals -extremely easy. The user can afford to draw very quickly and even carelessly because the initial positioning of an object need only be very approximate. The objects will be pulled into place. The control can be used for sizing as well as positioning and can be switched off at any time if necessary.

Attributes of objects Each geometrical object will have detailed characteristics which might be shared with other objects - such as colour, line-thickness and fill-pattern. These are called attributes and are 'attached' to objects before or after they are drawn. If they are chosen before an object is drawn it is simply a matter of changing the 'current value' of that attribute. It usually means selecting from a menu system the thickness of lines, the colour of lines or the pattern used to fill shapes. After that, all objects will be drawn with those chosen attributes until they are changed again. If the decision is taken after the object is drawn then changing the attribute is just like any editing operation. The object is selected and the attribute changed by clicking on the new value from a list. Figure 5.7 shows an attribute window which offers a choice of line types and line-thicknesses. This can be used as an alternative to the normal menu system and can be 'popped-up' on the screen and moved to a position near the objects concerned.

Figure 5.7. Graphic objects are considered to possess 'attributes' like line-thickness and line-type. Here the attributes of a selected object can be chosen from a floating menuin IMSI TurboCAD.

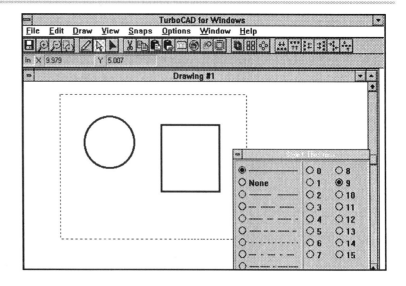

Figure 5.8 (a). A low-magnification CAD drawing of a building. This sample image is provided with IMSI TurboCAD.

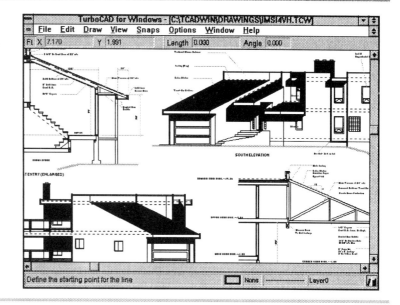

Editing

The facility to change objects after they are drawn, without any further drawing or redrawing, is one of the major advantages of vector (line) drawing methods over pixel-based drawing systems. It is a consequence of the process described already by which the computer keeps a record of each shape drawn, together with the current value of its attributes. The only record kept of a pixel drawing is the picture itself -all the pixels which make up the final screen image - regardless of how they came to be there.

Figure 5.8 (b). Part of the same drawing shown in Figure 5.8 (a), but at a higher 'zoom' level. The quality of the drawing is not lost in the process of magnification.

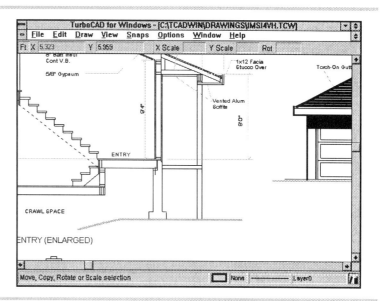

Zooming the picture

An important feature of vector drawing software is its zoom-facility. It is the equivalent of a powerful magnifying glass and makes it possible to draw pictures with the sort of fine detail which a laser printer can print, rather than be limited to the details which a computer screen can display. It follows that if an image is zoomed by a large factor (say x10) and small objects drawn at that magnification then, when the view is returned to normal, much of that detail may not be displayed because of the hardware restrictions already referred to.

This doesn't mean that the information has been lost. It simply means that the computer generates a picture which is based on its stored information but eliminates or approximates details which cannot be displayed by the hardware at that particular magnification. The details will 'return' when the picture is magnified again, or printed on a high-resolution printer. Figure 5.8 (a) and (b) shows two screen views, at two different magnifications, of the same drawing. It is clear that details can be seen in the more magnified view which do not appear at all in the lower magnification image. Plate 3(a) and (b) show similar views of a different object.

Zooming and panning, like editing, involves the software removing from the screen the previous version of the image and then redrawing it under different circumstances. In the case of a zoom, this means a much smaller part of the picture at a higher magnification. In the case of a pan, it means a shift of the centre of the image to bring into view part of the object not previously displayed. These tricks are a way of dealing with the fact that a picture which can be printed or drawn in detail on a piece of paper cannot be displayed in the same detail on a screen.

Front and back

When an object is drawn on top of another it will obscure or totally hide the one underneath. However, there is no reason why the positions should not be reversed and the one which was underneath be brought to the top. Because the computer keeps a record of both objects, whether or not they can be seen, it can easily redraw the picture in a different order, bringing one to the top. This usually involves selecting the object and then using a menu option ('Send to back' or 'Bring to top').

CAD *What is CAD?*

CAD (Computer Aided Design) was the earliest application of the vector drawing methods already described. CAD software is a computerised version of the engineering design drawing methods used engineering draughtspersons. Newer variations of CAD software

are now available for designing buildings, gardens, kitchens, offices and many other objects. The CAD software described in this section is of the traditional type which is limited to the production of 2-D images. Most modern professional-level CAD software can also generate 3-D images; this type of package is described in a later chapter since it has much in common with other 3-D software.

Drawing to scale

The special features of CAD software naturally derive from the special needs of engineering design. Diagrams of objects which are to be manufactured must be drawn to a clearly specified scale. A number of techniques are available for helping the user draw objects to scale. It is normal to choose the working scale of the diagram at the outset and this can then be reflected in the grid points and the screen rulers. It means that either the grid points or the rulers can be used in creating objects of a specified size. Alternative methods are to use the digital read-out of the cursor's position or to type in the dimensions of an object from the keyboard. The important point is that the user can work 'in the real world' - using the dimensions of the actual final object - and let the computer do all the calculations necessary to display a scale drawing on the screen or the printer.

Illustrating sizes

It is important not only to draw the objects to scale but to illustrate the actual dimensions of an object on the drawing. This is done by printing the dimensions by the side of the objects, using arrows to

Figure 5.9. The size of an object in a CAD package is shown by means of dimension arrows and witness lines. The software in this example is IMSI TurboCAD.

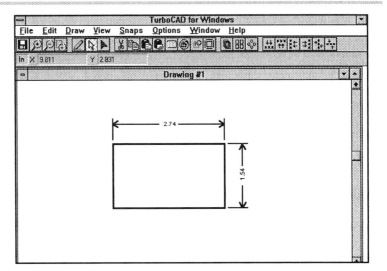

Figure 5.10. In CAD software, right-angled intersections between lines are often given a 'chamfer' or a 'fillet'. A chamfer is a straight-line drawn obliquely across the corner. A fillet is an arc of a circle which gives the join a rounded effect. The software in this example is IMSI TurboCAD.

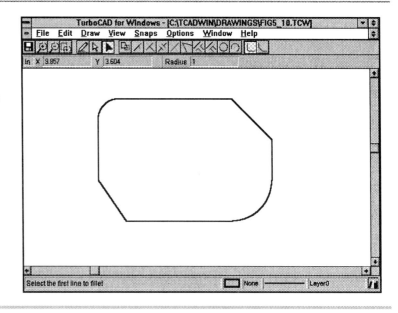

indicate where the measurements begin and end - see Figure 5.9. The numbers and arrows are drawn some way from the object, for clarity, but attached to it by 'witness lines' which extend from the object to the ends of the arrow. CAD software can automatically generate the correct dimension numbers, based on the scale of the drawing, and also draw the arrows and lines. The user selects a particular line in the drawing and then chooses the 'dimension' facility from a menu, and the software does the rest. Arrows and witness lines can also be 'associated' with an object in such a way that, if the object is then edited and the dimensions change, the number and the length of the arrows will be updated automatically.

Fillets

Manufactured objects do not have razor-sharp edges. Where two faces meet the edge must be rounded or 'filletted' and in the drawing this means that where two right-angle lines join, the ends of the lines must be replaced with an arc of a circle. It can also be done automatically by CAD software. The user simply chooses which edges are to be filletted and what radius of curvature is to be used. A similar automatic editing process is the 'chamfer' in which two right-angle lines are joined by another oblique line to produce the effect of a sharp edge in an object which has been shaved off. Figure 5.10 shows pairs of right-angle lines and both fillets and chamfers.

Levels

The complexity of CAD drawings can make it necessary to be able to isolate parts of the drawing from each other - particularly on the screen, which is so small compared with a final drawing and where so little detail can be shown. This is done using a number of 'levels'. Each level can be thought of as a separate drawing, on some transparent material, so that some or all of the levels can be overlaid on top of each other when needed, but can also be viewed on their own. Different levels might be also be assigned different colours to make it clear which object is part of which level when one or more are viewed together.

Snapping options

A sophisticated variation on the idea of snapping to a grid is particularly useful in CAD where precise geometrical shapes often need to be created. A type of snapping is used to automate the joining of geometrical shapes to each other according using one of a set of rules. For example, it might be necessary to draw a straight line from a point to another line in such a way that they meet at right-angles. This is called 'near-point' snapping since the right-angle condition is met by drawing to the nearest point on the existing line.

Other examples are 'intersection-snapping' (drawing to the intersection of two lines), 'midpoint snapping' (drawing to the midpoint of a line) and 'end-point snapping' (drawing to the end of a

Figure 5.11. Intersection snapping in CAD software (IMSI TurboCAD). Two intersecting lines (A & B) have been drawn. The software automates the process of drawing a third line, from a point X, to the intersection of A and B.

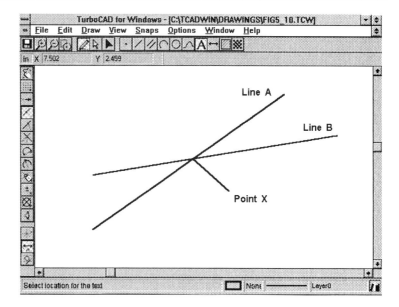

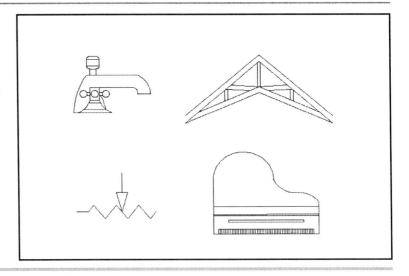

line) but there are many more possibilities. Figure 5.11 illustrates intersection snapping. All of these methods can be used to speed up the drawing process and to eliminate human error by removing at least some of the element of judgement which is needed when making precise drawings.

Symbol libraries

These are a very important feature of CAD. All drawing packages can supplemented with libraries of standard images (often called 'clip-art' in non-technical software) but CAD is, by its technical nature, particularly dependent on standard symbols. Different users need very different libraries. Architects need symbols for doors, windows and cavity walls. Electronic engineers need transistors, resistors and integrated circuit symbols. Mechanical engineers need hexagonal bolts and cog wheels. Figure 5.12 shows a small set of symbols taken from such a library. An important extra feature of a symbol library facility is the ability to create special symbols and add them to the library and to modify existing ones. In recent years, drawing software has become popular which is based entirely on the clip-art library concept. Virtually all the drawing is done by combining preexisting shapes chosen from extensive libraries.

Plotter fonts

CAD packages traditionally have been supplied with very few fonts and those that are provided are usually of a very simple design to make them suitable for pen-plotter output. Figure 5.13 shows examples of a typical plotter-font. However, the competition from electrostatic and ink-jet printers now means that engineering drawings need no longer be restricted to simple line-fonts, designed for pen-plotters.

Figure 5.13. Characters from a
'plotter font' suitable for use with a
pen-plotter.

> Plotter fonts have
> to be of a very
> simple design in
> order that they
> can be drawn with
> a moving pen.

CAD packages

PACKAGE	COMPUTER	COMMENTS
AutoCad (AutoDesk)	PC, Mac & Sun	The market leader; very powerful & expensive; highly customisable; has its own programming language; many 3rd party add-ons; 2D and 3D; Boolean operations only via extensions.
AutoCad LT (AutoDesk)	PC	Cut-down version of AutoCad; limited 3D facilities.
AutoSketch (AutoDesk)	PC	Cheaper still, 2D-only product
Microstation (Intergraph)	PC & Mac	Even more expensive than AutoCad; better interface; more drawing tools and 3D facilities as standard; Boolean operations.
DrafixCad (Manhattan)	PC	2D only; budget software
FastCad (FastCad)	PC	Two versions - 2D and 3D; very fast; budget software
DesignCad 3D (DesignCad)	PC	3D; budget software
TurboCad (IMSI)	PC	2D only; budget software
MacroModel (Computers Unlimited)	PC & Mac	An example of Mac modelling software; most Mac packages are aimed at designers rather than engineers; this aims at both.

Illustration software

What is illustration software?

Illustration software can be thought of as a CAD package for artists. It lacks some of the specialist facilities required for engineering drawings but has extra features which are useful when producing the sort of illustrations which might be used in textbooks or advertisements. In this context, while it might be necessary to produce technically accurate diagrams it is just as likely that aesthetic considerations will be important. The pictures must be attractive and pleasing to the eye. It usually means, for example, that a wide variety of decorative fonts is needed. In fact text may have just as important a part to play in illustration software as it does in DTP (see chapter 4) and so many of the features provided will be similar - a choice of fonts, character sizes, inter-letter and interline spacing, justification, for example.

The two main differences between the text facilities of this type of software and DTP are that relatively small quantities of text will be involved and that the text will therefore be less 'routine'. The fonts provided will include many more decorative ones than those used in DTP. Figure 5.14 shows some of the decorative fonts supplied with CorelDraw!. Decorative fonts are those which are suitable for headlines and large type sizes but not for large amounts of normal-sized 'body-text'.

Special Text Features

There is also a requirement to create eye-catching effects with the text. Examples of this type of effect include the facility to fit text along a curve or around a circle, to stretch text to fit it into an 'en-

Figure 5.14. Examples of decorative fonts for use in Illustration software. These fonts are some of those provided with CorelDRAW!

Figure 5.15. The top of the figure shows text which has been fitted to a curve in CorelDRAW!. The bottom of the figure shows text which has been distorted to the shape of an 'envelope'.

velope' (any boundary shape) or to fill the outline of the characters with patterns or colour-gradients. Another facility which is useful is the option to create simple 3-D features which allow flat characters to be extended ('extruded'), with or without perspective effects, into the third dimension so that they look like solid blocks. Figure 5.15 shows some examples of these effects. Another useful manipulation of text is to allow the user to change the shape of individual letters. This is a special type of editing feature which converts the outline of a character into a series of separate lines which can then be distorted in a variety of ways to produce a desired effect. Figure 5.16 shows how letters can be stretched to produce a desired artistic effect.

Colours and gradations

It will also be necessary to have a much wider range of colours and fill-patterns than would be needed in CAD software. CAD software makes limited use of colour and traditional pen-plotters are limited to six or eight colours. Illustrators can always make good use of a much larger range of colours and a modern computer sys-

Figure 5.16. A font which has been converted to a set of curves can then be distorted into new shapes.

Normal Font

Distorted Font

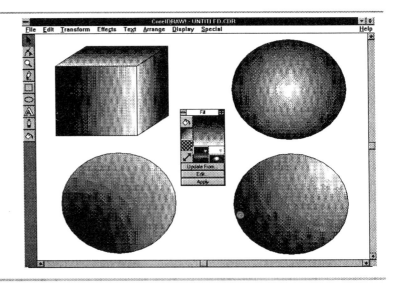

Figure 5.17. Simple 3-D effects (in CorelDRAW!) can be achieved by the use of gradients (shades of grey or other colours) which simulate the shading which is produced by light falling on a surface.

tem should be able to offer thousands, if not millions - an enormous advantage over conventional drawing techniques. One application of this huge range of colours is the ability to create interesting colour gradation effects.

Colour or grey-scale gradation is created by choosing two colours (or shades of grey) and then allowing the software to generate a whole series of intermediates. Some of these colour or grey-scale gradients can be used to create the effect of shading so that a flat circle with a radial gradient can be made to look like a ball or a drawing of a cube with a linear gradient made to seem to be more 3-D. Figure 5.17 shows drawings of a cube and a sphere created by the use of shading.

The same sort of principle can be applied to shapes. Two different shapes are drawn and the software then produces a series of intermediate shapes so that one seems to gradually change into the other. An extension of this principle (called polymorphic tweening) is used in animation software (see chapter 7).

Curves

There are four types of curved lines which can be drawn. Two are simple, well-defined shapes like circles or ellipses and their arcs (incomplete portions of these curves) are selected from a menu or icon, in the way already described. A third type, freehand curves can usually be drawn using the mouse, as in a pixel-based painting package. The fourth type - smooth, computer-generated curves - are drawn using a special system of fixed points and control points. This type of curve is both the most flexible and the most complicated to draw and alter. Figure 5.18 shows all four types of curve. Freehand curves cannot be edited except by the deletion or addi-

Figure 5.18. Four different types of curve which can be drawn with Illustration software (CorelDRAW!): the complete circle (or ellipse), the arc (a partial circle or ellipse), the Bezier curve and the freehand shape.

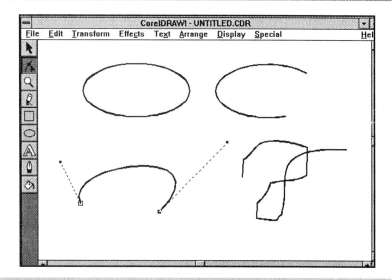

tion of pixels, usually done using a paint package. Circles and ellipses (and incomplete versions of these - arcs) can be redrawn using different parameters - for example their position or radius of curvature. The fourth type of curve (the Bezier curve) has two, more subtle, types of control which can be used to alter their final shape. One is the facility to move control points - points which lie on the curve - to any desired position. This drags that part of the curve with it and so changes the overall shape of the whole curve, since the software redraws the curves smoothly through these points. To make a more complicated curve, more controls can be added to it at any point. For a simpler curve, control points can be removed.

Levers

The second control feature involves the ability to change the tightness of the curve at a point of inflection. A point of inflection is a point in the curve where it changes the direction of curvature. Some software provides not only control points (which are really like handles, for pulling the curve about) but also a system of 'levers'. These short lines, which go through a control point, at a tangent to the curve, can be pulled away from, or towards, the curve. Because the levers are always at a tangent to the curve - never intersecting it - this alters the curvature at that point. The third curve in Figure 5.18 shows curves with these control points and levers.

Handling bit-maps

Sometimes it is desirable to scan an existing shape so as to incorporate it into an illustration. If the picture is to be used unchanged then all that is required is the facility to incorporate such a bit-mapped image into the vector image in a similar way that images

119

can be added to text in a DTP package. Sometimes, however, it is desirable to be able to manipulate the shape. For this to be done it is necessary to convert it into a vector description -a process called 'tracing'. For this, an extra piece of software is needed which detects the shapes of the individual lines or edges in the scanned image. It then converts them into vector lines, usually ironing-out the fine details of the original shapes and converting them into smooth lines in the process. The process is discussed further in chapter 6.

Illustration packages

SOFTWARE	COMPUTER	COMMENTS
Illustrator (Adobe)	Mac & PC	The first high-level illustration package; uses "plug-ins" (add-on modules); wide range of filters and DTP features; draws graphs; 220 fonts on CD-Rom
Freehand (Aldus)	Mac & PC	Major rival to Illustrator for Mac users; 120 fonts; no clip art; easier to use than Illustrator
CorelDraw! 5 (Corel)	PC	Market leader for PCs; includes huge variety of separate packages : DTP (Corel Ventura - see DTP section), presentation software, animation, photo-retouching etc. (on 2 CD-Roms); 800 fonts; 22,000 clip-art images
CorelDraw! 4	PC	Corel 5 without Ventura DTP
CorelDraw! 3	PC	Earlier version of Corel on 1 CD-Rom
Designer (Micrografx)	PC	Aimed at technical illustrators but not exclusively; includes 13,000 clip-art images and 500 technical symbols; export filters for CAD; 280 fonts; excellent interface; no colour separation
Windows Draw (Micrografx)	PC	Budget software from same source as Designer
Claris Draw (Claris)	Mac & PC	Upgrade to well established predecessor (MacDraw); no colour separation; simple slide-show facility; easy to use; too expensive to compete in PC market

Apprentice (Arts & Letters)	P C	Very cheap; crude drawing tools but has some sophisticated facilities also.
DesignWorks (GST)	P C	Excellent budget package; surprisingly, includes colour separation and range of gradations and blending facilities.
Professional Draw (Gold Disk)	P C	Good range of very versatile drawing tools; 150 fonts; budget price.

Presentation software

What is presentation software?

Presentation Graphics (or Business Graphics) Software is aimed at the business user who wishes to present business information in an attractive manner. The information will probably involve data as well as text which means that graphs and charts of all kinds are needed. Early examples of this type of software were mainly concerned with the automatic generation of bar charts, pie charts and line graphs. Modern versions have added considerable drawing facilities, extensive collections of clip-art and 'slide-show' facilities.

The typical user

The underlying assumption is that, more than with most types of graphic software, the user will have little specific expertise in design and is probably in a hurry to produce results. It is very noticeable how often the advertisements for presentation graphics software show the user as being pressurised by the boss to produce an instant report. The user is then shown to surprise everyone because, despite being no expert at graphic design, they can produce an attractive and compelling presentation of the data. The key to all this is speed and automation. Both the necessity for speed and for help with the design are usually covered by the use of 'templates' or style-sheets, concepts already mentioned in connection with DTP software. In this context, a template is a screen showing a carefully-chosen combination of a background colour or a picture, a choice of fonts and character sizes for the text and a set of suitable colours for the graphs.

Templates

The user is presented with a whole range of these templates (sometimes called 'Master Styles') - each supplied with dummy text and data so that the overall appearance can be judged. Sometimes this choice is helped by the display of a range of miniaturised samples displayed on the screen like photographic proofs. The user simply

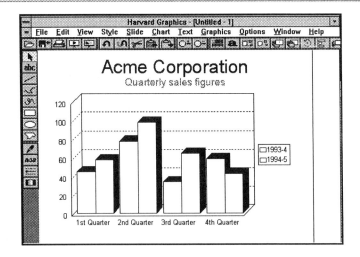

Figure 5.19. Screen shot of business presentation software (Harvard Graphics) being used to create a 3-D bar chart.

chooses one, changes the dummy text to something more suitable and changes the dummy data in the graph - if any - to the appropriate data which is to be illustrated. If a company wants to use a 'house' style in all its presentations it either chooses a template supplied with the software or designs one of its own which all employees then use.

Charts

The main style of data charts which are available include line, area, pie and bar charts but there are a huge number of variations possible and, again, a wide range of styles are usually presented to the user, into which the real data can be imported. Charts can be 2-D

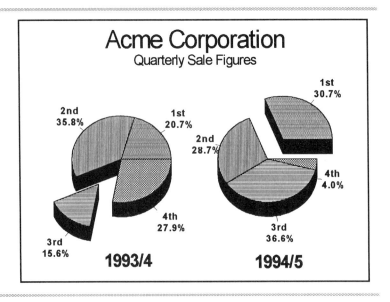

Figure 5.20. 3-D pie charts, automatically generated from eight data items using Harvard Graphics.

or 3-D, running vertically or horizontally. Figures 5.19 and 5.20 show two examples of the many types available. A wide range of colours and fill-patterns can be used. 3-D charts can be viewed from a wide range of angles. Labels can be placed automatically on bars and pie slices, and data presented in percentages or actual values. Linear or logarithmic scales can be chosen. All of these can be created from a set of data which is either typed in or imported from a spreadsheet.

Drawing
The charts, once generated, can then have extra information added by using the sort of basic drawing facilities found in an illustration package. An important feature of this process, particularly useful for the rapid presentation of results by someone without graphic art skills, is the clip-art library. The software will probably come supplied with anything from hundreds to thousands of clip-art images but there is a significant industry devoted to the sale of add-on libraries, increasingly supplied on CD-ROM (see chapter 8).

Clip-art consists of line-drawings, which vary from very detailed images of people, buildings, vehicles, etc., to very simple icon-like symbols. The drawings are free from copyright so that the user can incorporate them into their own work and even sell that work without incurring any further financial penalty. Because they are vector images they can be re-sized, distorted and added to if necessary. In some cases they can be un-grouped and have components removed also. Figure 5.21 shows a range of examples.

Figure 5.21. Three examples of business-oriented clipart.

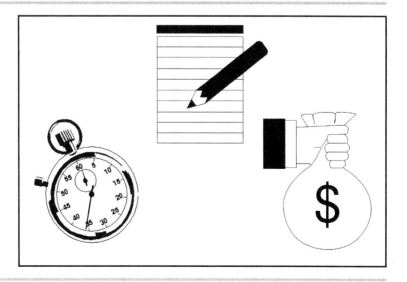

Text charts

The presentation of text can be just as important as the presentation of data. The choices here include organisation charts, simple lists, bullet lists and a variety of headings, subheadings and footnotes. Organisation charts are a system of boxes, representing either people or work-functions in an organisation, arranged in hierarchical fashion, connected by lines - see Figure 5.22. They show organisational relationships such as who is responsible to who or for what and how different sections of organisations are structured. They are generated automatically once the data and relationships are supplied.

Text charts, lists and bullet lists are ways of presenting small amounts of text, often as visual prompts to supplement a lecture or business presentation. The difference between this type of application and word processing or DTP is that small amounts of text are involved because of the nature of the presentation. The output must be often be suitable for projection on a screen and must be both easily readable from a distance and attractive to look at. Again, the use of well-designed templates discourages the user from trying to squeeze too much information on to a screen. It also discourages the use of inappropriate fonts or the use of too many fonts or sizes. Bullet lists are lists of items or headings which are preceded by a bullet - a symbol - which draws attention to the beginning of a new item in the list. Even text charts can be enhanced by the use of suitable background colours or images or decorative borders. Figure 5.23 shows an example of a text chart.

Figure 5.22. An hierarchical organisation chart, created in Harvard Graphics.

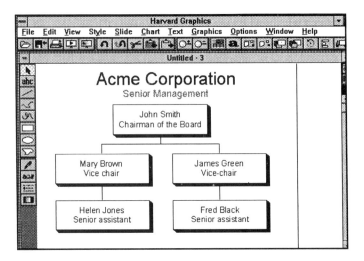

Figure 5.23. A text chart, created in Harvard Graphics.

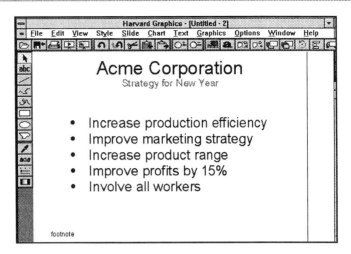

Slide shows

Although this type of software is used to produce illustrations for printing in brochures or for use in TV and video work, its main application is to produce 'slides'. A slide might be the traditional 35 mm photographic slide which is projected on to a screen but it might equally be for turning into an OHP slide or for displaying directly on the screen of the computer.

The latter use is increasingly a feature of exhibitions or for demonstrations of software or other products to be distributed on disc. A series of images can be presented as a 'slide show' - as if by conventional projection. The user is helped in organising the slides into suitable order by a slide sorter. This is a screen in which a dozen or more slides are displayed, reduced in size. The user shuffles them into the correct order by dragging them around.

The advantage of slide shows, apart from the ease with which the process can be automated, is that it is possible to use the dynamic nature of a computer display. Computer displays, unlike slide projectors, are updating their images dozens of times every second and this means that rapidly changing transition effects can be created between slides. An example of a simple transition is the 'wipe'. The image seems to be wiped slowly off the screen, as if with a cloth. In another, similar effect, the picture seems to slide bodily off the screen. New images can be loaded in a similar way. There are also more complicated effects like 'rain', in which the image appears to be washed away by rain drops and 'interlace' in which thin sections of the image slide apart in two opposite directions like interlaced fingers being pulled apart.

It should be possible to save the finished slide-show in a form that will not require the original software in order to run it (using a 'run-time' viewer). This means that in addition to the conventional presentations, to be given by the person who created them, advertising and training programs can also be created and distributed to any customer with the appropriate computer system.

Documentation

Because this type of software is designed to help the user make a 'presentation', it is increasingly common for these packages to help the user structure their accompanying talk or lecture and to automate the production of suitable material to accompany the talk. Help in planning the talk is provided by an 'outliner'. This a text editor into which the main headings of the talk are entered (the outline). More and more detail can then added, in a structured way, but can also be progressively hidden from view, so that the overall, structure of the talk is not lost in the detail. On the basis of this information the software can then be used to generate both notes for the speaker which show the connections with the individual slides in the presentation, and handout material suiting for giving to the intended audience.

Multimedia

The newest versions of this type of software include multimedia features so that animated sequences, sound and video material can be included. This means that this type of software can offer a simple alternative to fully-fledged multimedia authoring software (see chapter 8). Another feature is to build in viewer-driven explorations of the slide sequence, sometimes called 'hyper-links'. The designer of the slide sequence can provide a variety of ways of navigating through the slides enabling the viewer to exercise choice about the amount of detail they see (by omitting some slides or choosing to see extra ones) and the order in which they explore the information. Buttons are added to the screen images, as in a graphical-user interface, so that users can click on their choice and create their own sequence of slides.

Presentation packages

SOFTWARE	COMPUTER	COMMENTS
Harvard Graphics (SPC)	PC	One of the top PC products; only 2 fonts; 88 graph types; 31 templates; "special effects" and some multi-media facilities
Freelance (Lotus)	PC	Main competitor with Harvard for PCs; only 18 graph types; 65 templates; 13 fonts; very similar specification.
PowerPoint (Microsoft)	PC & Mac	Extremely easy to use; uses "Wizards" to guide the user in creating a presentation; 14 graph types; 23 fonts; 55 templates.
Persuasion (Aldus)	PC	Awkward interface; no multimedia or hyperlinks; 13 fonts; 37 templates; 10 graph types; limited drawing tools.
Persuasion (Aldus)	Mac	Mac version much better than PC version; 84 graph types; good colour handling; multi-media & hyper-links.
WordPerfect Presentations (WordPerfect)	PC	Awkward interface; 65 templates; 14 types, but many variations; 88 fonts; sound clips; 1000 pieces of clip art; multi-media facilities.
Stanford Graphics (Adept)	PC	Highly sophisticated modelling and data analysis tool; aimed at scientific and academic community; 160 graph types for business, statistical & technical use; no multi-media or spell checker.
Charisma (Micrografx)	PC	Very large package; 440 fonts; 7000 pieces of clip art; 75 templates; 76 graph types; large number of sound clips; excellent multi-media facilities; needs high-level computer
Astound (Gold Disk)	PC & Mac	Only 11 fonts but large number of clip art, video & sound files; good special effects and multi-media
Bravo (Alpha Software)	PC	Short of fonts & clip art but some good features and one of the cheapest.
Cricket Presents (Computer Associates)	PC & Mac	No "master-styles" (templates) or guided tour; 35 fonts; simple drawing facilities; separate outliner; no multi-media or hyper-links

Summary

1 There are a wide range of basic drawing and editing techniques which are common to all vector-based illustration software. These include the simple production of a variety of straight and curved lines and other geometrical shapes. Editing facilities include the deletion, moving, re-sizing, stretching and copying of these shapes.

2 Graphical user interfaces also offer the user a number of standard techniques for placing and manipulating graphic objects on the screen. These include 'rubber-banding', 'marquees' and a range of standard mouse operations for selecting and dragging objects.

3 There are special aids to drawing - such as on-screen rulers, non-printing alignment lines, grids and 'snapping'.

4 Graphic objects have their own special characteristics -such as the thickness of a line or the colour of a fill-pattern. These are called 'attributes' and can be specified either before or after that object is drawn.

5 In addition to the general drawing facilities now available in all vector drawing software, CAD also has special features which relate to engineering requirements. These include the need for visible dimensions, witness lines and fillets.

6 Illustration Software differs from CAD both in specialist engineering features which it does not have and extra facilities which are appropriate to the field of commercial art. These features include decorative fonts, 3-D fonts, fitting text to curved lines and envelopes, colour gradations and curve manipulation. 7 Business Presentation Software offers special facilities for the rapid production of graphics to illustrate business activities. These include graph and chart plotting, clip art and 'slide-shows'. Modern versions of this type of software are increasingly providing multimedia effects and so can be thought of as a simple form of multimedia authoring software (see also chapter 8).

Painting and photo-retouching

Key points
- *facilities offered by paint packages*
- *techniques which mimic traditional drawing and painting methods*
- *photo-retouching techniques*

What is paint software?

Previous chapters have been concerned with drawing packages which store and edit images in the vector format - sometimes called line-drawing software. In this chapter we are concerned with packages which store and process images as bit-maps -collections of coloured pixels. They are often called paint packages because much of their appeal is to artists for whom the software is a substitute for, or an extension of, traditional freehand painting and drawing systems. Thus the final product, the techniques used and the typical user are likely to be different from the more technically-oriented style of vector package. The important difference lies in the way that the images are created and stored as bit-maps. Unlike a vector image where the shape of the objects is stored as a mathematical description and can therefore be redrawn and edited in a geometrical fashion, with a bit-mapped image 'what you see is all there is'.

The interface

A first glance at the screen of this type of package (Figure 6.1) might seem to contradict these remarks because the software interface often looks very similar to those described in the last chapter. In fact, for many simple applications it may make no difference which type of package is used. The differences will only become apparent when the drawing tools are examined in detail or the image is magnified or edited.

The Tools

All drawing packages provide a basic range of drawing tools. Figure 6.1 shows a set of tools, represented by a group of icons. The term tool has come into use since the development of graphical

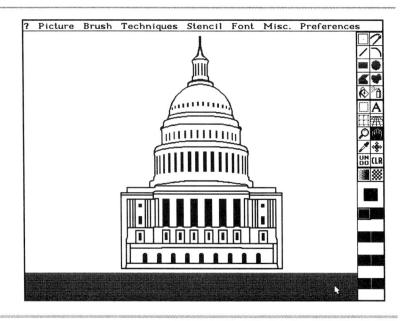

Figure 6.1. Screen-shot of a paint package (Deluxe Paint), with toolbox.

user interfaces (GUIs) and has been referred to already in the chapter on DTP. Icons, that is small drawings, are used to symbolise the range of facilities which are available to the user. In this case the facilities can be of a many different types. One type is the drawing tool. It is a replacement for an actual pencil, paintbrush or piece of charcoal. Another type of tool is really a pre-drawn shape. In normal traditional art, the artist uses skill to draw shapes like straight lines, squares or circles. In computer art these shapes have been stored in the software and the artist simply places, moves and re-sizes them. This is can be thought of as the electronic equivalent of a ruler or a template - a sheet of plastic with a series of geometrical shapes cut in it, for the artist to trace.

Palettes

A third type of 'tool' is a palette of colours and a fourth could be a range of line thicknesses. The term tool has been extended from its normal meaning of an object which is used to accomplish a special purpose, to a generalised computer software facility which can be chosen to help create the image. The tools may be grouped together into a toolbox, which is a rectangular window on the screen, sometimes moveable, made up from a set of icons. To choose and use a tool, the user clicks on it. Often the mouse screen cursor changes shape - becomes a sort of icon - to remind the user which tool it represents.

Drawing with a paint package

Paint programs have the same basic drawing tools for creating simple geometrical shapes, like circles and rectangles, as a vector drawing package. Drawing is done in the same way, by selecting the shape from a menu or icon and using the mouse to create a marquee. In addition, however, a good paintbrush package will often contain a range of other, more complicated shapes like stars, with different numbers of points, flower-like petal shapes and spirals. Figure 6.2 shows some of the variations which can be obtained with just one of the shapes available in Animator Pro. This petal shape can have a variable number of points (petals) and a variable ratio between the inner and outer radii. Another variation, for most closed shapes, is that they can be created empty or filled - with some suitable pattern or solid colour.

Drawing aids

Some of the tools are aids to drawing, rather than shapes in the normal sense. One example is a tool which will automatically add a thin boundary line round a region of one particular colour. This is used by first choosing a colour to use as the edge, then selecting the tool and finally choosing a screen colour which is to be surrounded. This will cause all blocks of that colour to be given a single-pixel edge of the current colour.

Colours

Colours are chosen by clicking the mouse cursor on the appropriate colour, displayed in a palette. A palette of colours is represented in a rectangular array, like the colours in a child's paintbox. Sometimes only a small subset of colours is displayed permanently on the screen to avoid the palette taking up too much space. This is more likely to be the case if a very large number of colours is pro-

Figure 6.2. Some of the many variations that are possible with one basic shape - the petal. The two variables are the number of petals and the distance from the centre of the pattern to the start of the petals.

vided. The solution to this problem is to display a smaller subset of colours and a means of choosing which set that is at any one time.

Brushes

Even a simple drawing package will have a number of basic 'brushes' - shapes with which to draw. The term brush, as used here, is really an alternative to the 'tool' concept. It is an analogy, based on the fact that a real artist has a range of different types and thicknesses of paintbrush to paint with. The two basic shapes of brush are likely to be a small circle and a small square and the size of the shape should be user-definable. Similarly there should be a variety of line types - a variety of thicknesses and type of dotted patterns with which the artist can draw. Figure 6.3 shows a range of brush sizes, chosen from a floating palette. The shape of the brush can also be chosen from a second palette.

User-defined brushes

A good package, however, will also have user-defined brushes. At it simplest, this means that the user can choose any region of the screen, of any size, shape and colour - or colours - and define that as a brush. These can be saved in a library for later reuse. A library of pre-defined brushes is sometimes supplied by the software manufacturer also. When drawing with such a brush a whole variety of effects can be achieved. For example, if the pen or mouse is positioned and clicked once, one copy of the brush is 'stamped' onto the screen. If the brush is moved slowly over the screen a smeared effect is produced as multiple copies of the brush shape

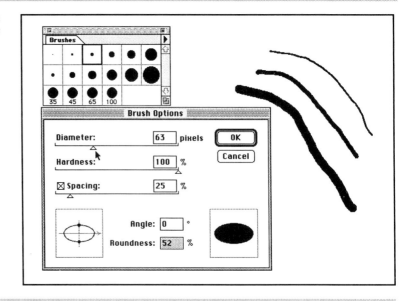

Figure 6.3. A floating window gives a choice of brush sizes and shapes in a paint package (Adobe Photoshop). Three freehand lines have been drawn using different brush sizes.

are placed on the screen, each one on top of the previous one and slightly displaced from it, as the cursor moves. If the brush is moved very rapidly over the screen, multiple separate copies of the brush shape are left behind, like an elaborate dotted line.

Special brushes
Other complicated brush effects may be provided by the software. These are designed to simulate the wide range of drawing and painting tools which are available to the artist - pens, pencils, chalks, spray-cans, palette-knives and paint brushes. Some of the effects are designed to provide the direct equivalent of a particular artistic medium, such as oil paint or watercolour. Others simulate a technique such as the blending together of two different colours at the boundary where they meet or the use of tiny dots of paint, as in Pointillism. Some of the techniques require the use of a graphic tablet with a pressure-sensitive stylus to allow the artist to work in a more natural way, the pressure exerted by the stylus determining the amount of 'paint' laid down. Some packages simulate the effect of drawing on different types of paper or canvas with a variety of surface textures and absorbencies. Some provide the visual equivalent of coloured glass and other substances like marble. One package provides facilities for artists who specialise in black and white sketching and drawing using hard and soft pencils, charcoal, felt-tips and crayons.

Other effects Most of the tools described so far are computerised equivalents of traditional artistic tools. The only exception is the user-defined brush. This has no real equivalent in traditional art; if the artist wants many copies of the same shape he has to draw them over and over again. There is another tool which is rather like this, in its usefulness in automating a repetitive process.

Flood-fill
The lood-fill tool, already referred to above, does exactly what its name suggests - it floods an area until it is full. This tool supplements the facility already mentioned of drawing certain regular shapes in such a way that they are filled as part of the drawing process. Flood-fill is used to fill irregular shapes, which have already been drawn. It can also be used regular shapes which were drawn empty, if the artist has a change of mind, since such a shape cannot be edited by changing its attributes, as in vector software.

It its simplest form, a complete boundary is drawn and then filled with a single colour. The user simply chooses a fill-colour, selects the tool and clicks anywhere inside the shape which is to be filled. The computer then examines every pixel inside that shape

Figure 6.4. A number of freehand drawn boundary shapes, flood-filled with six different patterns.

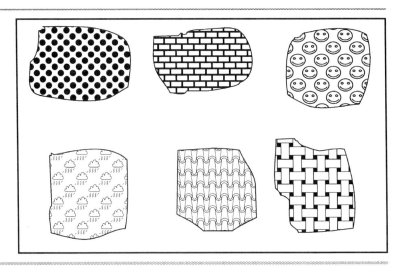

in a regular fashion, by searching along the scan lines of the display and changes the colour of each pixel to the new flood colour. It detects where the boundaries of the shape are by recognising the colour of the boundary. If the boundary has not been drawn very well, and there are one or more pixels missing - sometimes undetectable to the eye - the colour leaks out and flood fills the rest of the screen.

Fortunately a good paint package will also have an Undo tool which will reverse the last action! If not, an enormous amount of work can be lost - especially if the work has not been backed-up at regular intervals. A good flood-fill tool is not restricted to filling shapes with a single colour. Shapes can be filled with patterns also, so that a drawing of a brick wall, for instance, could be created in seconds if a brick pattern is available in the pattern library. Figure 6.4 shows some examples of freehand drawn shapes which have been flood-filled with a variety of patterns.

Tiling
The example of a wall, drawn by flood-filling, leads naturally into a related idea - the tile tool. This is a facility for creating patterns of the sort which are found in tiled walls, carpets, curtains and other fabrics in which a motif is repeated over and over again. The tile tool enables the artist to draw the motif once and then automatically create a screen full of repeating copies of that motif in one of a variety of tiling patterns. The simplest pattern would place the motif side-by-side and one above the other in a rectangular grid. More usually, each row is displaced with respect to the row above - normally by half the width of the motif. Other patterns are obviously possible. Figure 6.5 shows some examples of different tiling effects, all based on the same basic pattern.

Redefining palettes

This theme of automating processes which would be tedious if done 'by hand' is at the heart of computer art. Another example, which might be particularly relevant to the sort of tiled fabric design just described, is the facility of palette redefinition. The colours used by the artist in any particular image are a small subset from a much larger palette of possibilities. If the colours which are provided in a palette offered by the software designer are not suitable it is very easy to change some, or all of them - so creating another palette which can be saved and used again. Usually this involves selecting the colour - in the usual way, by clicking on it - and then calling up the appropriate tool. This might be done by selecting an item from a menu, by choosing an icon or by double clicking the colour. This will present a set of three slide-bars, one for each primary colour. See the later section ('Redefined colours') for an account of the use of the new colours.

Colour systems

These colour controls can be one of a number of different colour systems and good software will offer a choice. One is the RGB (Red, Green and Blue) system, associated with colour monitors. Another is the CMYK (Cyan, Magenta, Yellow and Black) system associated with printing inks. Another is the HSB (Hue, Saturation and Brightness) system which is more closely related to the way that we think of colours - not as a combination of primaries but by name (orange, purple or green, for example). Another possibility is a commercial colour-matching system like Pantone. This is intended to

Figure 6.5. A number of different tile effects, created from the same repeating pattern.

help designers be sure of the way that colours will look when finally printed - by providing printed samples of a wide range of colours, identified by codes (see chapter 2 for more details). The RGB, CMYK and HSB systems all involve the user adjusting the three or more components of the colour, either by typing in percentage values or, more easily, by sliding simulated slider-bar controls using the mouse (see Figure 1.7 in chapter 1).

Colour solids

Another approach is to represent a large range of colours on a colour solid. This is a 2- or 3-dimensional object whose different dimensions represent colour variables. One such solid is a colour triangle which illustrates, for one colour or hue, the differences as that colour loses brightness and shades into black, as it mixes with other colours and becomes closer to white or grey. Another solid is the colour wheel which is rather like a spectrum wrapped round a circle.

Because of the number of variables required the most comprehensive models involve 3-D shapes. The best-known of these is the CIE system (named after the Commission Internationale de Eclairange. Because of its complexity this is often reduced to a 2-D chromaticity chart.

Redefined colours

Whatever system is used the resultant colour, created by changing one or more of its components, is instantly displayed on the screen. There are two different approaches to the use of these new colours. In some software, particularly where the palette contains a small number of colours, the new colour is substituted in the palette in place of the one which was originally selected.

So, for example, if the palette has only 32 colours, all 32 possibilities will have been already defined and if a new one is created an old one must be lost. The result is that if the old colour has already been used in a picture, the new colour will replace the old one wherever it has been used on the screen. This can have a simple application. If a commercial artist has designed, say, a fabric or wallpaper design, using one set of colours it is possible to rapidly duplicate the design using another set of colours, without any further drawing, simply by redefining one or more of the colours in the design. Both old and new palettes can be saved so that nothing is lost in the process.

If the system can cope with a much larger range of colours then it is not necessary for the software designer to specify every possible colour in a palette. Some can be left blank for the user to define. In this case new colours can be created without losing any of the old ones.

Zooming

The magnifying glass (sometimes called a zoom facility) is an invaluable drawing tool. A similar tool, when used in a vector drawing package, produces the effect of seeing part of a drawing in much more detail - perhaps seeing details which were not displayed at all in the lower-magnification view. The effect in a paint package is quite different - see Plate 4. The individual pixels which made up the normal view, and were too small to see, now become clearly visible.

At very high magnification the pixels may be displayed as very large squares. The main use of the zoom tool is to enable the artist to do delicate work - to work on fine detail which is difficult to do and easy to spoil. The nearest equivalent for traditional art would be to paint using a magnifying glass to aid the eye. The magnifying glass does not aid the hand, however. The computerised zoom facility does. It is as if the artist is actually shrunk to a smaller size and can work with individual pixels, if necessary.

Editing

When mistakes are made it is necessary to draw over the old image and change the colour of pixels concerned. For small mistakes it may be enough to use the magnifying glass and alter the colours of a few individual pixels. For larger-scale problems the Undo facility could be used to reverse the last action so that it can then be repeated.

A third approach is to use the 'rubber' tool - the electronic equivalent of the sort of rubber which is used to rub-out pencil marks. The beauty of the electronic rubber is that no damage is done to the 'paper' and that the colour is completely removed. Another bonus is that it is possibly to rub-out colours selectively. This means that the rubber can be set so as to rub-out only one colour, and no other. This means that a much higher degree of precision can be achieved without the laborious process of changing individual pixels using the zoom facility.

Tracing

One final drawing tool which can be of considerable value in solving certain drawing problems is the Trace facility. This is often a separate piece of software which converts a paintbrush style, bit-mapped image into a vector image. The software identifies the shape of component groups of pixels and converts them into a vector line description. One simple example of its use would be a line-drawing in which the lines have been drawn by the artist with a rather thin brush. Perhaps it becomes necessary to scale the image down. The problem is that the lines become too thin to print cor-

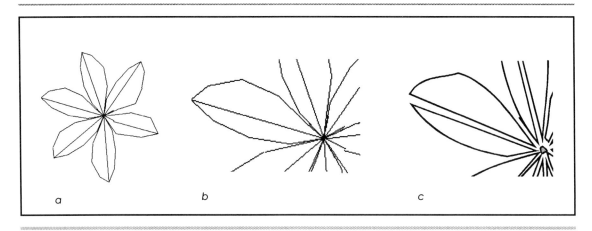

a   b   c

Figure 6.6 (a). A bit-mapped flower shape; (b). The same figure enlarged; (c). After tracing, the flower shape can be enlarged without showing the original pixel structure.

rectly or be seen easily. To thicken the lines in a paintbrush package, the artist would have to go over the drawing again with a thicker brush, adding extra pixels to all the lines and effectively redrawing the picture. A trace program could convert the drawing into a vector description and then import the drawing into a vector drawing package. All that would then be necessary would be to select some, or all the lines, and redefine them as thicker lines. The software would then redraw the image in the new version. If the lines were still not right, the process could be repeated as many times as necessary, using different thickness values, until it looked right. Figure 6.6 (a) and (b) shows a bit-mapped image, one magnified so that the pixels can be seen clearly. Figure 6.6 (c) shows a traced version of the same shape.

Other useful transformations that can be easily achieved with the trace facility include enlarging an image without loss of quality, distorting it in ways that are not possible with bit-mapped images, smoothing roughly drawn curves and changing the shape of component parts of the image without affecting other parts. All of these are ways of having your cake and eating it. It is possible to get the benefit of painting and line-based software systems at the same time.

Pixellating
The techniques called pixellating is a widely-used effect in TV and video applications and is sometimes available in paintbrush packages. This involves deliberately degrading the spatial resolution of an image by amalgamating groups of adjacent pixels into one. This effectively reduces a 640 x 480 pixel image into a 320 x 240 pixel image of the same size. Each group of four small pixels becomes a single large pixel, occupying the same space and in a colour which is some sort of average of the four original colours in those pixels. Figure 6.7 shows a series of stages in this process. The process can then be repeated over and over again until the whole image is re-

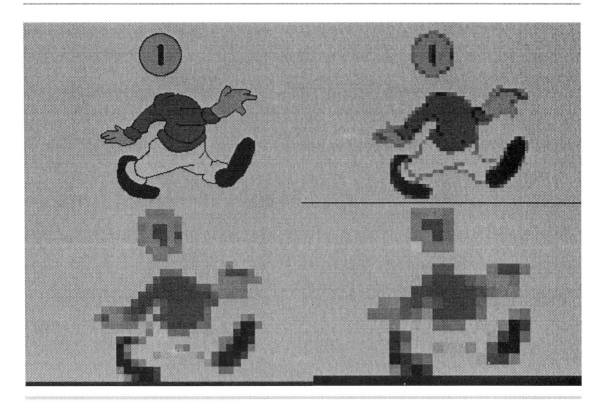

Figure 6.7. Four stages in the 'pixellisation' process. The original image (a sample image from AutoDesk's Animator Pro) becomes progressively less recognisable as first 4, then 8 and finally 12 of the original pixels are averaged.

duced to a handful of pixels. Before this stage is reached the image will have become unrecognisable. In fact, in addition to its use for artistic effect, it is also used for hiding details in an image. Usually it is done in such a way that the image is still recognisable in a general way but so that specific features have been lost. For example, if people are interviewed on TV but it is not desirable that their identity should be known, then their faces can be reduced to a relatively small number of pixels so that it is clear that it is face, but that no one could recognise them as any particular individual.

Special effects Some of the effects which are provided go beyond the mimicking of non-electronic artistic techniques. These include the facility to draw with coloured glass so that those parts of the image which are beneath, appear in colours which are modified as if the light had actually passed through a transparent but coloured material like glass. Another example is the use of colours which change with time. This can have no equivalent in traditional art because the computer display is used to constantly change colour values in a part of the image in a cyclical fashion. It is a dynamic redefinition of colours at one point, cycling through a user-defined range, either chosen from the available colour palette or by redefining one colour.

Shading

Other effects are designed to automate artistic techniques to reduce time and labour. For example, shading a surface of an object, like a cube or sphere, is conventionally used to show the effect of illumination and emphasise its three-dimensional shape. This can be done instantly by using a gradation facility. The artist chooses two extreme values of a colour - usually a dark version corresponding to the appearance of the colour under low illumination and a light version. The computer then generates a range of intermediates and fills the outlined shape with them, starting at one end with the darkest version and gradually changing the colour until it reaches the other end.

For a shading effect the colours must be the same but the same technique can be applied producing a whole range of intermediates between two quite different colours. The form of the gradation can vary also. For the shading of a flat surface, a linear effect is needed but is it also possible to produce a radial (semicircular) effect - suitable for shading a sphere (see Figure 5.17, chapter 5).

Colour editing

A whole range of effects are available to simulate the way that artists will blend colours, either by placing them side-by-side and merging them in some way, or by modifying colours already on the canvas by combining them with new ones, placed on top. One example of the first group of techniques causes adjacent coloured pixels to be jumbled up in a randomised fashion to produce an impressionistic effect. Another example blurs sharp divisions between colours to create a softer line and a greater sense of realism. Examples of the second group include a facility to place colour on top of an existing background and then 'scrape' away some of the 'paint' to partially reveal the image underneath. This sort of facility involves the computer keeping a separate record of two different 'planes' of images - as if one was on a sheet of paper and the other on a transparency, placed on top. Other examples involve the computer adding or subtracting the drawing colour from the one already laid down, to produce a third colour.

Photo-retouching The widespread availability of image scanners has led to the creation of a specialised type of paint-package, devoted to editing (or 'retouching') scanned images. Though this type of software offers most of the basic drawing tools found in a normal paint package the main emphasis is on facilities to manipulate the image - usually a photograph. In the same way that the original clear distinction between DTP and word processors has been blurred, the distinction between paint packages and photo-retouchers is also being gradually lost. The difference is becoming more one of emphasis. A paint package will concentrate on facilities which enable the artist to create images from scratch, a photographic manipulation package will concentrate on facilities to enhance existing -bit-mapped, often photographic - images. There are three broad areas of manipulation which can be applied to pictures - the removal of defects, the 'improvement' of images and the addition of special effects.

Correcting defects

The term defect usually implies technical faults associated with the photographic process, such as scratches or dust on the negative or unwanted colour or contrast effects introduced by faulty processing of the film. Figure 6.8 shows an example of an image with dust on the film. It is necessary to 'remove' the dust by superimposing on that part of the image, pixel colours which are like the surrounding area - the region where there is no dust. One method would be to simply copy a rectangle from an adjoining region on top of the dusty part of the picture.

This might, however, cause problems if there are noticeable differences in colour between the two regions caused, for example, by the lighting. An alternative, provided by PhotoShop is a special 'dust and scratches' filter which detects colour differences between adjoining pixels. In this case it responds to differences between the colour of the dark dust pixels and the colour of the surrounding ones - and eliminates the differences. Another example is of a picture which is not quite in focus. A special 'sharpen' filter can be

Figure 6.8. An enlarged portion of a scanned photograph showing dust marks in the bottom left corner. These can be removed by a process of copying a portion of the surrounding image on top of it. The sample image is provided with Adobe Photoshop.

a

b

c

Figure 6.9 (a). A scanned photograph of a flower (provided with Adobe Photoshop); (b). the same photograph with the blacks and whites reversed producing the effect of a photographic negative; (c). another way of processing the same image, by tracing the contours between some of the principle colours.

used to increase the contrast at the edges of the shapes - the regions where colours change. This has the effect of making the image seem better focused. Sometimes the filter is used to produce the reverse effect - to give a sharply-focused image a more soft-focus effect.

Improving the image

'Improvements' are changes to the image which make it nearer to some imagined ideal. This might mean removing wrinkles from a face or changing hair or eye colour. Plate 11 shows a photograph of a pear with a bruise. The bruise can be removed by a process of painting over it using a 'brush' copied from an adjoining region. Another example of this technique might be the case of a photograph taken of some beauty spot which is 'spoilt' by the presence of too many cars. Photo-retouching can be used to remove them. This involves copying parts of the road surface where there are no cars and superimposing these over the offending regions of road.

Both the types of image manipulations discussed so far involve changing the colour of selected pixels, either using sophisticated 'filters' or by carefully redrawing certain pixels using the zoom tool or by copying closely adjoining parts of the same picture. More drastic changes might involve copying patterns from a completely different photograph. An example of this would be to replace a grey cloudy sky with a blue, sunny sky, taken from another photograph. A simpler method, if clouds were not required, would be simply redefine the colour of the grey pixels to blue pixels. Even larger scale changes could involve rearranging buildings, replacing a road with a river or creating completely fake scenes by assembling items taken from many different photographs.

Special effects

The two types of manipulation described so far are designed not to be noticed. 'Special effects', however, usually implies changes which the artist definitely wants to be noticed because they are an important feature of the image. There is of course no limit to what these changes might be. Some of them might be 'realistic' in intention, like adding wings to a pig to create a mythical, but lifelike creature. Others will be non-realistic effects which are designed to

Figure 6.11(a). A scanned grey-level image (provided with Adobe Photoshop); (b). the photograph has been 'embossed'; (c) the photograph has been 'crystallised'.

a

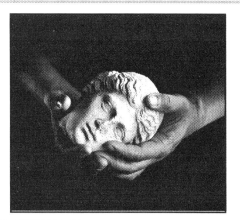

b

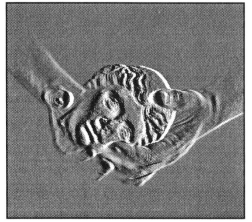

c

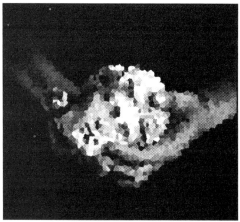

143

produce very stylised images. One example of this would be to reduce the number of grey-levels in a monochrome image to just two - black and white, to produce a high-contrast image of the sort made by a child's 'potato-print'. Another takes an image and produces a grey-level version of it in which the edges of the picture are enhanced to achieve an 'embossed' effect. Figures 6.9 - 6.12 show a number of these types of image processing : 'invert', 'trace-contours', 'emboss' and 'crystallise'.

Selecting areas

For some of the manipulations which have been described it is important to be able to select very precisely the region of interest in the photograph which is to be modified. It is unlikely that this can be achieved using the simple rectangle selection tool which is available in all paint packages because this will not be sufficiently selective. Two, more sophisticated, approaches involve either a more selective choice of geometry or choice by colour. The first method uses a selection by careful, freehand drawing round the area of interest, perhaps using the zoom facility to ensure complete accuracy.

The other method is selection by colour. The software automatically selects all pixels with a particular colour value. This second approach would make it easy to change the colour of the eyes in a portrait from, say, brown to blue. Because a colour photograph, digitised into thousands or even millions of colours, will contain many slightly different shades of any particular colour this type of selection tool is usually used to select all the pixels which have a closely similar, rather than identical, colour.

Choosing colours

Another aid in dealing with such large numbers of colours is the 'eye-dropper' tool. The artist will often want to add to some feature in a photograph and this involves drawing with the same colour as the feature. The question is 'What colour is it?'. With the aid of the eye-dropper the user can 'pick-up' the appropriate colour directly from the picture rather than by guesswork, from the palette.

Masks

Another useful aid to any type of operation which involves making small changes to a scanned picture, is the 'mask' which prevents the colour of a group of chosen pixels from being changed by the normal painting processes. This is like using masking tape when painting window frames; it protects areas, like the glass, from being painted accidentally. Masks can also be used to produce attractive design features. For example, a mask can be made of a set of large letters - perhaps the name of a product in an advertisement - and used to select appropriate parts of a photograph. When this is overlaid on top of the letters it creates the effect of looking through a window at the photograph, the window being the shape of the characters.

'Photographic' processing
Some tools are designed to be exactly similar in intention to methods used in conventional photography and keep the same name. Two examples of this are 'Dodge' and 'Burn'. When a photograph is printed it can sometimes be seen that parts of it are either too dark or too light, compared with the rest of the picture. A skilful photographer can compensate for this in the printing stage by placing a suitably shaped object in the path of the light from the enlarger during part of the exposure of the print. This has the effect of reducing the amount of light falling on the print. This makes that particular portion of the final image lighter since it is a negative process - light produces silver in the final image which darkens the image.

Dodging and burning In some cases the photographer's hand is used; sometimes it is necessary to cut out a piece of card into a suitable shape, mounted on the end of thin handle - a 'dodger'. In either case it is important to move the object about during the process so as to avoid clear-cut edges on the final print. 'Burning' is the equivalent process, using a hole in a large piece of card, which produces a darker area on the print. Using photo-retouching software, both of these techniques can now be done digitally.

Other techniques which have an obvious photographic equivalent include 'sharpen' and 'un-sharpen', already referred to earlier in the chapter. The difference is that in conventional photography these effects are determined during the exposure of the film. In the digital equivalent they can be done after the photograph has been taken. There are another set of techniques which emulate photographic processes after the picture has been taken. These are filters which change the lighting effects by adding shadows or lighter regions to edges in the picture. They can be used to make the picture look as if it had been taken using a strong spotlight or an ordinary light-bulb held close to the object or using general but very directional lighting.

Solarisation Another effect which can be achieved by clever manipulation of the photographic printing process - called 'solarisation' (see Figure 6.13) - can also be mimicked. This pro-

 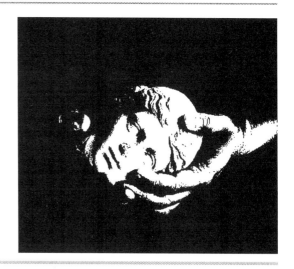

Figures 6.13 and 6.14. Two more 'photographic' processing techniques : solarising and posterising.

duces very high contrast images which look like line-drawings from black and white originals. In conventional photography solarisation involves a number of time-consuming processing stages but can be instantaneous by digital means. Figure 6.14 shows another technique called 'posterising'.

Wrapping images

There are also techniques which have no obvious photographic equivalent. Some involve geometrical distortion of the original photograph or scanned drawing. For example a picture can be distorted in such a way that it appears to be wrapped round a cylinder. This can be used to create the appearance of a drinks can, or any other cylindrical object, with the image printed on the side, or stuck on, like a label. Similarly a picture can be distorted, with or without perspective to so as to fit on to the side of a 3-D rectangular box (see Figures 15 a, b & c). Some techniques draw their inspiration from the world of television or other electronic media. An example of this is electronic 'noise' which introduces 'snow' - random dots of the sort seen on a TV when the picture signal is very weak and has then been amplified too much to compensate.

Figure 6.15 (a). A scanned photograph of a flower; (b). the same flower which has been 'skewed' so as to fit on the top of a 3-D rectangular box. (c). a similar process to the previous distortion except that perspective has been added.

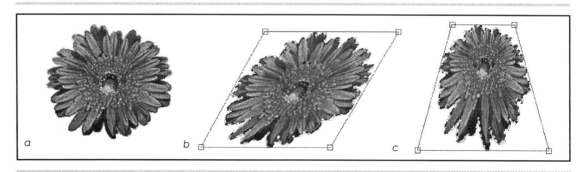

Software packages

SOFTWARE	COMPUTER	COMMENTS
Picture Publisher (Micrografx)	PC	Can load parts of images or low-resolution versions of images; has layers (like CAD); wide range of features.
Publisher's Paintbrush (ZSoft)	PC	Has 4 modes : B/W, 256 greys, 256 colours & 24-bit colour; blending & smudging tools plus some filters; poor support for fonts.
Deluxe Paint Enhanced (Electronic Arts)	PC	Low price product with slide-shows and animation.
Cricket-Paint (Computer Assoc)	PC	Full-featured package with 24-bit colour.
Fractal Design Painter (Letraset)	PC	Designed for painters; needs pressure-sensitive tablet for best results; more than 80 painting & drawing tools to emulate painting styles; 24-bit colour
Fractal Design Sketcher (Letraset)		Budget price; similar interface to Painter but designed for sketching in black & white.
Paintbrush (Microsoft)	PC	Limited features but provided "free" with Windows
Word, Ami-Pro, Works, Office etc	PC	Many wordprocessors and software "suites" are provided with built-in paint packages.
PhotoShop (Adobe)	PC & Mac	The market leader in photo-retouching; huge range of facilities; expensive; aimed at professional users.
PhotoStyler (Aldus)	PC & Mac	Main rival to PhotoShop; cheaper but a powerful package
PhotoFinish	PC	Best of the cheaper photo-retouchers
Photo-Paint (Corel)	PC	Photo-retouching software supplied with CorelDraw! but now available separately

Summary

1 Paint software includes many of the basic drawing techniques which are found in vector drawing packages but also include a range of freehand techniques which are characteristic of this type of product. These include a range of special drawing 'tools' which are called 'brushes'.

2 The term 'tool' is used in a variety of ways in drawing software. These include electronic drawing 'instruments' (such as spray-guns), object attributes such as colours and patterns and a variety of editing effects.

3 Some paintbrush packages offer a variety of facilities which help the user mimic traditional drawing and painting techniques, such as oil-paint, charcoal and water-paint. They can also mimic artistic styles like those used by the impressionists or pointillists.

4 There are a whole range of computer-based effects, such as flood-filling, tiling, colour redefinition, zoom, tracing and pixellating.

5 Some of these facilities, like grey-level gradation, can be used to speed up normal drawing techniques by automating shading effects.

6 An extension of some of the editing techniques of paint software have been developed to the point where a new category of software has merged. Photo-retouching software is used specifically for making modifications to scanned photographs and other bit-mapped images.

7 There are three main types of alteration which this software can make to photographic images - removing photographic defects, removing blemishes and special effects.

8 Traditional photographic effects such as solarisation and 'dodging' can also be mimicked electronically.

9 Image distortion can be used to appear to 'wrap' flat images around 3-D shapes like cubes and cylinders.

Animation and 3-D modelling

Key points

- *the principles of computer animation*
- *3-D modelling*
- *photo-realistic images*
- *virtual reality*

What is animation software?

All animation involves displaying slightly different versions of a picture in very rapid sequence. The eye cannot react sufficiently quickly to see them as separate images, and the brain interprets the sequence as a single, smoothly changing image. In the child's 'flicker' book, a set of drawings are made on the edge of the pages of a book and the pages rapidly flicked over (see Plate 12 and Figure 7.1). In the Hollywood cartoon, the pictures are drawn by hand, photographed by a special cine-camera using the 'stop-frame' method and projected on to a screen. Ever since raster-scan displays (see chapter 3) were first used, computers also have been involved in a form of animation. Because of the way that the fluorescent screen fades so rapidly it has always been necessary to keep a coded-version of the image in memory and send a fresh copy to the display at least 25 times per second. It is only necessary to send different images to the screen for a form of animation to take place.

Even in a simple text-only word processor, scrolling the text produces an animated effect - the text seems to move down the screen. The two factors which, until recently, held back the development of true animation software have been the problem of storing the large number of images and the lack of power needed to generate the images in a reasonable time.

The cel technique

Special paint packages are now available, however, which provide the electronic equivalent of the Hollywood animation studio. They offer all the standard drawing and colour facilities but, in addition, two broad categories of special tools for the job of animation. The first category is designed to help with the tedious process of

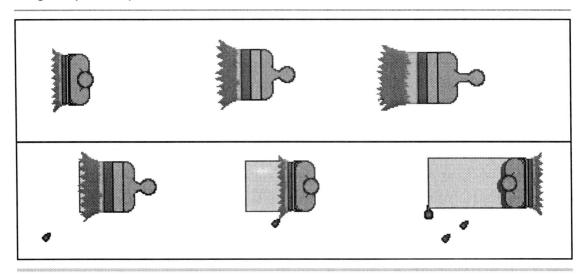

Figure 7.1. Six stages in a simple animation of a paint brush, from Autodesk's Animator Pro.

producing the huge number of separate images which are needed. In traditional animation the most important of these is the 'cel' technique. A cel is a celluloid - a transparency. The background for a scene is drawn on one sheet of paper and the foreground, the moving parts, on a series of sheets of transparent material - the cels (see Figures 7.2a & b).

The idea is that those parts of the image which will not change during an animated sequence need only be drawn once. Those parts which do change are drawn on the cels, which are placed in turn on top of the background and the whole is photographed as a single image. Even this process involves vast amounts of repetitive labour and the work is done by teams of animators. Some do the most creative work - executing the overall sequence of movements - others, are concerned with the details. These details are of two types. One is the drawing of all the small changes which occur in the course of an animated movement. This is called 'in-betweening' or 'tweening' because the artist draws large numbers of slightly different pictures, which are between the start point and the end point of a movement. The other is the colouring of the outline shapes in each picture. The computer can help in both these areas.

Digitised cels
The electronic basis of the cel has been described briefly in the previous chapter in the discussion of the scrape facility in some paint software. Two parts of an image are kept separately, in two distinct areas of memory and only brought together electronically at the display stage. This means that the software can be used to make changes to one part of the image without affecting the other. This same idea is used to create cels and backgrounds. One advantage that the computer has over conventional methods is that there is

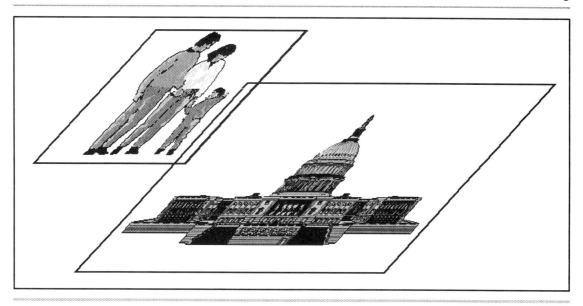

Figure 7.2 (a). The two parts of the image - foreground and background - are drawn on different transparent cels.

no theoretical limit to the number of transparent overlays that can be used. Real transparencies are not totally transparent. They absorb and reflect a small amount of light and if too many are sandwiched together the colour and detail in the ones at the bottom will suffer. The use of the flood-fill facility to fill a boundary with a colour or pattern, has already been described in the last chapter. A version of this technique can be used to automate the tedious process of colouring shapes which in traditional cartoons occupies teams of artists for many hours.

Figure 7.2 (b). What seems to be a single picture of a family sightseeing is in fact two separate images, overlaid. Changes can be made to the foreground cel without redrawing the background.

Tweening

Perhaps the most sophisticated facility the computer provides is in automatic tweening - sometimes called polymorphic tweening. The term polymorphic - 'many shapes' -emphasises the fact that the computer is being used to gradually change one shape into another, through a series of intermediate shapes. This requires the artist to draw the first and last image in the sequence, and also to indicate how the changes are to occur. The simplest way of doing this is to mark a series of corresponding points on the first and last images. The computer then calculates a series of intermediate values for each set of points and each frame in the sequence, and then draw suitable lines to join up those points. These then become the intermediate images.

Morphing Morphing is an application of this technique to realistic images - usually photographs - which has recently been used widely in films and TV advertisements. Simpler forms of this are now possible on microcomputers. The technique, again, uses the computer to generate a series of intermediate images which appear to show one object metamorphosing into another.

In its simple form two images are scanned - say a man's face and a lion's. The user must then identify a whole series of corresponding points on the two images. In this case, the corresponding points in the first and last images are not points which indicate how movement is to take place but points which indicate similar regions of the images which are to metamorphose, one into the other. In this example, there are obvious equivalent points in the two images -corresponding parts of the eyes, ears and nose, for example -the differences between them being those of size, shape and colour.

The software calculates a whole series of intermediate values of colour and position for each pair of points, so creating a series of complete images which gradually become less like one image and more like the other.

When the series is animated the 'morphing' effect is produced. The simple software which is currently available for microcomputers works essentially in two dimensions for static images - scanned photographs.

The more powerful software used in the cinema has to work on images of 3-D objects which have shading and lighting characteristics and are probably moving during the course of the metamorphosis. This type of morphing requires a type of 3-D modelling software - see the next section.

Geometrical effects

There are other computer-generated animation effects which though very simple in principle can produce very impressive results. They include geometrical changes like linear distortion, zooming and panning. Even with a 2-D drawing package these can produce effects which give the illusion of a 3-D image. For example, if an animation of a title is created by simply squeezing it in the vertical direction and then reversing the process it produces the effect of a solid object being rotated about a horizontal axis (see Figure 7.3). Distorting it by squeezing it horizontally makes it seem to be rotating about a vertical axis. If it is zoomed, it gives the impression of the object flying towards the viewer (see Figure 7.4). If the object is made smaller it seems to be flying away. The illusion is quite effective because the human brain is much more used to objects which are rigid and retain their dimensions, but move and rotate, than objects which change shape and size with no apparent reason.

Animation produces huge numbers of images and would very quickly fill the memory capacity of any ordinary computer. Fortunately, it is not necessary to store the whole of each image. In principle the computer, unlike cine-film, only needs a copy of those parts which have changed since the previous frame and so only saves the differences in each frame, as compared with the first.

Figure 7.3. Six images in a sequence representing a spinning title. The illusion is created by squeezing the title and then creating a mirror image and stretching it back again. In rapid succession the title appears to be spinning on a horizontal axis.

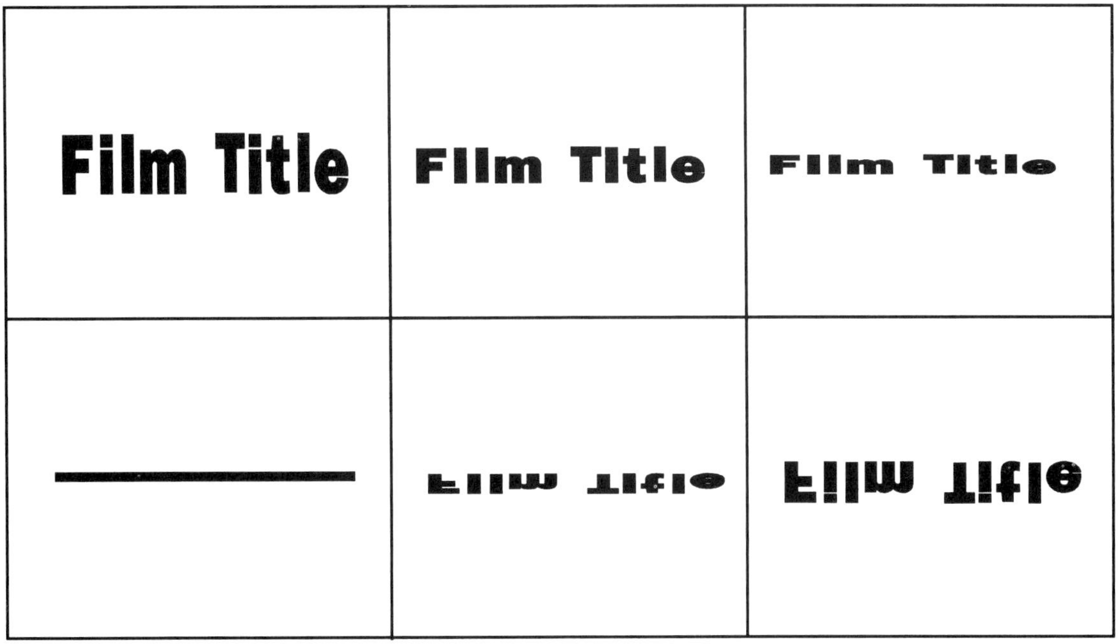

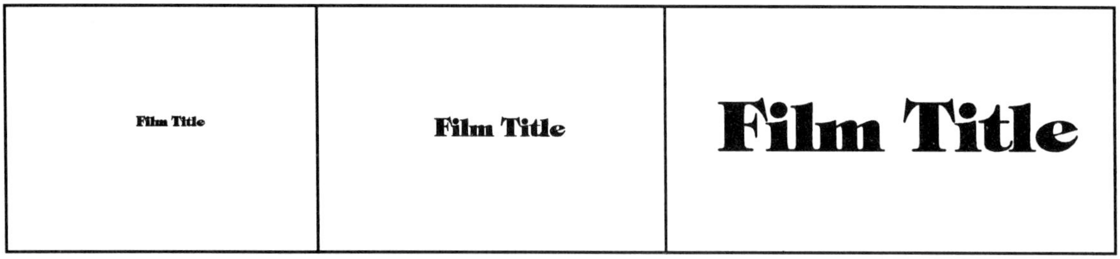

Figure 7.4. A simple animation of a title flying towards the viewer is created by progressively enlarging the text.

Video

Animated images can be displayed on the computer, but more often they are transferred to video tape via a special piece of hardware (see chapter 3). There are two major advantages to this. The first is that, once they are stored on tape, well-established analogue editing techniques, such as overlaying text onto background pictures or fading from one image to another, can be used. The second relates to the speed with which the computer can produce the images. If the computer is not powerful enough to generate all the necessary images in 'real time' (as they are needed) then they must be created in a separate operation and stored before they can be viewed. They can be stored as digital images on a magnetic disc but this will occupy an enormous amount of disc space. The alternative is to transfer them to analogue tape which is a much cheaper medium. It is, in any case, likely that the final images will be viewed on a TV system rather than a computer screen.

Frame-grabbing

The type of hardware which is used to transfer computer images to video tape can be designed to work the other way - by digitising analogue video images and transferring them to the computer. Such a device is often called a 'frame-grabber'. Using a frame grabber to transfer video to the computer offers the option of editing and mixing with conventional video on the computer instead of the normal analogue editing suite (using special software). In fact the power of modern computers is making this a much cheaper option than the traditional method. When the current generation of analogue TV systems are replaced by completely digital systems, as seems likely in the near future, then the differences between analogue TV and digital computer equipment described here will vanish.

Software packages

SOFTWARE	COMPUTER	COMMENTS
Animator Pro (AutoDesk)	PC	Very versatile paint package with a wide variety of tools and effects together with polymorphic tweening, traditional cel animation, colour cycling and text animation.
Animation Works (Gold Disc)	Mac	a simpler and much cheaper equivalent program for the Mac.
CorelDraw! 5 (Corel)	PC	(See chapter 5). Originally an Illustration package; now a collection, including some animation and morphing features.
Morph (Gryphon)	PC & Mac	Mac version is called Morph SFX; will create video sequences; needs a lot of (computer) memory and patience.
PhotoMorph (North Coast Software)	PC	Similar software to Morph; slightly cheaper.
Digital Morph (HSC)	PC	A low price combination of morphing and paint/re-touching

3-D modelling   *What is 3-D modelling?*

Producing 3-D images is one of the most demanding graphics tasks that a computer can be given. As outlined in the introduction, the computer is used to take a complete definition of the shape and position of the object, together with the laws of optics, and then to calculate what that object would look like under a given set of conditions. The conditions include the lighting, the position of the 'camera' and the type of materials which make up the outer surface of the object. This process involves calculating the behaviour of every ray of light which interacts with the object and enters the observer's eye - a process called 'ray-tracing'. Before that can be done, however, the object has to be described in a way that the computer can handle (and the user can understand). In fact two of the basic problems in designing software for the production of 3-D images are how the user is to specify the precise shape of a 3-D object on a 2-D screen, and how to see the result.

Figure 7.5 (a). The four conventional views of a 3-D object : front, side (left), top and isometric. These are 'wire-frame' views, from Strata Vision 3d.

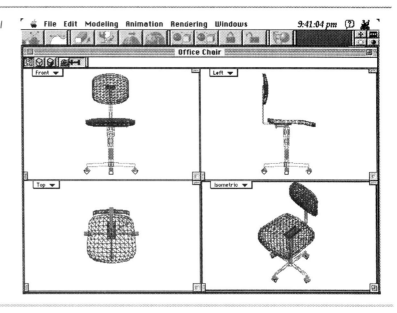

Creating a 3-D model   *Visualising the object*

Unlike all the other software described so far the user must get to grips with the second question, posed above (how to visualise a 3-D object). This always involves the display of two or more simultaneous views of the object on the screen - usually the traditional orthographic views of the front, the side, the top ('plan') and the isometric views, as used in architect's and engineers diagrams (see Figures 7.5a & b). These are the views which are constructed as if a transparent cube had been placed over the object and the object

Figure 7.5 (b). The same four views of the same object but displayed as a collection of blocks. Each of the major components of the object are represented by a rectangular block which indicates that component's position in space. The shape of the blocks is much simpler to calculate, when changes in the object are made, which speeds up the re-display process.

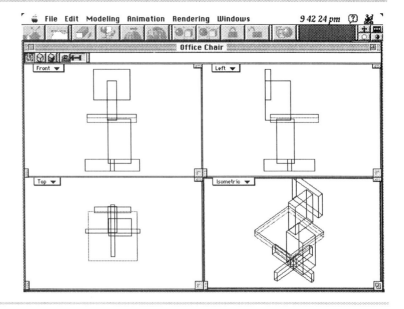

then 'projected' onto the cube's top, front, and right sides. A fourth view (the isometric) - drawn from a point which makes equal angles with all three of the orthographic planes - is often added, since this provides a more realistic general view of the object. It enables the viewer to see some, at least, of all three of the projected sides simultaneously.

Multiple views

These views can usually be made to fill the screen, so that only one can be seen at a time, but more often they will each fill one quarter of the screen so that the user can constantly refer to them to judge the overall position of the object in three dimensions. The user must learn the skill of working in these three different projections. When, for example, bringing two different objects together so as to touch, it is not enough that they seem to touch in only one projection. This might mean that the top of one object is in the same plane as the bottom of the other but that they are nevertheless a long way away from each other. Looking from the front, perhaps, they will seems to touch. Looking from above they will be seen not to.

Wire-frame images

The images of the object are usually drawn on the screen as simple wire-frame representations. A wire-frame image consists of lines which represent the edges of flat planes or follow the contours of curved surfaces (see Figure 7.6). There is no attempt to represent the colours of surfaces or the light and shade produced by illumi-

Figure 7.6. Three views of the same object : wire-frame, wire-frame with hidden-lines removed, and rendered.

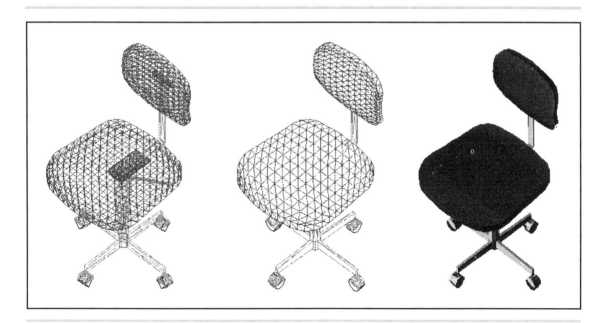

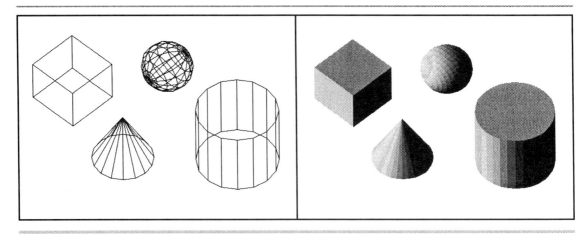

Figure 7.7. Four typical 3-D graphics 'primitives', in wire-frame and rendered view.

nation. A wire-frame view presents the minimum information which enables a viewer to see the shape and position of an object. For most objects such an image can be produced by a modern microcomputer almost instantly.

Even with the most powerful of current general-purpose microcomputers, however, a realistic shaded image can take many minutes or even hours of computation and so wire-frame images, however unrealistic, are used to provide the near-instant response which is expected in the early stages of the design process. Only when most of the design is done is it worth generating the more realistic images. This type of work is so demanding that serious professional work is often done on expensive work-stations which are fitted with specialised hardware, designed for the processes involved in 3-D image generation.

At the time of writing some of this special hardware is on the point of migrating to more standard computers because of the increasing interest in 3-D work. In time, it should be possible to dispense with the wire-frame views and work with more realistic images, as is already possible with top-end systems.

Creating the object

The first question, posed at the beginning of this section (how to specify the object) is much more difficult and there are a number of ways of performing this task. Different methods may be used for different parts of an image. The first method is useful for generating objects which have a simple regular geometry, like many manufactured objects. The 3-D software is equipped with a number of geometrical 'primitives' - basic 3-D geometrical shapes like rectangular boxes, spheres, cones, rods, tubes and pyramids (see Figure 7.7). The user selects the object from a menu and placed on the screen in exactly the same way that lines, rectangles and circles are drawn with 2-D drawing packages, using a marquee. The only extra complication is that to position the objects correctly in 3-D involves working, in turn, in the three different views, as described above. This is a skill which beginners sometimes find difficult to acquire and requires the facility to think in 3-D.

Adding shapes together

3-D primitives can be added to each other to build up more complex shapes, in the same way that 2-D primitives like lines and circles can. However, the extra dimension adds scope for much greater complexity in the creation of solid objects and the more sophisticated software allows for this by providing a wider range of ways for combining objects together. These are called Boolean combinations and in essence they all involve ways of selecting which parts of a combination of objects are to form the new object. The first stage of the process involves bringing two primitives together, usually in such a way that they 'overlap' (i.e. occupy the same region of space as if they were not solid). The next stage of the process involves choosing which Boolean operation is to be applied to the two objects. For example, an 'AND' operation means that the new, composite, object is made up of only those parts of the two original objects which occupy the same volume of space. Figure 7.8 shows two separate objects being brought to an overlapping state and then combined together. One uses a Boolean OR operation (which results in an object containing everything which

Figure 7.8. Boolean combination of 3-D primitives. The rectangular block and the cylinder (shown in wire-frame view) are first brought together so that they overlap. The first rendered shape is the result of an OR operation, the second of a subtraction.

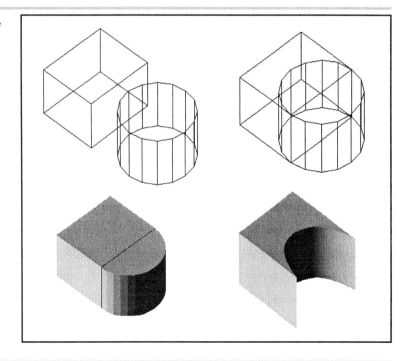

was present in either of the two originals). The other uses a sub-traction or 'cut' operation (where one acts as a cutter to subtract its shape from the other).

Extrusion

An alternative method of constructing objects is particularly suitable to those shapes which have some sort of symmetry. It consists of drawing a 2-D shape and then using the computer to extrude the shape into the third dimension, as if a soft substance were pushed through a suitably-shaped hole to form something like string. In fact wire is actually made by this type of process. It can be thought of as the reverse of the one in which a thin cross-section of an object is made by cutting a parallel-sided slice from it. Another name for the process is 'lofting'.

With a little ingenuity an enormous range of shapes can be created this way. For example, if a solid rod primitive were not available, it could be created by extruding a 2-D circle into the third dimension. A tube could be made by extruding a 2-D ring-shape. If the extrusion path is not a simple straight line, then more complicated objects can be made, like the exhaust-pipe of a car. Something like wooden beading or a picture rail can easily be created by simply drawing the cross-sectional shape and extruding it along a straight line (see Figure 7.9). Solid-looking letters for the titles of TV programmes or for use in advertisements are created by extruding 2-D vector fonts. One of the case studies in chapter 10 shows in detail how the outline of a word in 2-D can be extruded into a 3-D solid.

Figure 7.9. The outline shape acts as a 2-D 'cross-section' for the desired shape. This is then extruded or 'lofted' into a 3-D shape to create an object which looks rather like a piece of wooden beading.

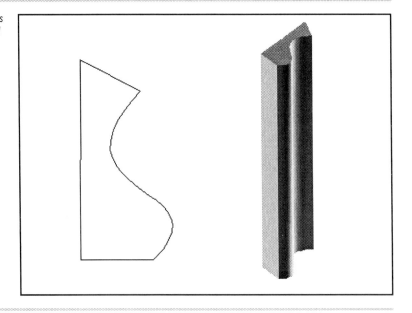

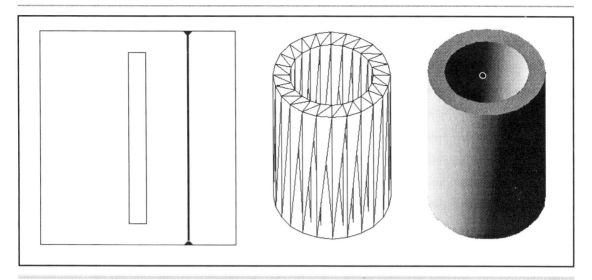

Figure 7.10 (a). A tall narrow rectangle is rotated around a vertical axis to produce a tube. The software used is Strata Vision 3d.

Figure 7.10 (b). The same technique is used to create a wineglass.

Rotation

The alternative to extrusion is rotation (sometimes called 'lathing'), which involves drawing a 2-D shape and then rotating it around a suitable axis in 3-D space. The simplest example would be the rotation of a narrow rectangle around an axis parallel to its long dimension to create a tube - see Figure 10 (a). A classic demonstration of this technique is the creation of a wineglass shape - see Figure 7.10 (b). Rotation involves drawing the 2-D shape, specifying the axis of rotation and choosing the number of turns the shape is to be given. This creates, initially, a large number of tiny flat surfaces (called 'facets'), each inclined at a small angle to the next. This is then usually turned into a smooth surface using a separate smoothing operation.

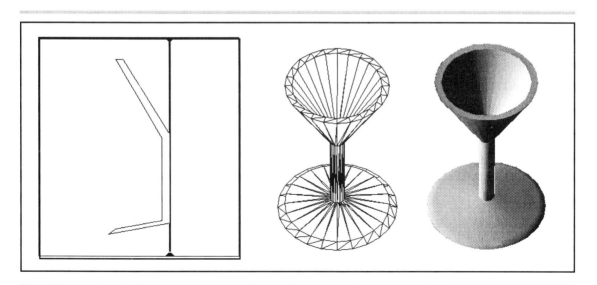

Irregular shapes

If a shape is too irregular to made by any of the techniques described so far then it may have to be created painstakingly using a large number of small faces (facets) which are drawn individually, oriented in 3-D space and then joined together. These basic surfaces are usually small triangles. Sometimes this process can be speeded up by drawing a crude representation of the shape out of a small number of large planes and then using the computer to break them down into a much larger number of small planes, inclined at small angles to each other, to make a smoother transition. With enough small planes it is possible to create what appears to be a smoothly curved surface like a human face or a car body.

Hidden-line removal

Once the basic shape has been defined there are two further tasks for the software. One is hidden-line (or hidden-surface) removal and the other is rendering. The first process requires the computer to calculate which parts of the object are visible to the observer and which parts are hidden. It must be remembered that an artist, in sketching an object, draws extensively on experience or direct observation to know exactly how that object should look from any particular position. The computer, on the other hand, only has data about the positions in space of all the surfaces which make up the object and the position of the observer.

When the object is displayed as a wire-frame, all the surfaces are usually displayed as if it were completely transparent. The computer must then use 3-D geometry to calculate for every surface whether or not the eye can see it, or whether another surface is blocking the view. This process of removing from the image all the hidden surfaces takes a considerable amount of calculation and can take many minutes or even longer. Figure 7.6 (a) and (b) shows an office chair in wire-frame view, both with and without hidden-lines.

Rendering

Even when the process is complete the image will not be very realistic. An even longer process - rendering - is necessary if the surface appearance of the object is to be lifelike. The appearance of a surface depends on four factors :

- the optical qualities of the surface
- the colour(s) of the surface
- the texture of the surface,
- the quality and type of the lighting.

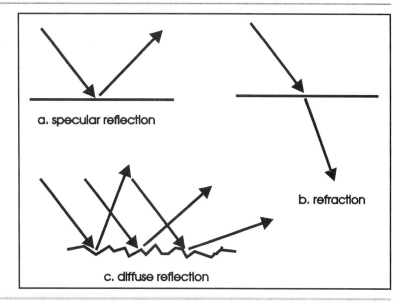

Figure 7.11. Three ways that light interacts with substances: 'specular' reflection from mirror-like surfaces, refraction through transparent materials, and diffuse reflection (scattering) from rough surfaces.

Many surfaces are opaque but in the case of transparent surfaces like glass the computer must calculate an additional set of ray-paths. Some light rays will reflect off the surface to produce a mirror-like effect, but some will refract through the material, being bent as they do so. If the glass is coloured this will change the colour of the light being transmitted through it. Figure 7.11 illustrates three basic effects on light of different types of surface : specular (glasslike) reflection, refraction and diffuse reflection (or scattering).

The colour of an opaque surface will not necessarily be uniform. Many manufactured objects have patterns printed on their surfaces. In the last chapter there was a reference to the process of wrapping patterns on to a curved surface like a drinks can and the same principle applies to wallpaper on the walls of a room.

Textures

To obtain the most realistic pictures - images which are often called 'Photo-realistic' - it is necessary to be able to create textured surfaces. Early attempts at 3-D modelling produced rather synthetic-looking images because the surfaces were too flat which often produced a bland, slightly unreal appearance. Many manufactured objects may be very smooth and uniform but other objects like knitted garments, tree trunks, carpets and bricks have a distinct and unique texture. Textured surfaces usually have a distinct repetitive quality, like the regular ribbing of a woollen garment but at the same time are not completely regular.

The most difficult surfaces to model are those which have some structure but also a large random element to them - like a rocky mountain face or a cloud. These are created using a branch of mathematics called fractals. Fractal formulae can be constructed which contain within them a description of the regular repeating aspects of a surface but also have an element of randomness which reflects the fact that very few real objects are entirely regular.

Surface libraries
The user specifies these three aspects of the object by choosing from a library - say, shiny blue plastic or coarse-grained dark brown wood or smoky green glass. The computer is then required to calculate the path of thousands of light rays from the various lights to the surfaces and back to the eye. This means that the user must also specify the fourth variable - the lighting. More skill is needed in choosing the lighting because the appearance of an object is critically dependent on it. Lights can be highly directional - like spot lights - or semi directional - like ordinary tungsten lamps - or very diffuse - like sunlight on a cloudy day or a set of long fluorescent lamps. Figure 7.12 illustrates the different types of light source. Lights can also be coloured and they can be placed at many different distances from the object and pointed in different directions. All these factors affect the light and shade effects and also the apparent colour of the objects being lit.

3-D animation   Animation of 3-D images can be done in two ways. The simplest approach is achieved by changes in the camera position, producing the effect that the observer is flying through space. The user specifies not one camera position, as in the normal static image, but a path. The computer then models a whole series of separately rendered images, one for each position on the path. The number of

Figure 7.12. Different types of illumination: a 'point' source (light-bulb), diffuse sunlight (scattered by clouds), a spotlight and diffuse light from a long tube source.

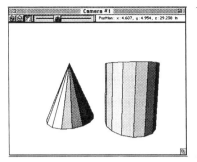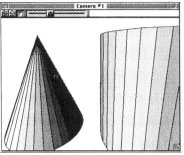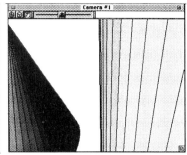

Figure 7.13. Three views of a pair of solids (created in Strata Vision 3d) as the camera moves towards them.

positions on the path will determine how quickly the observer appears to be flying when the animation is shown. Although the computer must perform a hugely-increased number of calculations in order to produce hundreds of separate images, the user only has to create the original model once and then specify the path along which the camera must move between 'shots'. Figure 7.13 shows a series of views as the camera is moved, forming an animated flying shot.

Title sequences

This technique is often used in TV programmes to produce an arresting title sequence. For example, the observer seems to fly towards the 3-D solid letters which make up the programme's title, rotate around it, then fly through or between the letters. It is also used to create 'walk-throughs'. A walk-through is an animated sequence of images created by moving the camera through a model of a structure such as a building. It gives the same impression that a person would obtain if they walked through the actual building and is an excellent way of demonstrating the main features of an architect's design. Similar methods can be used for training purposes, by showing the structure of a complicated piece of equipment, perhaps demonstrating it in detail by 'taking it apart', again by the use of animated sequences.

Animated objects

More sophisticated 3-D animation involves movements between individual objects and changes in the objects. The latter involves the user specifying the objects as a collection of parts - like a doll with moving arms and legs. The arms and legs must be created as separate objects so that they can be moved relative to each other. Types of possible movement must also be specified, such as rotation of an arm about the shoulder, so that the computer can automate the creation of the new position. Without this facility it would be necessary for the user to redraw each moving part for each picture, or at least, manipulate the position of the part manually to create the new pose. Techniques like this are used in some 3-D CAD

165

software to test the viability of the design of a piece of equipment before it is actually made. It can be used to demonstrate that when a component of the equipment rotates or slides it does not collide with other some other part.

Software packages

SOFTWARE	COMPUTER	COMMENTS
3-D Studio (Autodesk)	PC	The best general-purpose 3-D modeller for the PC; includes animation and Boolean operations
Topas (AT&T Graphics)	PC	2 versions; one designed for professional use and very expensive, the other a direct rival to 3-D Studio
Infini-D (Specular)	Mac	Relatively low cost but powerful 3-D modeller (all good 3-D software is expensive and needs high-powered machines)
StrataStudio (Strata Inc)	Mac	Expensive, high-end package for the professional
StrataVision 3D (Strata Inc)	Mac	Cheaper (half the price) package from same source; direct rival to Infini-D
Sketch (Alias)	Mac	Interface designed to be similar to 2-D illustration package; no animation
Dimensions (Adobe)	Mac	Limited to rotating & extruding 2-D images from Illustrator or Freehand (see Chapter 5); cheaper than normal 3-D software
Typestry (Pixar)	Mac	Limited to creating 3-D effects on type; simple to use
Renderman (Pixar)	PC & Mac	Rendering software which accepts images from other programs.

Virtual reality Virtual reality is one of the most exciting applications of 3-D modelling and animation. It was pointed out at the beginning of the section on 3-D modelling that the term 3-D image was being used in the limited sense that it might be applied to any realistic drawing or painting. The illusion of depth is created by means of perspective and shading. True 3-D images are those in which two slightly different views of an object are created and presented, one to each eye. The two views are taken from two points, a few inches apart, as if from two eyes. Figure 7.14 shows the two different views which are obtained of the same object when seen from a small distance apart. The brain has become very expert at interpreting these two simultaneous images in terms of depth.

Conventional 3-D

In the cinema, TV and photography, 3-D images are created using two different cameras, or one camera with two lenses. The major problem has always been that of presenting these two images separately to the two eyes. The solution has usually involved the use of special spectacles which use coloured or electronic filters to view a single screen on which both images are projected. Because of the filter effect each eye can only register one of the images.

Real-time images

Virtual reality is based on computer-generated 3-D images. Unlike TV or video images, which have been made at some previous time and recorded, computer images can be made of completely fictitious objects, specified in a computer program, and generated in response to input from the user. This type of interactive process is no different in principle from most other computer use. The big difference lies in the use of realistic 3-D images to create the impression that the user has entered a synthetic world. For this to be truly realistic, two things are necessary. First, the 3-D images must be believable. Second, the user must have suitable ways of interacting with this imaginary world. For example, when we turn ours heads in the real world, or walk forward, our eyes are given a completely different view of the world.

Figure 7.14. Two views of the same object (some 3-D text) - as if from the left and right eyes.

Sensors

Virtual reality systems must equip the user with suitable sensors to convey information about bodily movement to the computer.

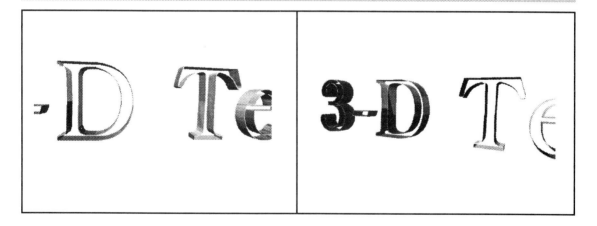

For example, the user will wear a headset which not only conveys two different views of the computer-generated world to the user's eyes through the special goggles which are needed for a true 3-D effect, but also signals movements of the user's head back to the computer. These signals are used by the computer to generate fresh images of the synthetic world, appropriate to the new viewing angle.

Similarly, if the user wears special gloves, which send signals to the computer about the movements of the hand and fingers, it becomes possible for the user to 'grasp' the imaginary 3-D objects which are seen in the goggles. Ideally the gloves would be able to exert pressure on the user's hands so that a sense of touch can be simulated. When a user grasps or pushes the imaginary object it should feel as if the object is solid. To allow complete freedom of movement in the virtual reality world it must be possible to walk and run. This is sometimes simulated by the use of an athlete's exercise treadmill. The speed of running or walking can be fed back to the computer so that the speed with which the user moves through the simulated world is also controlled by the user's movements.

Processing problems

At the moment the degree of realism which can be obtained in virtual reality systems is limited because of the immense amount of computer processing which is needed to create high-quality images in real time. However, flight simulators show that very realistic systems can be created. The realism is partly a reflection on the amount of money invested in these systems, and partly because they are highly-specialised virtual reality worlds, with limited options available to the user. The same principles could be applied to training systems for operators of any expensive or dangerous equipment, like nuclear power stations or chemical plants.

It seems likely that before long increasingly realistic virtual reality worlds will be developed for a whole range of other training, educational and entertainment purposes. One application which has been developed is for fire fighters who might be called to an offshore oil rig, but could be applied to any other unfamiliar environment. The fire officers can practice finding their way around a structure as part of their training without the expense and inconvenience of flying them out to the rig. Leisure applications which have been suggested include virtual-reality holidays. People can 'visit' and 'explore' the Grand Canyon or a famous museum. A recently-released CD-ROM contains 3-D models of hundreds of objects in a museum in the USA, which the user can 'pick-up' and rotate -something which, no doubt, would be forbidden in the real museum. It is also possible to imagine a whole variety of educational applications of this approach, including virtual science laboratories. where experiments can be performed without expensive equipment and without any risk.

Software packages
True virtual reality systems have, until recently, involved specialist hardware - high speed computers and headsets and have not been available to the ordinary user. The nearest that it has been possible to come to this on a PC has been by using software like **Superscape VRT (Dimension International)** which can be used with a virtual reality helmet or an ordinary monitor. Its high price suggests it is aimed at the professional user for visualising architectural designs and training and has a lot in common with the 3-D modelling/ animation software described in the previous section. Virtual reality headsets are now available at a reasonable price and it seems likely that there will be a consequent growth in software to take advantage of this hardware - probably in games initially.

Summary
1 The basic principle which lies behind all animated images is that of creating a large number of slightly different versions of a picture which are then viewed in rapid succession, creating the illusion of smooth movement.

2 The traditional 'cel' (celluloid) method of drawing 2-D animations involves drawing a single background image and a series of separate foreground images on transparent celluloid. The cels are laid on top of the background and the composite image photographed.

3 This method can now be computerised using a modified version of painting software. The two separate images are merged electronically and many more 'cels' used.

4 'In-betweening' (including 'polymorphic tweening') is the process of drawing all the slightly different intermediate images between the beginning and the end of an animated movement. Much of this can be automated by the computer. 'Morphing' is a variation on this technique where one image metamorphoses into a completely different one.

5 There is a range of simple geometrical distortions which can be used to produce the appearance of animated movements, like spinning and movements towards and away from the camera.

6 3-D modelling is the process of creating lifelike 3-D images using all the effects which artists traditionally have achieve by means of perspective, shading and their own observations. The computer uses the laws of physics to calculate the effects of reflection, scattering, absorption and refraction on rays of light which interact with the imaginary object and finally enter the observer's eye.

7 There are problems in providing a suitable interface which will enable the user to specify a 3-D object and visualise it on a 2-D display device. Usually the user has to work with three or more different projected views to visualise the object.

8 The problem of specifying the object is solved using a mixture of techniques, including 3-D primitives, Boolean combinations and the extruding and rotating of 2-D shapes into 3-D shapes.

9 There are four factors which determine the appearance of a surface - its colour, its transparency, its texture and the quality of the lighting. Each of these must be chosen by the user and each forms the basis of a set of calculations performed by the computer.

10 The overall appearance of the object is determined by the point-of-view of the observer. The computer must use this information to ensure that only those surfaces which will be visible to the observer are actually displayed - a process called 'hidden-surface removal'.

11 It is possible to produce animated 3-D sequences by repeating the above processes to produce many images, together with movement of the camera (the observer), the object or parts of the object.

12 Virtual reality is an extension of animated 3-D modelling which is created in 'real time' in response to actions and movements of the observer. This gives the illusion of living in the imaginary world created by the software. For a lifelike illusion it is necessary to provide stereoscopic images and detectors which monitor the movements of the user's body.

Multimedia

Key points
- *the advantages of combining graphics, animation, hypertext, video and sound*
- *technical limitations*
- *uses of multimedia systems*
- *multimedia authoring software*

What is multimedia?

For a number of years, cynics dubbed multimedia, a solution looking for a problem. This was because multimedia systems, representing a much-advertised convergence of three existing technologies - graphics, video and sound - seemed to offer all sorts of new possibilities but commercially viable systems were a long time in coming. Enthusiasts have always believed such a convergence would create exciting new ways of communicating - particularly in education, training and entertainment. In fact suitable, affordable hardware systems have only recently become available. Multimedia systems have finally crossed the boundary between technically-possible curiosities and commercially-viable, useful systems. As always in computing, however, though the technology is vital it is not sufficient. It is the software which transforms technical possibilities into useful systems and a huge range of CD-Rom based software is now flooding the market.

The technologies

The converging technologies which make up a multimedia system are high-quality graphics (including animation and 3-D modelling), video and sound. Until recently there were two methods for the mass communication of ideas and information - the traditional technology of the printed book and the newer technology of TV and video. The video has the advantage that it combines good-quality sound with moving images but any substantial amount of text must be spoken by a narrator. It is not practical for the viewer to read large amounts of information on a TV screen. A book, on the other hand, is an ideal way to communicate large amounts of text but

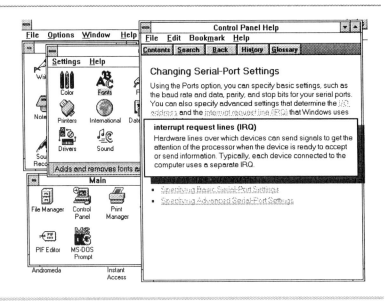

Figure 8.1. The hypertext help system in Microsoft 'Windows'.

the accompanying images, if any, are static and there is no sound. Books, however, are in principle an interactive medium. Readers can select which parts to read, can reread portions which are of particular interest and can navigate their way through the text by a variety of different routes. This selective type of reading is principally used with reference books, and for it to take place easily the author must provide aids to the process, in the form of cross-references and indexes. Some authors do provide detailed suggestions for a variety of alternative ways to use the written material, according to the reader's interest or background. In a highly developed form, this has acquired a name: hypertext.

Hypertext

In true hypertext, the text is not designed to be read in a simple linear progression, from start to finish, like a novel. Rather, information is seen from the outset as consisting of a large number of separate but related facts and ideas which have many cross-connections, some of which can be identified by the author. The author must try to foresee as many as possible of these connections and relationships, and to provide 'maps' in the form of a web of many cross-linking connections.

This way of allowing the reader to find their own way through a set of ideas - and to admit that there are many such ways - is an important element of an interactive system. The reader, to some extent, takes control, makes decisions about what they want to know and how they want to arrange the material. In a traditional book hypertext can be provided by a large number of cross-references but these are tedious to use. A computer, of the other hand, is an ideal technology for implementing hypertext connections. Words can be marked in another colour or font, inviting the reader to click on the word with a mouse. This then immediately brings up on the screen the related material - perhaps in a separate window, without losing the original text. The computer can be used to keep a track of many such jumps so that readers can at any time begin to retrace their footsteps, or go straight back to the start of the journey. All this can be done without the problems of marking places in a traditional printed book with bookmarks or trying to hold open a number of different pages simultaneously.

Hypertext help

Figure 8.1 shows part of the hypertext help system used in 'Windows' software. Technical terms in the body of the text are indicated by means of a dotted coloured underline. If the reader wants a definition, a click of the mouse brings up a small window containing an explanation of that term. Cross-references within the text are indicated by a continuous coloured underline. A click of the mouse on one of these will jump to the reference. A 'Back' button at the top of the screen enables the reader to jump straight back to the previous screen. If the reader gets confused after a number of jumps a 'History' button is provided to see a list of all the screens visited, in order, and a jump back to any of them is then possible. There is also a complete list of all screens which are available (using the 'Search' button) and a list of all technical terms in the 'Glossary'. This type of hypertext linking is now employed very widely, in such applications as electronically-published journals, in on-line

Figure 8.2. A hypertext style link to a digitised photograph in a multimedia encyclopedia (Software Toolworks Multimedia Encyclopedia).

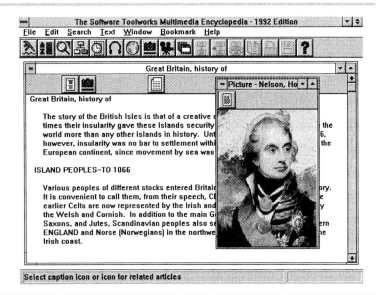

Figure 8.3. A hypertext-style link to an audio clip (from Software Toolworks Multimedia Encyclopedia).

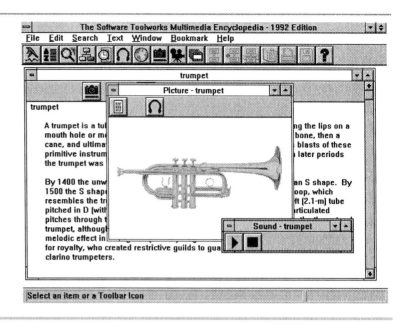

software help systems and in CD-Rom based reference books like encyclopedias.

Cross-referencing

The hypertext principle of cross-referencing can be extended to non-textual material. Modern multimedia encyclopedias commonly use small icons to indicate references to sound or video recordings, graphics, tables, captions or animations. A click of the mouse on the icon plays the sounds or creates a window on screen containing the graphic, animation or video clip. Figure 8.2 illustrates a link in an encyclopedia to a photograph. A click on the camera icon brings up a small window containing the photograph. A click on the text icon brings up another window, this one containing a caption to the photograph.

The same principle is used to link to video clips and animation sequences. Figure 8.3 shows a link to an audio clip. In this case, clicking on the earphone icon brings up a small control window containing the sort of controls used on stereo equipment to stop and start tape players. These are used to start and stop the playback of the sound clip. This example also has an illustration of the instrument.

A hypertext 'book'

With a multi media system it is possible to produce a 'book' which is more like a TV program, and a 'video' which is more like a book. The images and sounds of video are combined with the text (and the interaction) which are associated with a book. The computer also adds a third important element - the ability to calculate and to simulate in reaction to input from the reader, as is common in all computer games. Plate 6 shows some graphing software which uses the calculating power of the computer to help the user visualise mathematical equations by drawing 2-D and 3-D graphs. The user types in the equation of interest and the graph is immediately displayed. A slider bar at the bottom of the screen can be used to vary one of the terms in the equation to see what effect it has on the graph.

In principle, this type of interactive process can be used to demonstrate any process which can be modelled mathematically or by means of any set of clearly formulated rules. There is obviously enormous scope for all types of educational and training software.

Graphics Multimedia systems have become both possible and affordable because of a number of technical developments. In the field of computer graphics these developments have been the increasing number of colours, the improving resolution and the speed with which this information can be handled. Only a short time ago most users had to be content with a colour graphics system which was limited to 16 colours. In some systems these 16 colours could be chosen from a palette of 64, but this restriction meant that it was impossible to reproduce colour photographs. Today, 256 colours, chosen from a palette of a few thousand would probably be considered a minimum system and, even with this number, good colour images can be displayed. In a similar way resolutions of 640 x 480 and 800 x 600 pixels mean that reasonably detailed images are also possible.

Image archives
Though these figures do not in any way compare with high-quality colour printing they can supply adequate images which are acceptable if there are compensating advantages to viewing pictures on a screen. These advantages might be the number of pictures which are available, the price, the compactness of the storage medium and the speed of retrieval. A good example of what is possible is provided by a disc from Microsoft which contains scanned images of all the pictures in the National Gallery, London - over 2000 - for about £40. In fact the disc offers much more than a series of static images, but even if it did not, that still might be considered good value. Figures 8.4 and 8.5 show screen shots from the disc. The second example has two cross-references which offer the reader further information about the painter and the meaning of a technical term.

Figure 8.4. One of 2000 digitised paintings stored on a CD-ROM (The Microsoft 'Art Gallery' disc).

Displays

For multimedia systems to rival books in every respect it is necessary for the screens to be larger and to be capable of showing much more detail and many more colours than normal computers can currently display. For example a conventional atlas or book of art illustrations might have a two-page spread which is four times the area of a standard 14 inch computer monitor. It will also be printed at well over 1000 lines per inch in a vast number of colours and shades. The technology is already available for much improved computer images - 1600 x 1200 pixels and over 16 million colours

Figure 8.5. A hypertext-style link, to explain a technical term used in painting, and to biographical information about the painter. (Microsoft Art Gallery).

on 23 inch monitors, for example - but the price of such systems is still far too great for mass use and software houses will not produce multimedia packages for such hardware until its price drops very significantly. It is true that the price of '24-bit colour' systems (see chapter 3) is dropping and could soon be in widespread use but cheap large, higher resolution displays are probably still some years away.

Video

The term video, as commonly used, refers to an analogue technology in which a series of images is stored on magnetic tape and played on a TV set. In the context of multimedia it refers to material which has been generated in the same way, by a video camera, but then digitised for storage on a computer disc. This has two advantages. It can be handled easily by a computer, along with other information types -text and audio, for example. Secondly, it can be processed in some way. One way, is simply to use the computer to replace the traditional video editing and mixing suites. Another is to add new, computer-generated effects - changing colours, distorting images or adding parts of images to others, in a way which would be difficult by analogue methods.

Data overload

The main problem with digital video is the vast quantity of data that the computer is required to handle. A static computer image consists of anything from one third of a million to over one million pixels. If such an image has a large number of colours or grey-levels it will occupy about one million bytes of memory. Videos, by their very nature, consist of a large number of separate images (about 20-30 per second). This poses major problems both for storage and for throughput. Thirty seconds of full-screen video require nearly 1000 images and if each image were to need 1 million bytes of storage then the computer would need to store 1000 Megabytes. This is not impossible, but still highly impractical, if only because the computer would have to be able to process 30 Mbytes per second of data. So far this problem has been tackled in three way:

- degraded images
- compressed images
- more powerful computers.

The first approach is a simple economic compromise and means that the user must accept small, jerky images. Figure 8.6 shows a screen shot from a CD-based encyclopedia with an animation running in a small window. The standard micro computer simply can-

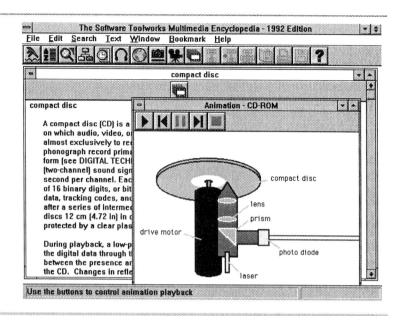

Figure 8.6. A screen-shot from a CD-Rom encyclopedia (Software Toolworks Multimedia Encyclopedia), showing an animation - How CD-Roms work!

not handle large detailed images which change rapidly, and so most current video applications, like this, only offer small images (a few inches square) and rather jerky transitions - which are the result of slower frame rates.

Compression

The second approach is to find ways of storing images more efficiently. Some of the techniques used for this have been indicated in chapter 2. All computer images are stored using one or other compression technique, but many traditional methods, particularly the loss-less ones, take some time to complete the process. The interest in digital video has sparked off considerable research and the development of more efficient processes which can also be implemented very quickly. These can be implemented using software but the most efficient way of implementing any computer algorithm is in specially designed hardware. The result is that chips are now available which compress images -by a factor of about 100:1 - and un-compress them, in real time (i.e. without imposing any delays on the screening of the video).

Fortunately, video images can be compressed more than static images because the quality of the individual pictures does not need to be so high. Traditional storage compression techniques must be loss-free; it must be possible to un-compress them and recover all the original information. Compression of video images, however, can be 'lossy' - some detail can be lost in the process. Individual TV or cine frames, when seen as static images are often of quite poor quality, and yet the eye does not notice this when those individual images are part of a stream of rapidly changing ones. This means that lossy compression of video images is perfectly acceptable.

Data flow

The third approach is to boost the capacity of the computer to store and handle large quantities of data. The modern storage medium - CD-Rom - is discussed later. Methods for improving the flow rate include faster signal buses, faster central processors and special co-processors designed to handle particular types of information. Currently, video processors are usually supplied on special circuit boards which have to be purchased separately and installed in the computer. Computers which are offered for sale as multimedia machines usually have these boards pre-installed but already the chips are being designed into the main board of some computers and it is not difficult to imagine a time when all computers will be equipped this way. The best systems can handle video information flow in both directions. With them it should be possible to feed in a video signal from a TV aerial or videotape, digitise it and compress it 'on-the-fly'. When such material has been processed by the computer it should also be possible to output it, and any other computer-generated images, back to video tape.

Audio Since the earliest days, microcomputers have been equipped with some sort of sound output. The purpose of this was to enable software to send simple warning signals - to attract the attention of the user. These devices have usually been very elementary, cheap electronic buzzers or small loudspeakers. They were not required to produce sound of high quality. Multimedia machines, however, need the capacity to produce music and speech of a quality at least as good as domestic radios and TVs and increasingly will be required to produce CD-audio quality sound. This needs loudspeaker systems, amplifiers and the capacity to deal with digitised music.

Sound cards

Sound cards, like video cards, are available as plug-in systems. At the simplest level a sound card will provide the computer with audio output from digitised sound stored on a disc. In addition the board should be able to synthesise sound - actually create a range of sounds under the direction of software, in much the same way that an electric organ creates a sound similar to a pipe organ. The board contains a ROM which when driven by a suitable program will synthesise a whole range of sound effects. Finally it ought also to be able to reverse the process - to digitise sound signals from a microphone or other sound input for storage in the computer. The output from the card is played through stereo loudspeakers. These are supplied as separate devices, but a true multimedia computer, which has been designed as such, will have them built into the body of the computer or the monitor.

Sound quality

Like digitised video, digitised sound can occupy a considerable amount of storage, the exact amount depending on the quality of the sound. It might be guessed that digitised colour images occupy more memory than sound and this is correct. Conventional CD audio discs can store a maximum of about seventy minutes of music, in un-compressed form, on a disc with a capacity of about 650 Mbytes. Un-compressed CD-quality audio is sampled at 44.1 KHz stereo and needs nearly 10 Mbytes per minute. 70 minutes of digitised colour videos can only be fitted on to one disc with modern compression and decompression technology. Consider the claims, then, of the publishers of a current CD-Rom encyclopedia who boast that it stores 21 volumes of text, over 3000 pictures, 250 maps, 30 animations and over 30 minutes of sound - all on a similar capacity disc! It is quite clear that these sounds cannot be of the same quality as an ordinary audio CD. Since the sound files are not compressed in any way, they would fill half the disc if digitised and stored at 'CD-quality'. In fact on such a disc 1 second of sound only occupies 22,000 bytes of storage and so a 650 Mbyte CD-Rom could store over 8 hours of music of this lower quality.

CD-Roms A number of technical developments have been necessary for the implementation of multimedia. Some have been mentioned already - larger memory sizes, faster processors and faster buses - but one of the most important has been CD-Rom. Compact discs were developed as a digital alternative to records for the distribution of music. They are made in a similar way to traditional records - by a pressing technique. The difference lies in the fact that the music has been digitised and the binary information (bits) stored as tiny pits in the surface of the disc, arranged in a spiral fashion. The presence, or absence of these pits is read by the reflected, focused beam of light from a small solid-state laser as the disc rotates.

Optical storage

For some time this type of technology had little impact on the computer world, partly because the discs are read-only devices (which is what ROM means: Read-Only Memory) and partly because few users had any need for the vast quantities of information which could be stored on such a disc. For some years it seemed that such systems would be of general value only if recordable versions could be developed. Much work has, in fact, gone into producing digital, nonmagnetic disc systems on which the user could record computer data and a number are now available and the prices are dropping rapidly. In the mean time, traditional magnetic technology has not stood still and it is not certain which technology will come to dominate for recordable systems.

However, it was the second assumption - that ordinary users had no need for a storage system which would record large amounts of data which they could not alter - which has proved to be wrong. Multimedia systems generate vast amounts of data in the form of digitised static images, video, animation and sound and a disc which can store 600 Mbytes of data and be mass-produced very cheaply has proved to a popular answer. Another, more recent development, has been the storage of feature films in digitised form on CD-Roms. The need to store 90 minutes or more of high-quality video and sound on one disc has led to the development both of CD-Roms which will store more than the current 600-700 Mbytes and of improved compression algorithms and hardware.

Data archives

The easiest starting point in the development of multimedia software has been to use the discs to reissue large quantities of existing text - with a collection of library images to add a little glamour. The best examples are encyclopedias, dictionaries and important archives of documents, largely for the use of scholars or for professional use (such as the complete works of Shakespeare, Law Reports, back numbers of newspapers and journals). True multimedia material implies a much more imaginative blend of text, images and sounds and this requires a significant rewriting of existing material or projects which have been conceived from the start in this new medium.

This move from text archives to true multimedia systems has forced the pace of development towards faster CD-Rom drives. For a scholar, searching for one document amongst thousands, an access and search time of a few seconds is trivial, compared with traditional methods which might take hours or days. For someone watching video clips, however, delays of fractions of a second can produce jerky, unpleasant results which compare very unfavourably with analogue video. Multimedia applications are already leading to a market for double-, triple- and even quadruple-speed CD-Rom drives so that the information can be accessed and downloaded at an appropriate rate.

The Uses of CD-Rom

What sort of use is being made of this new technology? It is important at this point to say that for commercial reasons the term multimedia is currently being applied to almost any software which is distributed on CD-Roms. However, publishing an existing reference book on CD-Rom with the addition of a few digitised images and sounds does not do justice to the concept. The quality, size and detail of colour pictures printed in a conventional book is far superior to a 640 x 480 pixel, 256 colour image on a VGA monitor and the text, even in a cheaply-printed book, of much better quality. As a result, some hastily cobbled-together multimedia publications would be better left as books.

Multimedia publications come into their own only when the subject benefits from the imaginative use of video, animation, simulation, sound and interactivity. Some of the best examples of multimedia software so far have been games, training manuals and reference works. Adventure and narrative-style games have been able to take advantage of the vast storage capacity of CD-Roms to include a huge range of choices for the player. The better ones include digitised video sequences, with actors playing characters in the game, a wide range of accompanying music and 3-D modelled scenes, particularly in the form of objects like buildings.

Training manuals have much in common with games since they also seek to offer a realistic, interactive environment with a large range of scenarios. Reference and educational works can add to the standard text and still images of an equivalent book, relevant video, sound and animation together with hypertext-style cross-referencing and, in some cases, interactive simulation.

Software It is in the nature of multimedia systems that the software situation is a little confused - both because this is a rapidly developing area and because it involves a variety of technologies. It is therefore convenient to divide the software into three categories. The first concerns the operating system itself and the newer devices for which the operating system must provide. Until recently computer operating systems made no allowance for the addition of peripheral multimedia devices such as CD-Roms nor for handling sound or video files. However, more recent versions of operating systems like DOS/Windows, OS/2 and Mac System 7 contain additional software facilities to enable the newer hardware devices to interface properly and sometimes provide simple applications also. In a similar way CD-Rom drives and sound and video interface cards are often provided with a range of free software applications.

If this 'free' software is not enough, more advanced packages must be bought and the second category comprises these specialist applications such as desktop video and sound editing software. Desktop (or digital) video software digitises video signals from a video camera or video recorder and provides a variety of editing facilities. 'First generation' software, designed to work either without specialist hardware or with limited hardware, provided rather small image sizes and slow frame rates but with modern hardware which can compress and un-compress video in real time, full-frame recording and playback is now possible.

Separate cards and software are available for handling sound and are aimed at users who wish to work only in this area but most of the modern video systems will cope with sound also. Unlike the other software dealt with in this book, multimedia software increasingly requires special hardware -unless the computer has been specifically purchased as a multimedia machine. Even so, most 'multimedia' machines are provided only with a sound card and CD-Rom and are not suitable for any serious video work. Good video cards can cost considerably more than the computer but usually include a range of good software.

Authoring
The key to producing good multimedia systems lies in realising that a considerable amount of work must be put into rethinking the process of authoring. Authors have traditionally thought largely in terms of text, together with a few static illustrations and a linear reading process. Multimedia authorship is more like the production of a film than the writing of a book and may well involve a team of 'authors' with experience in the different media. Since this team will be chosen for their knowledge of the subject rather than any technical computing skills, the production of multimedia software has stimulated the development of suitable authoring languages which enable the author(s) to specify how all the components of the production are to be assembled together, and how the user can interact with the final product. These packages usually take one of two approaches.

Language styles
The first approach is a natural development of traditional programming languages. The author must learn to write code which describes both the elements which make up the screen display (such as icons or buttons) and the actions associated with them. The second approach is much more visual and more suited to the non-programmer. The logic of the software is visualised by means of a flow chart. This is a chart in which each element of the final pro-

Figure 8.7. Screen-shot of a multimedia authoring package (Macromedia Authorware Professional). Icons are used to create a flow chart which describes all the options which can be chosen in the final software product.

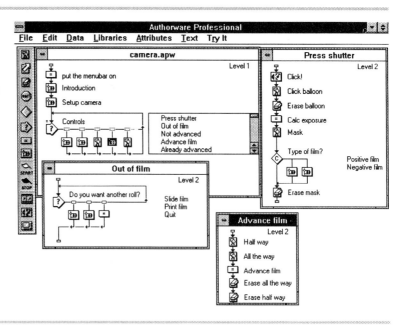

duction is shown as a small picture - an icon (see Figure 8.7). One type of icon represents elements like a picture, a video clip or a button - all those events which are seen or heard by the user. Another type of icon represents events which affect the flow of the program, such as a button being clicked by the user to signal that a choice has been made or a timer which determines how long a picture will be displayed. The design of the flow chart determines the logic of the program. For example, when a choice is offered to the user -perhaps to click a 'Yes' button or a 'No' button - the flow chart shows a branch. The two routes which flow from that decision show the results of the two possible actions. All the elements which make up a multimedia production, such as pictures, video or sound clips or blocks of text, are stored as separate files. The software controls how and when and if any particular element is actually called. The control icons in the chart are linked together by lines so as to represent the flow of control when the software is run. Even with the aid of this type of software, writing a multimedia program still lies within the province of a professional programmer. It remains to be seen if the process will become so simple that any author, teacher or trainer will be able to assemble a multimedia 'book' as easily as they can create a traditional book on a word processor or DTP package.

Software packages

SOFTWARE	COMPUTER	COMMENTS
Media Player and Sound Recorder (Microsoft)	PC	Simple applications provided "free" with Windows 3 to play video clips and sound files
Premiere (Adobe)	PC & Mac	Desk-top video software; allows for recording, editing & assembling video; poor preview facilities
VideoFusion (Computers Unlimited)	Mac	Desk-top video software; has some more advanced effects than Premiere; better previewing; titling feature
VideoShop (Avid)	Mac	Desk-top video software; not as many features as Premiere; large number of special effects
Authorware Professional (Macromedia)	PC & Mac	Authoring software; uses a graphical approach to programming by icons and flowchart; easy to use
Viewer (Microsoft)	PC	Authoring software; uses macro programming language; difficult to use for non-programmers
PictureBook (Digitalk)	PC	Authoring software; very simple to use; actions assigned to graphic objects by choosing from menu; not flexible enough for commercial applications
IconAuthor (IconAuthor)	PC	Authoring software; uses similar approach to Authorware Pro. except that no scripting language is used
InterActive (Xitan)	PC	Authoring software; a cut-down version of IconAuthor; much cheaper
Multimedia Toolbook (Asymetrix)	PC	Authoring software; screens created by dragging graphic objects onto page; "logic" of program written in code; relatively cheap and very flexible
Director (Macromedia)	Mac	Authoring software; uses icon-based approach; standard software for Macs

Summary 1 The term 'multimedia' has been given to a new combination of computer graphics, animation, digitised video and sound and hypertext. It has a number of advantages, as compared with traditional single-media systems like books and TV - notably the range of media which can be combined and the scope for interaction.

2 Hypertext systems are those in which many cross-references and interconnections between different parts of the text are embedded in the system. In traditional books this can only be done by footnotes, cross-references and indexes which can be very tedious to use. Computer systems can implement these connections much more rapidly and flexibly.

3 A number of separate technical advances have been necessary in computer graphics and digitised video and audio systems to make multimedia a practical possibility.

4 Because of the vast amount of data which is generated when video sequences are digitised, many computers cannot handle the flow of information at a fast enough rate. As a result, a number of unsatisfactory compromises still have to be made with video - such as small images and jerky animation. For satisfactory results, specialised hardware and very fast computer systems are needed.

5 CD-Roms have a crucial role to play in multimedia systems since they provide a means of storing the large amounts of data associated with digitised images and sounds.

6 The creation of multimedia software often involves a team of specialists, each an expert in the different type of medium involved, together with a computer programmer. For ordinary authors to be able to create multimedia 'books', easy-to-use authoring software is needed to enable them to bring together the different components and to describe the possible interaction schemes which the author wishes to offer.

Integrating software

Key points
- *combining different types of software*
- *graphics file formats and conversion*
- *problems of large files*
- *file compression*

Using more than one package

This book is designed to help the reader actually use computer graphics. It covers most of the important principles of the subject, but experience shows that there can be many problems which are often not discussed in books because they seem to be trivial details. It is usually the trivial details which are the biggest problems! This chapter attempts to bring together some of the practical issues which every user discovers in the course of using the graphics software.

For the purposes of explanation it has been convenient to divide graphics software into categories such as DTP and Illustration software. In practice many users find that they need to use more than one type of software on the same project. This book was produced on two different types of computer, using a text-based word processor package, an Illustration package and a DTP package and, for the screen dumps, at least half a dozen other pieces of software. This obviously raises the question of how easy is it to integrate different software from different computers? The following sections introduce the main practical problems which tend to boil down to the two issues of graphics standards and file sizes.

File formats and file compression

We have seen, in chapter 2, that vector images, by their very nature, can be stored very economically but pixel-based images are a different proposition. A high-resolution 24-bit colour image can occupy many megabytes of memory or disc space. Therefore, when this type of image is saved to a disc it is automatically stored using one of a number of proprietary file formats which are, in effect, a form of image compression. Most of them take advantage of the fact that there is a large amount of, so-called, redundancy in each image. This means that there are large areas of any picture which consist of many pixels of the same colour and it should not be necessary to store hundreds of copies of the same colour code.

One method, called Run-Length Encoding (RLE), simply counts how many consecutive identical coloured pixels there are on a particular scan-line and records that number, together with the corresponding colour code. For example, if all 640 pixels in one scan line were blue then a code like:

<blue><640>

would be used. This is much more compact than the code for blue being repeated 640 times. Another method uses the same principle to record how many identical consecutive scan-lines there are.

Most file compression of graphics therefore takes place without the user realising it, because the act of saving to disc in a standard graphics file format reduces the size of the file, as compared with the space it normally takes up in RAM. The only choice offered to the user is that many graphics packages can save files in more than one format.

Standard file types

One of the most irritating problems of computer graphics is the huge variety of proprietary formats for saving graphics files. Most of them have been developed by software companies - usually the one to be first in some particular field of graphics, so that their file format was adopted by later entrants into the field. For example, file formats designed for PC compatible software include: **PCX** files, developed for the paintbrush package 'PC Paintbrush', **IMG** files for the graphical interface 'GEM', **BMP** for the graphical interface 'Windows', **WPG** for the word processor 'WordPerfect', **DXF** for the CAD program 'AutoCAD' and **PIC** for the spreadsheet 'Lotus'.

File types developed specifically for Macintosh software are, fortunately, fewer in number than those associated with the PC. They include: **MAC** files, developed for MacPaint and **PICT** for MacPict. Some file formats are commonly used by both Macintosh and PC compatibles - for example **EPS** (Encapsulated Postscript), **PCX** and **TIFF** (see below). Some file formats are associated with pieces of hardware (like specialist display cards) - for example **TGA** (Targa boards). Another widely-used format (**GIF**) is associated with the CompuServe network information service.

Some file formats (like **CGM** - 'Computer Graphic Metafile') have been designed by non-commercial bodies like the American National Standards Institute. The idea was to create an independent standard which would make it easier for graphics files to be exchanged between applications. Some, like **TIFF** ('Tagged Image File Format') have been developed by more than one company for similar reasons. Most file formats are designed either for bit-mapped graphics or vector images but there are a few which are designed to handle both types of image. In practice these, so-called Metafiles, are usually only used to store vector images.

What format to use?

Every piece of graphics software will use a file format which the developers consider the most appropriate. This format will be the default which the software uses to save files, when the user does nothing to choose one of the alternatives which will almost certainly be offered. When a file is saved in a non-default format it is sometimes called 'exporting' the file rather than 'saving' it. There are reasons why the user might choose to use a non-default format. The format the developer considers appropriate might not be an industry standard but simply be the one they developed. The user, however, has other priorities and must consider how large the final file will be and how useful it will be.

The same image stored in different file formats may occupy different sizes. How much compression is achieved varies on the algorithm used and the efficiency of the algorithm can depend on the content of the image. Another factor may be speed; fast compression methods are often less efficient than slow ones. If disc space is at a premium then choosing a format which achieves the maximum compression can save valuable space.

For most users, however, the important consideration is what is to happen to the file. If it is to be imported into another package it is important what file filters that software has. Just as most software can save images in more than one form, most can load it in more than one. These operation use 'filters' - pieces of software which do the translation. Some software comes with so many different filters that the user is given, on installation, the choice of which are to be installed, to avoid wasting disc space with filters which might never be used. Clearly files must be exported in a format which is acceptable to the importing software and these might not include the format which is the default for the exporting package.

File conversion

The proliferation of graphics file formats has meant that built-in file filters will sometimes not cope with the problems of moving images from one package to another. This has led to the development of stand-alone file conversion software. These utilities are designed to take a graphics file in any one of a wide range of formats and convert into to another. They are not always satisfactory because there are often so many different versions of one file format; there are, for instance, five different, recognised types of TIFF file and six different TIFF file compression methods. In addition to properly defined and documented versions of a file type there is often enough flexibility in the general definition of that type for individual software designers to produce their own variations which may be particular to their company. As a result of these variations anyone working with graphics files will soon find the need for a conversion utility.

Fortunately file conversion software can be quite cheap because so many utilities are available as share-ware. Though not free, this type of software can be obtained from commercial suppliers, computer magazines (on cover discs) or from friends and then used on a trial basis for a limited period. If it seems suitable it can then be 'bought' for a small registration fee - about £10-25, usually. Two good examples are **Graphic Workshop (Alchemy Mindworks)** and **Paint Shop Pro (JASC Inc.)** but there are many others.

One of the best commercial utilities for the PC is **Hijaak (Inset Systems)** which is available in DOS and Windows versions. A good, and cheaper, alternative is **Conversion Artist (North Coast Software)**.

In the Macintosh world there are far fewer file formats being used and most good Mac packages have enough import and export facilities to cope with any problems which might arise. If not, there are graphics file management packages which, amongst other facilities, will have file conversions. **Pick Librarian (Iris)** is a good example of this type of composite program. Its primary function is to help the user display and browse through a large collection of files, in different formats, by displaying them as a catalogue of small-size images - about 50 to the screen. Many PC-oriented conversion programs, like Hijaak, will cope with Mac file formats also.

Vector and bit-mapped files

Most graphics software is designed to handle either vector images or bit-mapped ones and some users always use either one or the other but never both. Engineers using CAD software work entirely with vector images and vector files. Some artists, using paint packages or retouching software work only with bit-mapped images. Increasingly, however, it is advantageous to use both forms. Good illustration packages, though primarily designed to handle vector images will allow the importation and incorporation of bit-mapped images into a design. Sometimes it is necessary to convert images from one form to the other, normally from bit-mapped to vector.

For more details of this, refer back to the section called 'Tracing' in chapter 6.

Different computers

It is sometimes important to be able to move files between two different types of computer. One method is to use removable (usually floppy) discs. The bridge between the two major computer types - the PC and the Mac - is now easily bridged, mainly because of facilities provided with the Mac. The Mac is supplied with a software utility (called **Apple File Exchange**). When it is run, the Mac floppy drive will read PC discs and can copy PC files onto the hard disc of the Mac (and vice versa). There are also utilities (like **PC Exchange**, also from **Apple**) which run in the background and will automatically detect PC discs and treat them in the same way as a Mac disc.

File sizes

The problem with using floppy discs for transferring files between any two computers is the size of discs. The standard maximum disc capacity, both for PCs and Macs, is 1.4 Mbytes and this is simply not enough for many graphics files. There are three possible solutions to this problem: higher-density discs, better compression or networks.

There have been a number of technological advances which make it possible to store much more than 1.4 Mbytes on a removable disc. Some are developments of the current magnetic technology. Some are optical systems (effectively 'writable' CD-Roms, if that is not a contradiction in terms). Some are hybrid magnetic/optical systems. Some are called floppy discs and some, removable hard-discs. All are capable of increasing the capacity of a disc to between 10 and 600 Mbytes. Unfortunately none of them is yet an agreed standard so prices tend to be higher than would be necessary if they were standard fittings and made in large numbers. The other problem is that they can only be used when the same system is known to be fitted to both machines concerned.

For the moment it is more likely that file transfers will be possible via a network, since so many computers are now networked. The only drawback here is that of transfer times. Some networks are slow and many are subject to large amounts of traffic. This means that whether a network is being used to send graphic files between computers or from a computer to a printer it might take some time.

More on compression

The third option mentioned above was better compression. Graphics files, like all computer files, can be compressed using general-purpose compression methods and smaller files can speed network transfer and save disc space. It might be that a compressed version of a file will fit on a floppy where the uncompressed version won't. This type of compression is sometimes called 'archiving' because it is used to store material in a small space, but at the expense of the time taken to do the compression (and the uncompression when the file is needed again).

Many file compression programs are distributed as share-ware products. The best known ones for the PC are **PKZip** and **PKLite (PKWare)**, **ARJ, Zoo (Ronald Gas Software)** and **LHA ('Yoshi')**. The latter is said to have a better compression factor for graphics files than any other general-purpose compression product and the author requires no registration fee.

DiskDoubler (Symantic) is an excellent commercial product for the Macintosh.

On-the-fly compression

Another category of file compression software is 'on-the-fly' compression. These are programs which compress all of the files on a hard disc (or a floppy) and then run in the background, un-compressing them and re-compressing them as required, without further intervention from the user. The best do this in such a way that the user has no awareness that anything is happening, other than the fact that up to twice as much information can be stored on the disc. There are a number of well-known examples of this for PCs including **Stacker (Stac Electronics)** and **SuperStore (AddStor).** There are similar products for the Mac, such as **AutoDoubler (Fifth Generation)** and **StuffIt (Aladdin)**. A recent trend has been to incorporate this type of product into the operating system itself. **DOS 6 (Microsoft)** for example now provides such a utility.

Lossy compression

The types of file compression referred to so far in this chapter are 'loss-less'; no information is thrown away in the process. In some contexts, however, it is acceptable to compress images in such a way that information is lost. These are called 'lossy' methods. The advantage of these methods are that the process of compression and decompression can be speeded up and high higher compression ratios can be achieved. The two standards which have emerged are **JPEG** and **MPEG**. These letters stand for the Joint Photographic Experts Group and the Motion Picture Experts Group and they are used as a short-hand for two compression algorithms - one for static images and the other video (or moving) images. The subject of lossy compression, in the context of video images, has been referred to briefly already in chapter 8.

Screen grabbers

One final graphics utility which can be of great value is the 'screen grabber'. It is often important to be able to incorporate a copy of the screen display of a piece of software into a printed document - as in magazine articles and books, like this one. At first sight this might not seem to be a problem since virtually all graphics software will have a 'Print' facility, intended to allow the user to output a hard copy of their work. There is a problem however. It is sometimes necessary to take a copy of everything on the screen, including the menu bar, the icons or other software control features, and not just the image which is being created. A screen grabber is a piece of software which runs invisibly 'in the background' - it is runs in addition to the graphics application. When the user wishes to take a copy of the screen it is activated, usually by means of a sequence of keystrokes, and copies the contents of the screen into a graphics file. This can then be incorporated into a document in the same way that any other illustration would (see for example chapter 4, on Desk-Top Publishing).

Screen grabbers for PC compatibles are not usually sold as separate items, except as share-ware - for example, **Screen Thief (Nildram)**. They are, however, often supplied as extra utilities with graphics applications packages or word processors or as part of other graphics utilities like **Hijaak**. **Exposure Pro (Baseline)** is a very versatile screen grabber for the Macintosh.

'Windows' (Microsoft) has a built-in screen grabber that can be used to grab images from any Windows application. It is operated simply by pressing the 'PrintScreen' key on the keyboard. This copies the screen into the clipboard, from which it can then be pasted into any suitable Windows paint package and saved. Similarly, the Macintosh operating system provides a built-in screen grabber which is operated by the key combination: Command+Shift-3.

Summary

1 It is common to use more than one type of graphics package in working on a particular project. This usually means transferring files between packages.

2 There are many different types of file format. A file format is the precise way that a package stores data when it is saved.

3 Most modern software can load and save graphics files in more than one format - though one particular format will be the normal, or default, for that package. This process is sometimes called 'im-

porting' and 'exporting' and uses special pieces of conversion software called 'filters'.

4 Special utility packages are also available, whose function is to convert graphics file formats.

5 Because images contain a lot of information, involving both spatial detail and colour, they occupy a large amount of memory. The size of graphics files can be a major problem. Some files will not fit on a normal floppy disc and so cannot be easily transferred from one computer to another. They can also occupy a lot of space on a hard-disc.

6 There are three ways of tackling the problem of file size. One is to use one of the many types of high-capacity, removable disc systems. None of them yet are supplied as standard. Another is to transfer files between machines over a network. A third is to use file compression.

7 Most forms of file compression are 'loss-less' (no information is lost in the process). However the greatest compression can be obtained by using 'lossy' methods and for some purposes it does not matter if some of the detail in the image is lost.

8 'Screen-grabbers' are software utilities which will copy a complete screen display into a graphics file, for printing as illustrations.

10 Case studies

Key points
- *putting principles into practice*
- *setting out a page using DTP*
- *manipulating text in a drawing package*
- *using a paint package to manipulate a screen grab*
- *creating 3-D modelled text*

Why case studies? It is a well-established principle in computing, as in many areas, that there is no substitute for trying it out for yourself. There is a limit to how much you can learn from reading a book but it is hoped that reading this book will make the reader want to go and try for themselves. The trouble, sometimes, is that however clear the principles of the subject may have become, it is difficult to see how to put them all together to produce something useful. This final chapter tries to do just that for four of the areas discussed in the book: desktop publishing, vector drawing, paint packages and 3-D modelling. In each area a sequence of images is used to show step-by-step how some simple result was produced.

Desktop publishing The first steps in producing a simple document using PageMaker on an Apple Mac have already been outlined in chapter 4. Figure 4.2 shows the general layout of the screen, including the pasteboard facility. Figure 4.6 shows the dialogue box which is used to define the setup of the page. Figure 4.7 shows how the magnification of the view can be changed. The illustrations in this case study begin after a page has been defined. Figure 10.1 shows how it is possible to choose to lay out the text in columns. The number of columns are chosen from a dialogue box, as is the separation between those columns. Figure 10.2 shows an empty page with column 'guides' displayed. These are used to line up the text properly. Figure 10.3 shows how to begin the process of 'placing' a text file - which has been created already in a word processor. When the text is ready, the mouse cursor is clicked on the page which causes the text to be placed, flowing into the columns. Figure 10.4 shows the text, magnified a little. The boundaries of the text are shown by a 'roller-

Figure 10.1. Column guides, in
PageMaker, are chosen via a
dialogue box which offers the
option of how many columns are
required and what the separation
between them (the 'gutter') should
be.

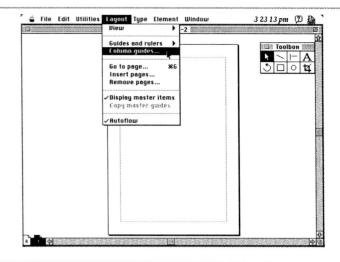

Figure 10.2. The empty page now
shows the column guides - text can
be made to flow into these
columns automatically. If columns
of different widths are required the
column guides can be dragged to
new positions using the mouse.

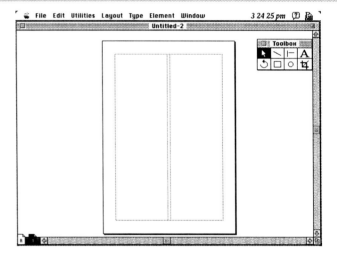

Figure 10.3. Text is then 'placed'
onto the page. The text file, already
created in a word processor, is
selected - again, via a dialogue
box - and the mouse cursor clicked
on the page where the text is to
begin. It 'flows' into place between
the column guides and the
margins.

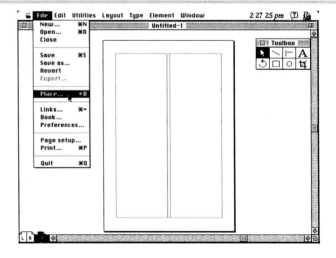

Figure 10.4. The text is shown in a 'roller-blind' frame. This frame can be moved and re-sized at will whenever the pointer-tool is selected (see the Toolbox). It can also be rolled-up - like a blind - by dragging at the semicircular handles at the top and bottom of the frame. The plus symbol (+) at the top of the blind in the second column shows that the text follows on from the bottom of the blind in the first column (which also has a + symbol in its handle, which cannot be seen in this screen shot).

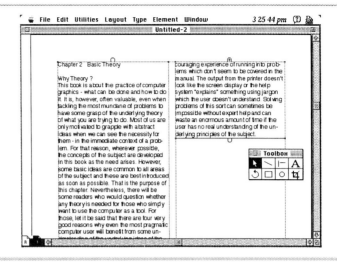

Figure 10.5. In this magnified view the main heading has been selected by dragging the mouse cursor over it. To do this, the text tool must be selected (see the 'Toolbox'). The selected text is shown in inverse video. Text can also be selected by double or triple clicking with the mouse button. Double clicking selects a word; triple clicking selects a paragraph.

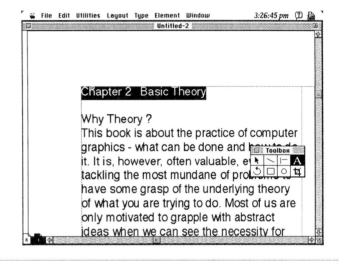

Figure 10.6. The size of the selected text is then altered by means of the 'Type' menu. In this screen shot a size of 18 points is being chosen.

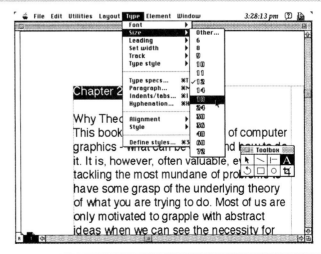

Figure 10.7. The selected text is now made bold using another option chosen from the 'Type' menu. Many common choices, like bold, can be selected more quickly using keyboard short-cuts. The screen shot shows the short-cut for bold which is indicated on the menu as a reminder to the user that there is another way of performing the operation : the shift key (shown as an up-arrow) in conjunction with the 'command key' and the B key.

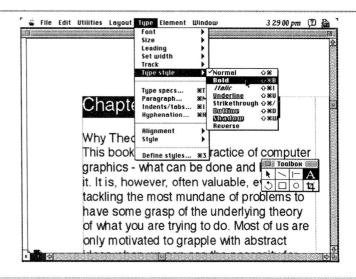

blind' frame. The next steps involve specifying the appearance of the text. Text is chosen by dragging the cursor over it, in Text Mode. In Figure 10.5 the heading has been selected and is therefore shown in reverse-video. Figures 10.6 - 10.8 show the point size (18), the weight (bold) and the alignment (centre) being chosen.

The next step is to make similar choices for the main text. Figure 10.9 shows this text being justified. Finally Figure 10.10 shows the columns being pulled into position using the mouse cursor. The top of the text blind in the second column is being pulled down to match the text in the first column. Now that the text looks right, a graphic is added. This is placed using exactly the same method that was used to place the text. After selecting the file (see Figure

Figure 10.8. The selected text is centred within the boundaries of the column using another option from the 'Type' menu. This involves using a sub-menu since all the alignment choices are grouped together in the 'Alignment' option. Again, a keyboard short-cut is available. The tick against 'Align-left' shows that currently the text is left-aligned - until another choice is made.

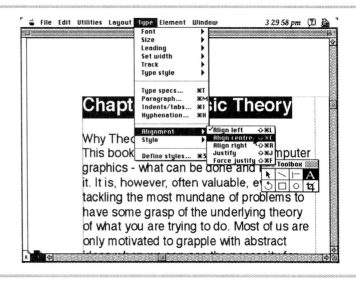

Figure 10.9. The main body of the text is now selected and justified using exactly the same methods as were used for the heading.

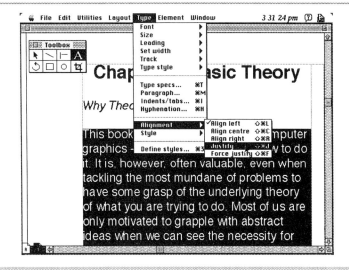

Figure 10.10. The top of the roller-blind frame in the second column is pulled down (after selecting the pointer tool) to make the text match up with the text in the first column.

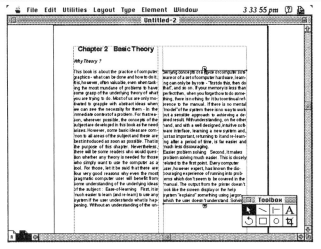

Figure 10.11. The final process is to 'place' a graphic in the middle of the text. The first stage is identical to the process of placing text (see Figure 10.3). When the cursor is clicked on the page the graphic appears, on top of the text (covering some of it).

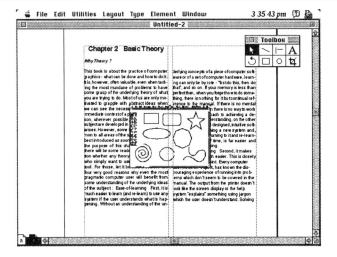

Figure 10.12. The graphic is selected and then the 'text-wrap' option is chosen. This is the option which makes the text wrap around the edges of the graphic instead of over or under it.

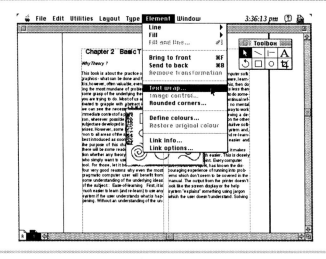

Figure 10.13. The text-wrap option provides three alternatives. The default (first icon) is no-wrap. The second (being chosen in the screen shot) is a rectangular wrap. The third allows for the text to wrap round a graphic which is not rectangular. The second row of icons offers three types of text flow. The first will stop the text above the graphic. The second continues the text underneath the graphic. The third flows the text round the edges of the graphic where there is space free. The amount of margin ('standoff') round the graphic can be chosen also.

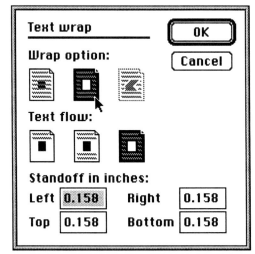

Figure 10.14. The final appearance of the page. The margin and guide lines will not appear in the final printed copy and they can be turned off in the screen view also to provide a more realistic result.

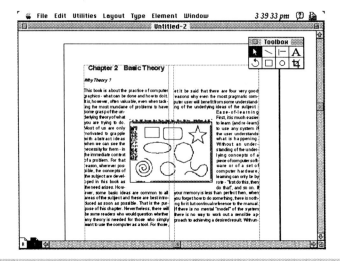

10.2 again), the cursor is clicked in the middle of the page and Figure 10.11 shows the result.

The graphic, however, sits on top of the text and obscures some of it. Figure 10.12 shows the menu item 'text-wrap' being chosen and in Figure 10.13 a dialogue box is presented which allows one of a number of types of text-wrap to be chosen. In Figure 10.14 the final appearance of the page is shown. The text has wrapped its way around the graphic, allowing a small amount of margin - the amount having been chosen in the dialogue box.

Vector drawing   In this case study, CorelDRAW! is used to produce two different effects, both involving text. The first involves choosing two graphic objects and then creating a series of intermediate shapes such that one object seems to change slowly into the other. In the process, those stages are swept out across the page along a path. In this example the two objects chosen are the words COMPUTER and GRAPHICS, one in black and the other in white. Other colours can be chosen and the colours can be blended gradually from one to the other as well as the shapes.

Figure 10.15 shows the two pieces of text and Figure 10.16 shows the path which has been drawn from one to the other. The exact shape of the path can be adjusted by pulling at the handles connected to the control points (see chapter 5). Figure 10.17 shows the 'blend' dialogue box (called a 'roll-up' in Corel because it can be reduced in size by rolling it up into the title bar). The number of intermediate steps is chosen and then the 'apply' button is clicked. This causes the selected conditions to be applied to the chosen ob-

Figure 10.15. Two pieces of text have been chosen to act as the start and finish points for a blending procedure. They are created by choosing the text icon (the icon on the left based on the letter A), clicking the mouse cursor on the screen and typing the characters. The size and font are chosen from the text menu. One word is left in an outline font and the other filled using the paint-bucket icon on the left. This 'pours' ink into the outline font in a flood fill operation.

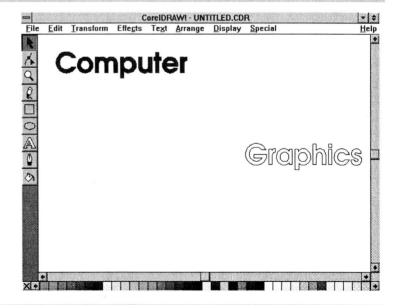

Figure 10.16. The curved line which has been added to the screen is the 'blend-path'. This is the path that the blend operation will eventually follow. It is drawn using the standard curve-drawing facility - see also chapter 5, Figure 5.18.

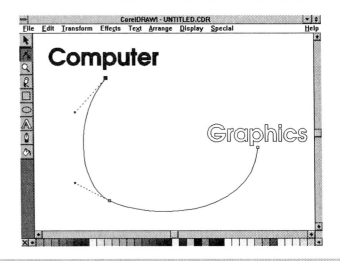

Figure 10.17. A blend dialogue box is used to specify the details of the blending process - in particular the number of intermediate shapes (the number of 'steps') which are to be created.

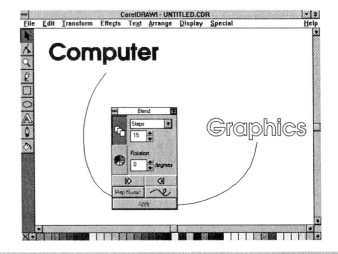

Figure 10.18. When the 'Apply' button is clicked in the blend dialogue box a number of intermediate shapes are created - initially on a straight line joining the start and finish shapes.

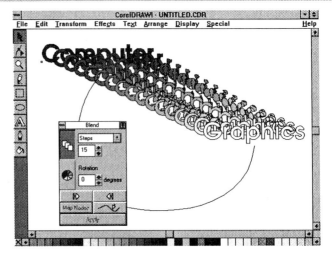

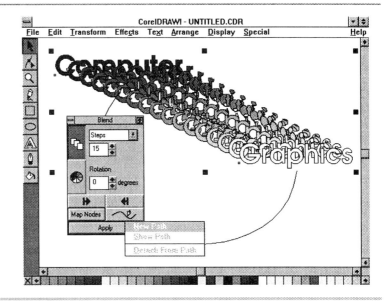

Figure 10.19. The next stage is to adapt the blend path to the curve which has been drawn. The path icon (the curved line) on the dialogue box is used to give access to the 'New Path' option.

jects. The result can be seen in the background of Figure 10.18. It can be seen that at this stage the blending is in a straight line connecting the first and last stages of the process. The next step involves modifying the blend to fit the chosen path. Figure 10.19 shows the menu which is pulled down when the path icon is clicked. When 'New Path' is chosen, all that is then necessary is to click on the path which is to be followed. Figure 10.20 shows the result. The only remaining task is to remove the drawing of the path from the image. Since the path is treated by the software as part of a unified whole, it is necessary to separate out the path from the rest

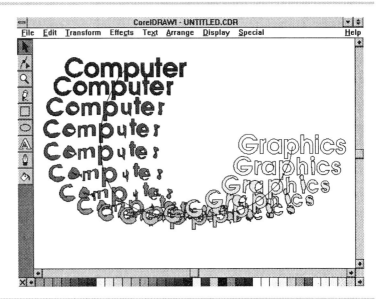

Figure 10.20. When the new path is selected (by clicking), the blend is redrawn along that line.

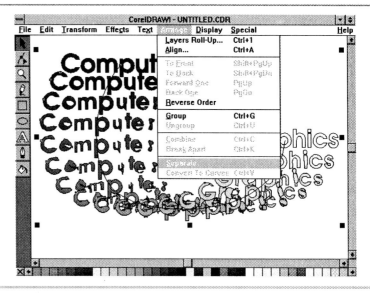

Figure 10.21. The final stage in the process is to remove the curved line from the image. The line, which is an integral part of the image, must be separated from it before it can be deleted. A menu option ('Separate') is used to do this.

of the image. This is done by using the Separate option (see Figure 10.21) which allows the path to be deleted, leaving the blended graphics unaffected. The end result is shown in Figure 10.22.

The second effect created in CorelDraw! is to wrap text along a path. This is extremely simple. In Figure 10.23 a large letter S shape is placed on the screen. This will be converted into a path, but any line drawn with the pen tool will do. In Figure 10.24, a long line of text is typed, in a suitable small typeface. Because the letter S is not considered to be a line, it is converted using the 'Convert to curves' option (see Figure 10.25). This makes no difference to the display. Finally the 'Fit text to path' option is selected (see Figure 10.26).

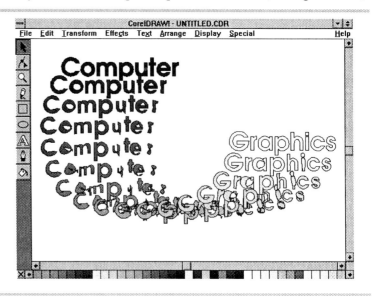

Figure 10.22. When the curved line is deleted the final blend is obtained.

Figure 10.23. A large letter 'S' - in outline - is chosen to act as the path, around which the much smaller text will be fitted. In general, any smooth curve can be used.

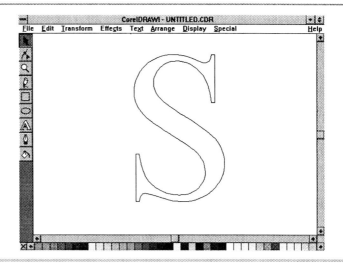

Figure 10.24. A long line of much smaller text is now added. This is the text which will be fitted to the curve.

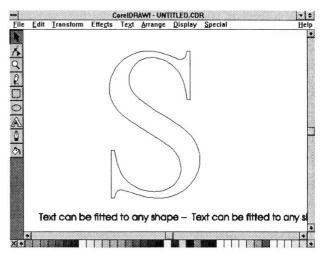

Figure 10.25. Text characters are treated by the software as a different category from curves, and so if the letter S is to be used as a curve it must be converted. See also chapter 5 and Figure 5.16 where a font is converted to curves and then distorted. The 'Convert to Curves' option is chosen from the menu.

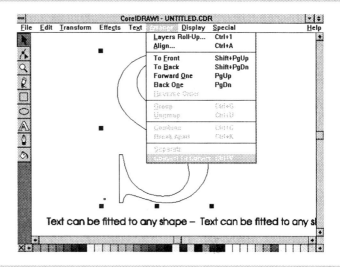

Figure 10.26. Both the 'S' shape and the text are selected and the 'Fit Text to Path' option is then chosen.

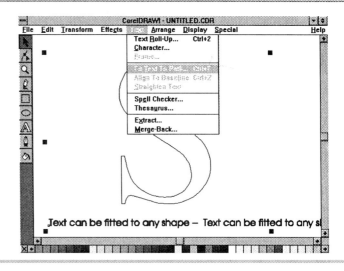

Figure 10.27. The 'Fit Text to Path' dialogue box offers a number of options which determine exactly how the text will be fitted to a curve.

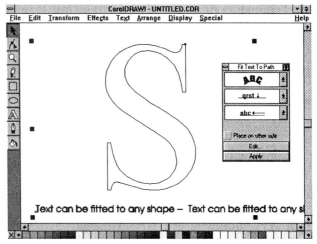

Figure 10.28. When the choices are made and the 'Apply' button is clicked, the text is redrawn around the outline 'S' shape to produce the final result.

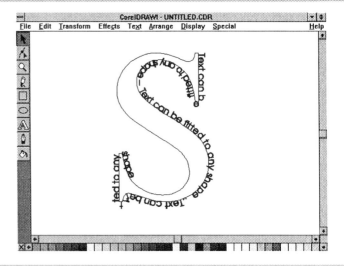

This produces a dialogue box, offering a choice of methods, but the default is chosen in this case -the text is fitted along the top of the curve (see Figure 10.27). Figure 10.28 shows the result.

Paint software Paint software is used to create and manipulate bit-mapped images, including images created by document scanners and by screen-grabbing. This little case study shows how one of the illustrations in chapter 2 (Figure 2.8) was created.

The point of the illustration is to show that the system font of an IBM-PC is a bit-mapped font - by enlarging a view of the screen so that the pixels can be seen clearly. The first stage involves running a screen-grabbing program so that any screen can be grabbed into a file by pressing the appropriate key combination. This was done while using WordPerfect 5.1, a text-based word processor, to produce Figure 10.29. The file created was in the PCX format and was then loaded into 'Paintbrush' - a paint package supplied with Microsoft Windows. At that stage the image looked like Figure 10.30. Using the zoom facility a portion of the image was magnified to look like Figure 10.31. This was then screen-grabbed so that the zoomed image was saved as a new file.

Screen grabbing can be done very easily in Windows by pressing the PrintScreen key on the keyboard. This grabs a copy of the screen - but unfortunately does not save it to disc as a normal screen-grabber would. It is temporarily stored in the 'Clipboard'. This is an area of memory used for cutting and pasting material from one application to another. The grabbed image has to be pasted, from the clipboard into a paint program and then saved.

In this context, 'pasting' simply means running the paint software and selecting the Paste option in the Edit menu and a copy of

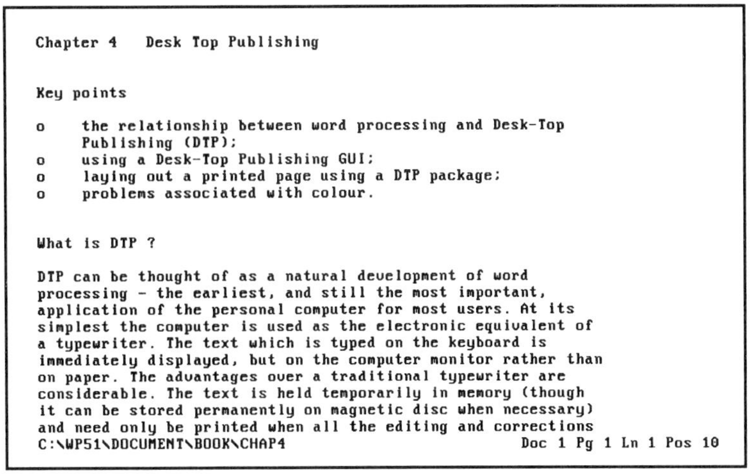

Figure 10.29. This is the screen of a text-based word processor (WordPerfect 5.1). It has been 'grabbed' using a screen grabber - a piece of software which runs in the background and which, when activated, takes a copy of the screen and saves it as a file.

```
Chapter 4    Desk Top Publishing

Key points

o    the relationship between word processing and Desk-Top
     Publishing (DTP);
o    using a Desk-Top Publishing GUI;
o    laying out a printed page using a DTP package;
o    problems associated with colour.


What is DTP ?

DTP can be thought of as a natural development of word
processing - the earliest, and still the most important,
application of the personal computer for most users. At its
simplest the computer is used as the electronic equivalent of
a typewriter. The text which is typed on the keyboard is
immediately displayed, but on the computer monitor rather than
on paper. The advantages over a traditional typewriter are
considerable. The text is held temporarily in memory (though
it can be stored permanently on magnetic disc when necessary)
and need only be printed when all the editing and corrections
C:\WP51\DOCUMENT\BOOK\CHAP4              Doc 1 Pg 1 Ln 1 Pos 10
```

Figure 10.30. The file, created by the screen grabber, has now been loaded into a paint package (Microsoft Paintbrush) so that the zoom facility can be used and the individual pixels shown much more clearly.

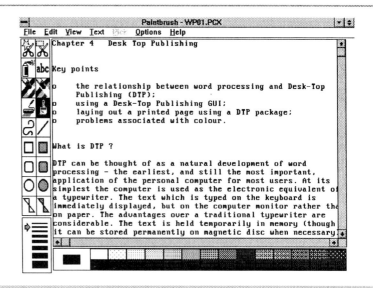

Figure 10.31. The zoom facility shows part of the original image at a high magnification and the pixels which make up the system font can now been seen very clearly. The effect is helped by the fact that this particular package (Microsoft Paintbrush) puts a grid on the screen in zoom view and this shows the positions of the pixels even more effectively. This zoom view is then screen-grabbed.

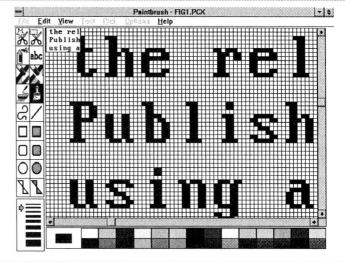

Figure 10.32. The final illustration consists of the screen grab which has already been used as Figure 10.31, but enlarged a little further, and with the edges of the picture removed. This can be done using a 'clipping' facility available in PageMaker (which is used to produce the final publication).

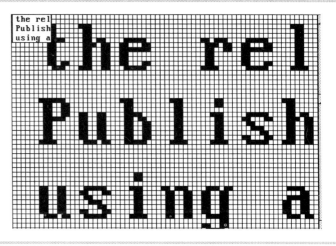

the image appears. 'Paintbrush' does not, however, manage to re-cover all the image - a strip at the bottom and right side is always lost in the process, presumably a 'bug' in the software. To avoid this it is necessary to use some other Windows paint package. If this is not available then the Clipboard Viewer (a utility also provided with Windows) can be used in similar way. This has the disadvantage, however, that the Clipboard Viewer can only save files in the 'clip' format and so it is usually necessary to then use a file converter to change the file into a PCX file or other suitable form.

Finally the image is incorporated into a document and printed - in this case using PageMaker. Since the screen-grab has material at the edges that is not wanted (the 'Paintbrush' parts of the image) some means must be used to remove them to get the final result (Figure 10.32). PageMaker, which is used to produce the final copy, has an image clipping facility which will do that, or it can be done within 'Paintbrush' itself before saving and placing in PageMaker.

3-D modelling   The last case study illustrates the steps needed to produce 3-D solid text by a process of extrusion. Figure 10.33 shows the first stage - choosing a font and some suitable text to place in the 2-D modeller. The 2-D modeller is that part of the software which is used for drawing 2-D shapes ready for extruding ('lofting') or rotation. Figure 10.34 shows the 2-D modeller with the text in place. The next stage is to choose the extrude option (see Figure 10.35). This produces a dialogue box (see Figure 10.36) which offers the choice of profile (i.e. the shape of the cross-section) of the 3-D object which is

Figure 10.35. The first stages of the process of producing 3-D images by extrusion involve using a 2-D modeller to create the 2-D shape which is to be extruded. In this case a suitable font is chosen, the characters are typed and the result loaded into the 2-D modeller. This, and all the following figures, are from Strata Vision 3-d.

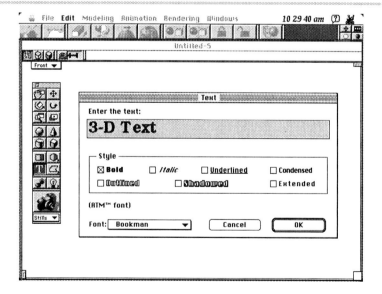

Figure 10.34. This is how the text looks in the 2-D modeller.

Figure 10.35. The next stage is to select the text and choose the 'extrude' option from the modelling menu.

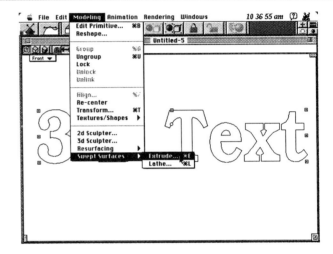

Figure 10.36. The two basic variables that must be specified before the extrusion can be done are the depth and the profile. The depth determines how far the extrusion is to go - and, therefore, how thick the 3-D letters will be. The profile affects the exact shape of the 3-D blocks which are to be created. The simplest profile, which is chosen in this case, is a rectangular shape - which means that the letters will have a uniform cross-section.

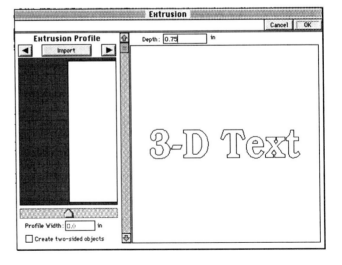

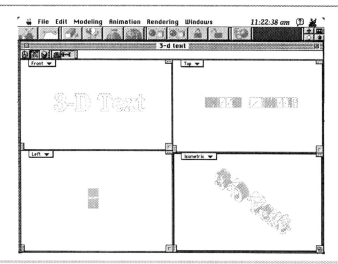

Figure 10.37. The usual four views of the extruded text.

to be created. It is also used to choose the depth -how far the extrusion is to go. In this case a simple rectangular profile is chosen - but there are a number of others available.

Figure 10.37 shows a four-window view of the newly-created 3-D object and Figure 10.38 shows an enlargement of the isometric view. Figure 10.39 is another view which is available - a view with the hidden-lines removed. All these views are easily obtained by selecting the right icons and require no operator skill. The last stage in the process is to place some lights into the scene, together with a camera to 'take the picture'.

Figure 10.40 shows a camera which has been placed by selecting a menu item and then dragging its image into place using the mouse. Figure 10.41 shows the view that the camera sees - a view that depends entirely on the position in which the camera is placed

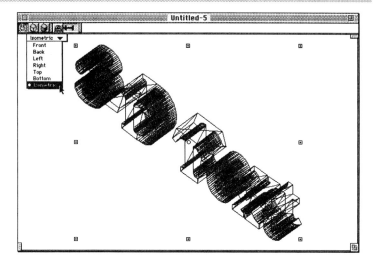

Figure 10.38. The isometric view, enlarged to fill the screen.

Figure 10.39. An isometric view of the extruded text with the hidden-lines removed.

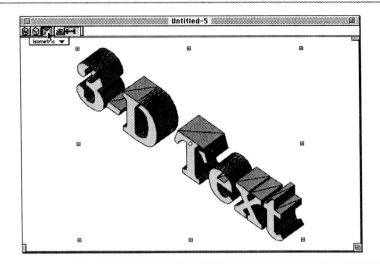

Figure 10.40. The last stage in the process involves places lights to illuminate the object and a camera to view it. This view shows a camera being positioned with the aid of the usual four views.

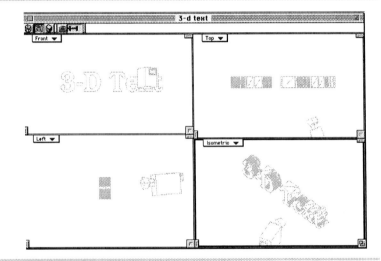

Figure 10.41. This view shows what the camera 'sees'.

Figure 10.42. When the camera angle is right, the surface of the object is assigned a colour and texture - chosen from a library - and a final view is then rendered, in this case against a background, also chosen from a library.

and the way it is pointed. After choosing a suitable colour for the surface of the text and a background colour, the software then renders the final view - Figure 10.42.

Glossary

A **Accelerator card (or board)**
Printed circuit card which plugs in to the computer main board and speeds up the performance of graphics operations. Many use a special graphics 'co-processor' which performs graphic operations more efficiently than the general-purpose microprocessor which is at the heart of the computer and to which all graphics operations can be delegated.

Active matrix LCD
An LCD display (q.v.) which has a transistor connected to each liquid crystal whose function is to turn the crystal on and off. The LCDs are more difficult to manufacture than 'passive matrix' LCDs and therefore more expensive but achieve higher contrast because the crystals do not begin to relax between refresh cycles.

Active window or frame
When one of a number of windows or graphic frames or objects is selected, by clicking on it with the mouse, it is considered to be active. This means that any activity, like text typed from the keyboard or a graphic file loaded from a disc, will take place in this window or frame. Its status is usually indicated, to distinguish it from an inactive one. A window usually has a different coloured title bar. An active frame or object usually has small black squares (handles) at its corners.

Additive colour
Colour monitors and colour printing processes create a wide range of colours by combining three primary colours in various proportions. Colour monitors use an emissive process, in which the primary colours (red, blue and green) are emitted by coloured dots on the screen. When these three different coloured rays of light combine, they do so by a process of addition. The light which enters the eye is a mixture of the three primaries. For example, when red is mixed with blue and green, white light is produced. Colour

printing, however, uses an absorptive process. Natural or artificial illumination, in the form of white light (which is a mixture of all the colours of the spectrum) is reflected off a mixture of primary coloured dots on the paper. In doing so some of the spectral colours are absorbed and the perceived colour depends on whatever wavelengths are not absorbed. When absorptive primary colours (cyan, magenta and yellow) are used to produce secondary colours they mix by a process of subtraction, each removing different wavelengths from the, originally, white light. For example, when cyan is mixed with magenta and yellow, black is produced (see CMYK).

Algorithm
A procedure, or series of steps, for solving a problem or producing a desired result.

Aliasing
The result of digitising a continuous shape into a series of discrete dots. For example, an oblique straight line becomes a series of small steps. Anti-aliasing techniques are methods of reducing this effect.
Alphanumeric A graphic shape which is either a letter of the alphabet or a number.

Ambient light
That part of the illumination of an object which applies equally to all surfaces in the object (as opposed to directional light which illuminates some surfaces more than others). It is caused by diffuse illumination (q.v.).

Applications software
A piece of software designed to be applied to the purpose of producing a particular end result, like a word processor or drawing package. See *Software* and *Systems software*.

Archiving
The process of producing a backup copy of some important data, which can then be used if the original is lost.
ASCII code A numerical code for storing alphanumeric characters; the letters stand for: American Standard Code for Information Exchange.

Aspect ratio
The ratio of the width to the height of a graphics display or other image.

B **Background colour**
When graphic objects are created they are said to placed on top of a contrasting colour, by analogy with paint placed on a canvas. The colour of the 'canvas' (those parts of the screen where there are no graphic objects) - is the background colour. The colour of the graphic objects is the foreground colour.

Backup
A copy of an important computer file which is made in case the original is lost. See *Archive.*

Balloon help
A help system used in some graphical user interfaces (q.v.) in which a cartoon-like speech bubble (balloon) appears on the screen whenever the mouse is pointed at an object, to explain the function of that object.

Bar chart
A graph in which the data points are represented by rectangular bars.

Batch processing
The processing of a number of computer programs (usually for the calculation of data) which are done, one after the other, in a single operation. This was a non-interactive, early style of computer usage. See *Interactive graphics.*

Binary
A number system which uses only two symbols. In mathematical jargon it is said to have a 'base of two', as compared with the normal decimal system which has a base of ten. See *Bit.*

Bit Short form of 'Binary digit'. The smallest unit of data, which can exist in two forms, usually designated 0 and 1 or off an on. See *Byte.*

Bit-map
A way of representing a digitised image in the memory of the computer. In its simplest form, each pixel in the image is represented by one bit in memory. For example, a bit set to 0 indicates a black pixel and a bit set to 1 indicates a white one. If more colours are used then more than one bit is needed for each pixel. The term 'map' indicates that a simple one-to-one relationship exists between the object being represented (the image) and the representation (in

memory), as in a geographical map.

Bit-mapped font
A font which is represented as a set of bits, rather than as a more general description of the shape of the letters. See *Scalable font* and *System font*.

Body text
The type of font which is used for the majority of the normal text in a document - the 'body' of the text.

Bold
A thicker, blacker version of a font (q.v.) which causes the characters to stand out from the surrounding normal text.

Buffer
A section of computer memory set aside for storing information on a temporary basis. See *Refresh buffer*.

Bus
A set of electrical wires which carry digitised information within the computer.

Byte
A number expressed as a fixed number of bits - normally eight. For example the decimal number 255 can be expressed in one byte because it consists of 8 binary digits (11111111). See *Bit* and *Binary*.

C ### CAD
Computer-Assisted (or -Aided) Design. Software used for designing and drawing, usually in the context of engineering design.

Cathode-ray tube (CRT)
A glass vacuum vessel used in traditional computer displays and TV sets. A beam of electrons is fired from an electron gun, through a vacuum, and is absorbed in a fluorescent layer on the inside of the face of the tube. This layer emits light to form a glowing image. The beam is scanned across the face of the tube in a 'raster' pattern - a series of closely-packed parallel lines, its brightness being modulated to form the bright and dark regions of the image.

CCD
Charge-coupled device. A semiconductor device which is sensitive to light. They are used in document scanners and digital cameras.

CD See *Compact disc*.

CD-Rom
A CD which is used to store computer data, as opposed to music.
See *Compact disc* and *Rom*

Cel
A component of an animated image. In traditional animation, parts of the image are drawn onto transparent celluloid (hence the short form: cel). A number of cels can be placed on top of each other and the result photographed. By this means, unchanging parts of the animation can be separated from the changing parts and only drawn once.

CGA
Colour Graphics Adaptor. The first graphics system used in IBM-PC computers. Had a maximum resolution of 640 x 200 pixels (two colours). At a reduced resolution of 320 x 200 pixels, four colours were available.

CGM
Computer Graphics Metafile. One of the many standard ways of storing a graphic image.

Character set
A complete set of alphanumeric characters in one particular font.

Clip-art A collection of digitised images which can be incorporated into a computer graphic image.

Clipboard
A temporary store for a portion of an image which has been 'cut' (removed) from one image, ready to 'paste' into another.

Clone See *IBM-PC*.

Compact disc
A small circular disc which stores digitised data as a series of tiny pits, arranged in a continuous spiral, in its surface. The pits are detected by reflected laser light and converted back into a binary signal.

CMYK
Cyan, magenta, yellow and black. The first three are the absorptive primary colours used in printed images (see additive colour).

Black should not be required in printing because a mixture of the first three should produce black but in practice the quality of the black produced this way is unsatisfactory.

Colour separation

The process of separating the three primary colour components from a colour image, in preparation for the printing process. See *Additive colour* and *Process colour*.

Colour look-up table (LUT)

A table which relates the colour codes, stored in the refresh buffer, to the specification of the colours, in terms of their R, G and B components (see *RGB*).

Compression

A technique for storing computer data in a smaller amount of memory than would normally be required. Some compression techniques are designed so that no data is lost in the process (loss-less compression). Some are designed to achieve higher levels of compression at the expense of losing data ('lossy' compression).

Continuous tone image

An image, like a photograph, which consists of such a large range of 'tones' (shades of grey or colour) that they shade imperceptibly, one into another. In contrast, a digitised image consists of a limited number of distinct shades. See *Grey levels*.

Contrast

The ratio of the maximum to the minimum intensity of an image.

Control code

A computer code which is used to control peripheral devices like a printer. For example, a code might be entered into a line of text which, though invisible to the user, will have the effect of instructing the printer to print all subsequent text in bold.

Control points

A set of points which is used to control the exact shape of a curve.

Coordinate system

A way of specifying the position of a point in space. The perpendicular distances (the x and y distances) to two right-angled axes are used in the 2-D Cartesian coordinate system. A third distance (the z distance) is used in a 3-D version of this method.

cpi
Characters per inch. Used to specify how close together printed characters are.

Cursor
A small graphical symbol, used in conjunction with a pointing device, like a mouse, to indicate a position on the computer display.

D **Descender**
The tail-like part of a character like p, y and j which descends below the line which designates the bottom of the majority of other characters.

Desktop publishing
The use of special software and high-quality printers (like laser printers) to produce printed material using a desktop computer. For best results the laser printer is used for the production of proofs (q.v.) and the final result is produced on a commercial-quality printer like a typesetter.

Desktop video
By analogy with DTP (desktop publishing), this is the production of video by means of desktop computers which take the place of the much larger and more expensive video editing suites.

Diffuse illumination
Light which, because it has gone though a series of reflections or scattering processes, shines in all directions and so illuminates objects very evenly. Natural light is diffuse when the sun light is scattered by clouds. Artificial light is diffuse when special glass diffusers scatter the light and when there are many different lights illuminating the same object. See *Directional illumination.*

Digital
General term applied to any situation where data is stored as a set of numbers (almost always using the binary system) as compared with 'analogue' systems where the data is stored in continuously varying voltages whose size is proportional to the original data.

Digital camera
Camera in which the film has been replaced with a 2-dimensional array of CCDs (q.v.). This produces a digital representation of the image which can be stored on a floppy disc. It requires no intermediate processing of film or secondary digitisation process.

Directional illumination

Illumination, usually from a small source of light or spotlight, which illuminates some surfaces much more strongly than others because of its very specific direction.

Disc (disk)

Small circular magnetic recording medium used in computers to record computer data. Removable discs are often referred to as 'floppy' discs (or occasionally as a 'diskette'). Non-removable ones are called 'hard' discs.

Disc drive

The device which reads and writes information to a floppy (removable) disc.

Display buffer

Another term for a refresh buffer (q.v.).

Display device

A device, such as a CRT monitor (q.v.) which produces images based on computer data.

Dithering

A method, used by computer printers, of simulating grey-levels based on the use of large numbers of tiny black dots. Those areas where there is a high density of dots look darker than areas where the density is low. The method depends on the use of dots which are too small to be seen individually. Colour tones can be simulated in a similar way using cyan, magenta, yellow and black dots. See *Halftones*.

Dot matrix

A rectangular array of dots. Most computer printing and display devices produce images based on such an array. One particular type of printer has acquired the name of 'dot-matrix printer'. It uses a vertical column of tiny metal pins, fitted to a moving head, to impact, via an inked ribbon, onto paper.

Dot pitch

The pitch of a CRT display (q.v.) is a measurement of the separation of the coloured phosphor dots or stripes which are used to create the image. The closer the dots are together, the more detail that can be displayed on the CRT. The best CRTs have a dot pitch of about 0.26 mm (millimetres). This means that the red phosphor dots repeat themselves every 0.26 mm.

Dots per inch (dpi)

The number of dots which are printed or displayed by a computer printer or display device per inch. For example, a standard laser printer produces 300 dpi but a standard CRT monitor operates at about 60-72 dpi.

Drum plotter

A pen plotter in which a pen is moved over a piece of paper fixed to a cylinder (drum). See *Flatbed plotter*.

DTP See *Desktop publishing*.

Dye sublimation printer

A printer which produces very high quality continuous tone colour images by a process of subliming dyes which mix and condense on the paper to produce intermediate tones. Sublimation is the process whereby some substances, when heated, turn from the solid phase directly to the vapour phase without melting to form a liquid.

E   EGA

Enhanced Graphics Adaptor. An improved display interface for the IBM-PC computer which superseded the CGA. Resolution of 640 x 350 (16 colours).

Electron gun

The device in a CRT (q.v.) which produces a high-velocity stream of electrons. These are fired at the face of the CRT and are absorbed in the phosphor layer, which then gives out light.

Electronic publishing

The production of printed documents using computer techniques (a more professional version of DTP). OR the production and distribution of documents in electronic form (e.g. on floppy discs, CD-Roms or via networks).

Encapsulated Postscript (EPS)

A file which contains a description of an image in the page-description language Postscript.

Extended Graphics Adaptor (XGA)

A graphics adaptor for the IBM-PC which extends the resolution available in the VGA standard (q.v.). The resolution is 1024 x 768 pixels.

Extended light source

A light source which, because it is long (for example a fluorescent strip light) produces a diffuse illumination because each surface on an object receives illumination from some point on the source. See *Point light source*.

Extrusion See *Lofting*.

F **Face**

A flat surface which forms part of a 3-D object.

File

A set of computer data which is saved as a single entity, under a 'file name'. For example an image saved as a graphics file or a document saved as a text file.

File extension

When files (q.v.) are saved using IBM-PCs the form of the file name is restricted to a maximum of eight characters plus a maximum of three further characters (the file extension), separated from the first eight by means of a full-stop ('period' in the US). For example a file could be called 'myfile.doc'. The three file extension characters are often used to identify the type of file, and are sometimes added automatically by the applications software (q.v.) being used to create the file. For example, a '.PCX' extension signifies that the file is a graphics file saved in the PCX format (q.v.).

File format

The particular way of saving a file. Graphics files are saved in many different formats. See *CGM, PCX, TIFF*.

Fillet

A term used in CAD (q.v.) to describe the process of turning a right-angle join between two straight lines into a curved edge.

Filter

An algorithm (q.v.) which is used to process computer data. Photographic retouching software can be used to apply filters to images which change their appearance. In this case the term is used by analogy with a coloured filter which can be used to change the appearance of a photograph.

Flat-bed plotter

A pen plotter in which a pen is moved over a piece of paper fixed to a flat surface (bed). See Drum Plotter.

Flood fill

A process used in drawing or painting software in which a colour or pattern is used to fill all the space enclosed by a chosen boundary of a specified colour - as if water were filling a container.

Folder

A term used in the Macintosh GUI (q.v.) to describe a symbol which represents what would be called a 'sub-directory' in most other, non-graphical operating systems. The analogy is with a cardboard folder, used in a filing cabinet, to store a number of documents which are to be kept together.

Font

A set of typographic characters with the same style or design. The term is often confused with the similar term 'typeface'. A font is usually taken to be a particular subset of a typeface. For example the typeface called 'Times' exists in many different sizes and in both bold and italic forms (q.v.). One complete set of characters in the Times typeface, of one particular size and form (for example italic), is a font.

Foreground colour See *Background colour.*

Fractal

A type of mathematical function which is used to produce graphic shapes of a natural kind - for example to model the shapes of trees, rocks and clouds in computer-generated images. Fractal equations have also been used to produce very elegant abstract patterns which contain endless detail as they are magnified.

Frame

A rectangular shape which is used as a border for a graphic.

Frame-grabber

A hardware device which is used to digitise an image from the stream of images produced by TV and video systems.

G   GEM

Graphical Environment Manager. A GUI (q.v.) produced by the Digital Research Corp. The term is now used to designate the graphic file format (q.v.) used by it to save images (with the file extension IMG).

GIF

Graphics Interchange Format. A graphic file format (q.v.) developed for use by CompuServe for storing and interchanging images.

Graphic tablet

Flat drawing surface, attached to the computer, which detects the position of a special pen (a 'stylus'); used for inputting drawings and other graphic information. A special version of the stylus - called a 'puck' because of its resemblance to a hockey puck - equipped with a transparent plate and cross-hairs, can be used to input position more accurately.

Grey-levels

Tonal variations of grey between the two extremes of black and white.

Grid

A rectangular array of dots or lines on a screen which can be used to help align objects drawn on the screen. See *Snapping*.

Graphical User Interface (GUI)

A pictorial system which enables a computer user to control software by means of small images (called icons) by means of a pointing device (usually a mouse). The ideas were developed by the Xerox Corp. but were first commercially successful in the Apple Macintosh.

Graphics mode

Many computers can operate in two different modes. In one, only a limited set of characters can be displayed on the screen. This is called text-only or character mode. In the other, every pixel on the screen is under software control and so a wide range of graphics can be displayed. This is graphics (or 'true graphics') mode.

Greeking

When text is displayed by DTP software at such a low magnification (or with such small characters) that the screen is not able to reproduce it in readable form, then it can be 'greeked'. This means that the outline of each line of text is displayed as a grey bar, in order that the layout of the page can still be seen even though the text cannot be read. Greeking text will speed up the display of a page whenever changes of view are required.

GUI See *Graphical User Interface*.

Gutter
The white space between two columns of text.

H   Halftone
An image which is reproduced using dots to represent continuous tones (q.v.). This is the normal method of printing photographs in books, magazines and newspapers. The halftone is created from a continuous tone image by photographing it through a fine mesh (a screen) which breaks it up into dots. See *Dithering*.

Handle
A small black square at the corners of a selected graphic object, frame or window. See *Active window or frame*.

Hard copy
A copy of a computer graphic image (or other file) which has been printed on paper.

Hard disc See *Disc*.

Hard return
The 'return' key on a computer keyboard (often marked as 'Enter' instead) is used by a typist to indicate the end of a line of text and (usually) the beginning of a new paragraph. This puts a control code (q.v.) into the text file. A 'soft-return' is an end-of line code which is entered by the software, and can be moved automatically if extra characters are added to, or subtracted from the line.

Hardware
The electronic circuits and other equipment which makes up a computer system. See *Software*.

Hertz (Hz)
A measure of frequency. One Hz means one cycle or operation per second.

Hidden line
A line which is part of a drawing of a 3-D object but which should be hidden from the observer because other parts of the object obscure it. In using a computer to create an image of a 3-D object, initially all the lines are drawn, and then the computer calculates which lines should be hidden, and removes them from the display. In different views of an object, different lines are hidden. The same terminology is applied to surfaces - for example, 'hidden surface' removal.

Hidden surface See *Hidden line.*

High resolution
An image which is displayed in very fine detail is said to be a high-resolution image. The same terminology applies to displays and printers. See *Resolution.*

HSB colour system
A method of specifying colour which uses three variables: Hue, Saturation and Brightness. Hue corresponds to the wavelength of the light and therefore to the name of the colour (e.g. red, blue, etc.); Saturation (or chroma) represents the strength or purity of the colour, sometimes called the purity or intensity (as if mixed to varying degrees with white); Brightness corresponds to the relative lightness or darkness of the colour (as if mixed to varying degrees with black). There is a similar system called the HLS (or HSL) colour system which uses Hue, Lightness and Saturation. See CMYK and RGB systems.

Hue See *HSB colour system.*

I **IBM-PC**
A type of personal computer designed by IBM and widely copied. Copies are sometimes known as 'clones', PCs or IBM compatibles. The term 'PC' is sometimes applied to any personal computer, for example an Apple Macintosh.

Icon
Small stylised picture used in Graphical User Interfaces (or GUIs - q.v.). An icon is usually used to represent a piece of software or hardware and is used by clicking, double-clicking or dragging. Clicking makes the object associated with the icon active. Double-clicking will run the software represented by the icon. Dragging the icon over another icon causes it to interact in some way with the function associated with that icon. For example, dragging the icon representing a file, over the waste-basket icon, causes the file to be deleted (thrown away).

Impact printer
A printer which produces its output by a process in which an object hits a ribbon onto a piece of paper, so transferring ink. See *Dot matrix.*

In-betweening
Part of the process of producing animated pictures which involves

creating large numbers of images which correspond to small stages in between the beginning and the ending of a movement of one of the cartoon characters.

Ink-jet printer
A printer which produces images by spraying very fine jets of ink from a large number of tiny nozzles in a moving head.

Input device
A computer peripheral (q.v.) which is used to enter information into the computer. Examples include the keyboard, mouse and scanner. See *Output device*.

Interactive graphics
Computer graphics in which the user sees an almost instant response to any input. All modern graphics systems are designed to be interactive although some systems still have an appreciable time-lag between input and system response (usually seen on the screen).

Interface
Any part of a computer system (whether hardware or software) which is designed to enable the user to communicate with the computer. See *GUI, Input device* and *Output device*.

Interlacing
A system used in many CRT monitors (q.v.) and TV sets in which the raster lines which create the image are not laid down in strict sequence. All the odd lines are first laid down, followed by all the even lines, interlaced between them.

Inverse video See *Reverse video*.

Isometric projection
A type of perspective drawing of a 3-D object in which the lines are drawn parallel to each other, rather than to a vanishing point, as in true perspective.

Italic
A font (q.v.) in which the, normally, vertical components of the characters are slanted.

J Joystick
An input device (q.v.), looking like the joystick of an aeroplane, used to position the cursor on a display device.

JPEG
Joint Photographic Experts Group. Name of a standards' body which has given its name to a lossy compression standard. See *Compression*.

Justification
The process of introducing small extra spaces into a line of text to make it line up at the right hand end. Typewritten text is left justified only, leaving the right end ragged, so no extra spaces need be introduced. Printed text is frequently right justified also (often simply referred to as justified but more properly, fully-justified). Text can also be right justified (or aligned) with a ragged end at the left. Text which is force-justified is fully justified even in a line which ends with a hard return (q.v.).

K **KByte**
Kilobyte. In binary arithmetic the use of the symbol k (kilo-) corresponds to 1024, not 1000 as it would be in decimal arithmetic. See *Mbyte*.

Kerning
A term used in typographer to designate the moving of certain character pairs closer together than they would be to other characters. This is done when the shape of certain pairs is complementary, so that they naturally fit closer together, and look better, especially in large font sizes, as in headlines.

L **Landscape**
The orientation of a rectangular document or display when the width is larger than the height - as in a landscape painting. See *Portrait*.

Laser printer
High-quality printer which uses a computer-controlled laser beam and optical scanning device to discharge a charged light-sensitive drum. The drum attracts toner (special ink particles) to the charged regions which is then transferred onto paper to form the final image.

LCD See *Liquid Crystal Display*.

Leading
Pronounced 'ledding'. The space between lines of text. Derives from traditional printers' method of separating lines of moveable metal type with thin strips of lead.

LED
Light-emitting diode. A semiconductor device which emits light. Is used in certain types of 'laser' printer as a replacement for the laser.

Line art
A graphic which consists of lines and is stored in a vector format. See *Vector*

Liquid crystal display
An alternative to the CRT (q.v.) as a display screen in computer monitors. The screen consists of thousands of tiny separate liquid crystals which can be individually turned off or on. The crystals act as a type of light-switch or gate. When light is let through, a pixel is lit. Otherwise the pixel is dark. For colour screens, each pixel has three liquid crystals, each with its own red, green or blue filter. See *Active matrix*.

Lofting
The process by which a 2-dimensional shape is extended into the third dimension to produce a 3-dimensional shape. Also called 'extrusion'.

Look-up table See *Colour look-up table.*

Loss-less See *Compression.*

Lossy See *Compression.*

LZW
Lempel Ziv Welch. A type of loss-less compression (q.v.).

M **MByte**
Megabyte (Mbyte). In binary arithmetic the use of the symbol M (mega-) corresponds to 1024 x 1024 (1,048,576) not 1,000,000 as it would be in decimal arithmetic. See *Byte*.

Mac
Short for Macintosh (an Apple computer widely used in computer graphics).

Mask
A method, used in graphic drawing and painting software, of protecting parts of the image from being changed.

Menu
A series of options which can be chosen from a list.

Mono-spaced font
A font (q.v.) in which all the letters have an equal spacing. Those letter which are naturally thin are artificially widened by the use of large serifs (q.v.). These fonts are designed for systems, like type-writers, which can only place characters in fixed positions regard-less of the actual character being printed. They tend to be harder to read than proportionally spaced fonts (q.v.).

Morphing
The process of gradually changing one image into another by a series of small steps.

Mouse
A small plastic box which can be moved over a flat surface. The movements are conveyed to the computer and used to move a cur-sor (q.v.) on the screen.

Multimedia
The combination of a variety of different media of communication, such as graphics, sound, video and animation to enhance the qual-ity of communication.

O

OCR
Optical Character Recognition. The process whereby a piece of soft-ware interprets the graphic file created when alphanumeric char-acters (q.v.) are scanned using a document scanner (q.v.), recog-nises the shapes and identifies the characters.

Operating system
The software which looks after all the regular operations of the computer, such as interpreting the input from the keyboard, con-trolling the display system and handling the saving and retrieving of files from the hard and floppy discs (q.v.).

Optical disc
A storage system which stores and reads data using a laser beam rather than the magnetic method used in floppy and hard discs (q.v.). See *CD-Rom.*

Orphan
A typographer's term for one or two lines at the beginning of a paragraph which occur at the end of a page or column and so look unsightly. See *Widow.*

Output device
A computer peripheral (q.v.) which is used to present information to the outside world. Examples include the screen and a variety of printers. See *Input device*.

P **Page description language (PDL)**
A type of computer language which is concerned with specifying the layout of a page of text and graphics. The description of the page is independent of the exact characteristics of the printer which will produce the hardcopy (q.v.). This means that a graphic file, which contains the computer code, can be sent to a variety of printers and in each it will produce an identical image, within the limits of its capability. The printers must, however, contain a language interpreter which can translate the code. The best known example of a PDL is Postscript.

Page printer
Unlike many printers which use a small moving head and lay down text and graphics in a series of horizontal bands, a page printer produces the whole page in one operation.

Paint software
An application package which is designed to enable an artist to create paintings electronically, using a mouse.
Palette A collection of colours which is available within a graphics package. The number depends on the hardware and can vary from 16 to 16.8 million. Often more than one palette is available, but only one can be used at a time. Each palette corresponds to a different colour look-up table (q.v.)

Pantone colour system
A system of standardising printed colours by the use of 'swatches' of colour cards which show how the chosen colour will look when printed - often quite different from its appearance on a computer display.

PC
Personal computer See *IBM-PC*

PCX
A widely-used graphic file format (q.v.).

Pel
A short form of 'pixel'. See *Pixel*.

Pen-plotter
A device which draws lines under computer control using a mechanical arm and a pen. See *Drum plotter* and *Flatbed plotter.*

Peripheral
Any device connected to a computer, such as a printer or mouse, but which is not absolutely essential for its operation.

Persistence
The time that the glow on a CRT (q.v.) lasts before fading away. Because of the fading effect the display must be regularly refreshed.

Perspective
The effect whereby objects appear to get smaller as they recede into the distance. See *Isometric projection.*

Phosphor
The special lining on the face of a CRT (q.v.) display which glows when irradiated by an electron beam.

Photo-typesetter
A device for producing high-quality output, suitable for use as a printing master, using a laser to record directly onto photographic emulsion.

Pica
A measure of the size of type. One pica is equal to 12 points; 72 points are equivalent to 1 inch.

Pie chart
A chart in which the relative sizes of a set of data are expressed as slices of a circular pie.

Pixel
A picture element. One of the many dots used in forming a computer graphic image.

Pixellisation
A graphic effect in which a digitised image is represented with fewer than the original number of pixels. Each of the larger pixels is derived from a number of smaller, original, ones by an averaging affect.

PKZip and PKUnzip
A widely-used program for loss-less compression. See *Compression.*

Point See *Pica*.

Point light source
A very small source of light which gives very directional illumination. See *Extended light source* and *Diffuse illumination*.

Pointing device
A peripheral input device which can be used to point to the display.

Polyline
A series of straight lines joined end-to-end.

Portrait
The orientation of a rectangular document or display when the width is smaller than the height - as in a portrait painting. See Landscape.

Postscript See *Page description language*.

Primitive
A basic geometrical shape from which more complicated shapes can be constructed.

Process colour
The combination of cyan, magenta, yellow and black 'separations' to produce intermediate colours in the printing process. See *Spot colour* and *Colour separation*.

Proof
A low-quality print which is produced for careful inspection and correction before the higher-quality final product is made.

Proportional spacing
Spacing between individual letters in a typographic font which is appropriate to their natural shape. See *Monospaced font*.

Puck See *Graphic tablet*.

R   RAM
Random-Access Memory. All semiconductor memory is random access (each memory element can be accessed in any order) but RAM refers to memory chips which can be written to as well as read from. A better name would be read-write memory. See *Rom*.

Raster

A method of placing information on the screen of a CRT (q.v.) display device. The electron beam is moved across the screen in a series of closely-packed horizontal parallel lines (a raster) and pixels are illuminated or switched off in a rectangular array.

Ray tracing

A process used to create a realistic image of a 3-D object. The laws of optics are used to calculate the paths traced by a large number of rays of light as they reflect and scatter off the object and enter the eye of the observer. The colour and intensity of the rays when they finally enter the eye are calculated from the types of interaction they undergo in the process.

Real time

A computer process which happens without any perceptible delay and can therefore simulate events as they might happen in the real world.

Refresh

The images created by most computer display systems fade rapidly and need to be recreated or 'refreshed'. See *Refresh buffer*

Refresh buffer

That portion of the computer's memory which is set aside to store data specifying the image to be displayed on the screen. This information is needed in order that the screen, as it fades, can be refreshed regularly. See *Refresh.*

Registration

When colour images are printed by repeated application of the four primary colours (cyan, magenta, yellow and black) to a sheet of paper it is important that the colours match exactly. Special marks called registration marks are printed on the edge of the paper which can be cut off at the end of the process, and are used by the printer to adjust the machine to ensure that this matching process is exact. See *Additive colour.*

Render

A term used to describe the process in which software creates a realistic image of a 3-dimensional object by ray-tracing or other methods. See *Ray tracing.*

Resolution

A general term used in science and technology to describe the amount of detail to be found in a set of data. In computer graphics it is used of the amount of spatial detail in an image and is therefore one measure of the quality of that image.

Reverse video
Also called inverse video. Characters have their normal foreground and background colours reversed. For example, white-on-black characters become black-on-white.

RGB colour model
Red, green, blue. A method of specifying additive colours by the proportion of the three primaries which combine to create it. See *Additive colour.*

Rom
Read-only memory. Semiconductor memory chips which store information which can be read by the computer but not changed or deleted. See *CD-Rom.*

Rubber-banding
An aid to drawing objects on a screen with a mouse. A flexible line or rectangle is displayed on the screen to show where the object will be placed. The rubber-band shape is fixed at one corner or end but can be stretched by dragging the mouse until a suitable position is reached.

S Sans serif
A serif is a term used in typography to describe the small hooks and decorations which are placed on the end of characters in certain typefaces. These are called serif typefaces. Plainer typefaces which have no serifs are called sans-serif typefaces (sans means 'without' in French).

Scan
A rather general term which means to move methodically over something. Used in the context of a document scanner to digitise a printed image. Used of the electron beam in a CRT (q.v.) to move in a raster fashion over the face of the tube.

Scan conversion
The process whereby a vector description of an object is converted into a form suitable for use in a raster-scan display device or printer which needs a bitmap of the image. See *Bit-map* and *Vector.*

Screen capture
Sometimes called screen dumping. The process in which a copy of what is seen on the screen is captured in a graphic file for printing (as in a manual or textbook).

Screen font
A font which is used to display on the screen a good imitation of the font which the printer will use in producing hardcopy.

Scroll bars
Bars on the side of a scrollable window which can be dragged using a mouse to cause the contents of the window to scroll.

Seed-fill
Another term for flood fill.

Serif See *Sans serif.*

Shading The use of different tones to create the natural effect of light and dark on a solid object.

Snapping
The effect in which objects which are drawn on a screen are attracted to a rectangular grid pattern in order to automatically ensure good alignment. See Grid.

Soft return See *Hard return.*

Software
Computer programs. A set of instructions which control the computer to produce some desired effect. See *Applications software* and *Systems software.*

Spatial
Relating to space. See *Resolution.*

Spot colour
An alternative to printing colours by the mixture of three or four primaries in different proportions. A spot colour is a specific colour, chosen from a range of printing inks, which is used either in addition to process colours, or as a substitute, where only a few colours are required. Spot colour is a better method of producing solid blocks of colour. Process colour is better at producing a large range of shades. See *Process colour.*

Subtractive colour See *Additive colour.*

Super twist
An improved type of liquid crystal which produces more contrast in LCD displays (q.v.).

Super-VGA See *VGA.*

System font
The bit-mapped font of characters which is supplied with the computer hardware and used for routine display of text.

Systems software
Software whose function is to assist the general operation of the computer. See *Applications software.*

T **TIFF**
Tagged Image File Format. A widely-used graphic file format.

Text-only mode
A mode in which the computer displays only text, and a limited range of other characters, in the system font (q.v.). See *Graphics mode.*

Thermal wax printer
A dot-matrix printer which uses a ribbon with a special waxy ink which is melted by heating the pins in the print head. See *Dot matrix* and *Impact printer.*

Tiling
A way of arranging windows in a GUI (q.v.) so that they do not overlap but sit side-by-side like tiles.

Toner
A special type of ink, in the form of a powder, which is used in laser printers. The toner is attracted to charged regions on the photosensitive drum. See *Laser printer.*

Toolbox (or Toolkit)
A small 'floating' window made up of icons in a rectangular array. Each icon represents a tool or utility for use in a graphics program. See *Icon* and *Window.*

Touch-screen
A transparent screen which is placed over a computer monitor and which is sensitive to touch so that choices from a menu can be made

without the need for a keyboard or mouse.

Tweening
Short for in-betweening (q.v.).

Typeface See *Font.*

V **Vector**
In mathematics: a straight line defined by its end points. More generally, in graphics, a line of any sort. Hence vector images are stored as a set of lines, as opposed to bit-mapped images which are stored as a set of dots (pixels) in a rectangular array.

VESA
Video Electronics Standards Association. A body which sets standards associated with video which has given its name to a way of interfacing video cards (q.v.) to a computer via a bus.

VGA
Video Graphics Array. A display interface for the IBM-PC computer which superseded the EGA. It has a standard resolution of 640 x 4890 (16 colours). Has largely been superseded by an enhanced version called Super-VGA (S-VGA) which offers a number of higher resolution modes and more colours, the exact number depending on the amount of video buffer RAM supplied. All S-VGA cards offer at least 800 x 600 resolution and most offer 256 colours. Some also implement the XGA standard also. See EGA and XGA.

Virtual Reality
A form of highly-realistic simulation of a 3-D world created by a computer. 3-D stereoscopic vision involves the use of special helmets which present slightly different views of this imaginary world to each eye and also provide the computer with feedback as the user moves his/her head. Some systems use special gloves to provide feedback of hand movements also.

W **Widow**
A typographer's term for one or two lines of text at the end of a paragraph, which occur at the top of a new page or column and so look unsightly. See *Orphan.*

Window
A rectangular, re-sizeable frame which contains text or graphics and is an important feature of GUIs (q.v.). 'Windows' is the trade name given by Microsoft to its GUI which operates in conjunction

with its MS-DOS operating system. See *Operating system*.

Wire-frame
A simple representation of a 3-D object in which the edges of the planes which make up the object are shown as lines, as if made from wire.

WYSIWYG
What You See Is What You Get. A type of display which attempts to represent exactly what the final printed graphic will look like.

X **X-axis**
In the Cartesian coordinate system, measurements in the horizontal plane are designated with the letter x and the corresponding axis called the x-axis. See Coordinate System.

XGA See *Enhanced graphics adaptor.*

X-Y Plotter
Another name for a pen-plotter. See *Flatbed plotter* and *Pen plotter.*

Index